Psychology:
A New Introduction
for AS Level

Richard Gross
Rob McIlveen
and
Hugh Coolican

London: Hodder &
Stoughton, 2000

0340776900

Hodder & Stoughton

A MEMBER OF THE HODDER HEADLINE GROUP

DEDICATION

To J.G., T.G. and J.G. The love just goes on and on.
R.G.

To Gill, William and Katie, with love.
R.M.

To Rama, Kiran and Jeevan for their continuing love and support.
H.C.

British Library Cataloguing in Publication Data

A catalogue record for this title is available from the British Library

ISBN 0 340 77690 0

First published 2000

Impression number 10 9 8 7 6 5 4 3 2
Year   2004 2003 2002 2001 2000

Typeset by GreenGate Publishing Services, Tonbridge, Kent.

Printed and bound in Spain for Hodder and Stoughton Educational, a
division of Hodder Headline plc, 338 Euston Road, London NW1 3BH,
by Graphycems.

Contents

Preface

Our aim in this book is to provide a comprehensive and detailed, yet readable and accessible, account of the major areas of psychology that are covered in the new AQA (A) Advanced Subsidiary (AS) specification. The book consists of seven chapters, divided into three main sections (Chapters 2–7), plus an introductory chapter (Chapter 1).

Unit 1 (*Cognitive and Developmental Psychology*) comprises Chapter 2 (Human Memory) and 3 (Attachments in Development).

Unit 2 (*Physiological Psychology and Individual Differences*) consists of Chapters 4 (Stress) and 5 (Abnormality).

Unit 3 (*Social Psychology and Research Methods*) comprises Chapters 6 (Social Influence) and 7 (Research Methods).

Whilst the sequence of chapters and much of the content is based on the new AQA (A) specification, we believe that the book will also prove valuable for those studying the AQA (B), OCR, and EDEXCEL specifications.

For each chapter there is an introduction and overview, an end-of-section summary, and a conclusion.

Within each chapter 'Pause for Thought' features are designed both to help students working through the text individually to digest and understand the material, and for use as class discussion points and activities. There are also self-assessment questions, based on the question format used in the examinations (short-answer questions). In Chapters 2–6, these appear at the end of each main section, whilst in Chapter 7 they come at the end of the chapter. The self-assessment questions are designed to assess the student's knowledge and understanding, and also to help revision. The overall approach is designed to be interactive and user-friendly.

For revision purposes, the index contains page numbers in bold which refer to definitions and main explanations of particular concepts for easy reference. Chapters 2–6 also have several website addresses for those who wish to research material further via the Internet.

We won't pretend that psychology is easy, and there is no substitute for hard work. We hope – and believe – that this book will make the task of studying psychology both less arduous and even a little more enjoyable than it would otherwise be. Good luck!

Richard Gross
Rob McIlveen
Hugh Coolican

Acknowledgements

We would like to thank Dave Mackin, Anna Churchman, Celia Robertson and Denise Stewart at GreenGate Publishing for the excellent job they have made of preparing the text. Also, thanks to Greig Aitken for his co-ordination of the project and his helpful, often imaginative, artwork suggestions. Finally, thanks to Tim Gregson-Williams.

PICTURE CREDITS

The publishers would like to thank the following for permission to reproduce photographs and other illustrations in this book:

Page 1, Wide World Photo, Inc.; p.2, (Figs 1.2, 1.3) Corbis-Bettman; p.5, Corbis-Bettman; p.25, Imperial War Museum; p.27, Mirror Syndication; p.30, www.CartoonStock.com; p.33, Telegraph Colour Library/Daniel Allan; p.37, Bubbles/Loisjoy Thurston; p.38 (Figs 3.2, 3.3), Harlow Primate Laboratory, University of Wisconsin; p.39, Science Photo Library; p.46, Associated Press/Topham; p.47, Concord Films Council/Joyce Robertson; p.49, The Ronald Grant Film Archive; p.54 (Fig 3.12), Press Association/Neil Munns; (Fig 3.13) Life File/Nicola Sutton; p.64, from *Psychology in Perspective* by James Hassett. Copyright © 1984 by Harper and Row Publishers, Inc. Reprinted by permision of Addison-Wesley Educational Publishers, Inc.; p.67, Sheila Hayward from *Psychology Review*, 1998, 5 (1) 19; p.73, Press Association/Jim James; p82, Life File/Jeremy Hoare; p.85, Science Photo Library/Sheila Terry; p.86, Northants Press Agency/Steve Nicholson; p.87, Big Pictures/© Jamie Budge; p.89, Press Association/Peter Jordan; p.90, Life File/Nicola Sutton; p.101, Rex Features, London; p.116, Associated Press/Itsuo Inouye; p.119 (Fig 6.6) Pinter & Martin Ltd, HarperCollins Publishers Inc., New York; (Fig 6.7) from the film *Obedience*, copyright © 1965 by Stanley Milgram and distributed by Penn State Media Sales; p.121, from *Psychology* by Zimbardo, P.G. and Weber, Ann L. Reprinted by permission of Prentice-Hall Publishers Inc.; p.125, Associated Press; p.126, from *Psychology and Life* by Zimbardo, P.G. Reprinted by permission of Philip G. Zimbardo, Inc.; p.136, www.CartoonStock.com; p.144, Camera Press/Homer Sykes; p.146, www.CartoonStock.com; p.152, Format/Joanne O'Brien.

Index compiled by Frank Merrett, Cheltenham, Gloucester.

1 An Introduction to Psychology and its Approaches

INTRODUCTION AND OVERVIEW

Clearly, the first chapter in any textbook is intended to 'set the scene' for what follows, and this normally involves defining the subject or discipline. In most disciplines, this is usually a fairly simple task. With psychology, however, it is far from straightforward.

Definitions of psychology have changed frequently during its relatively short history as a separate field of study. This reflects different, and sometimes conflicting, theoretical views regarding the nature of human beings and the most appropriate methods for investigating them. Whilst there have been (and still are) many such theoretical approaches, two of the most important are the *behaviourist* and *psychodynamic*. These, and the *neurobiological* (*biogenic*) and *cognitive* approaches, together form the core of what is commonly referred to as *mainstream* psychology.

Before looking at these approaches in detail, this chapter considers the discipline of psychology as a whole by looking at major areas of academic research and applied psychology.

WHAT IS PSYCHOLOGY?

The word *psychology* derives from the Greek *psyche* (mind, soul or spirit) and *logos* (discourse or study). Literally, then, psychology is the 'study of the mind'. Psychology's emergence as a separate discipline is generally dated at 1879, when Wilhelm Wundt opened the first psychological laboratory at the University of Leipzig in Germany. Wundt and his co-workers attempted to investigate 'the mind' through *introspection* (observing and analysing the structure of their own conscious mental processes). Introspection's aim was to analyse conscious thought into its basic elements, and perception into its constituent sensations, much as chemists analyse compounds into elements. This attempt to identify the structure of conscious thought is called *structuralism*.

Wundt and his co-workers recorded and measured the results of their introspections under controlled conditions, using the same physical surroundings, the same 'stimulus' (such as a clicking metronome), the same verbal instructions to each participant, and so on. This emphasis on measurement and control marked the separation of the 'new psychology' from its parent discipline of philosophy.

For hundreds of years, philosophers discussed 'the mind'. For the first time, scientists (Wundt was actually a physiologist by training) applied some of scientific

Figure 1.1 *Wilhelm Wundt (1832–1920)*

investigation's basic methods to the study of mental processes. This was reflected in James's (1890) definition of psychology as:

> ' ... the Science of Mental Life, both of its phenomena and of their conditions ... The phenomena are such things as we call feelings, desires, cognition, reasoning, decisions and the like'.

However, by the early twentieth century, the validity and usefulness of introspection were being seriously questioned, particularly by an American psychologist, John B. Watson. Watson believed that the results of introspection

Figure 1.2 *William James (1842–1910)*

could never be proved or disproved, since if one person's introspection produced different results from another's, how could we ever decide which was correct? *Objectively*, of course, we cannot, since it is impossible to 'get behind' an introspective report to check its accuracy. Introspection is *subjective*, and only the individual can observe his/her own mental processes.

Consequently, Watson (1913) proposed that psychologists should confine themselves to studying *behaviour*, since only this is measurable and observable by more than one person. Watson's form of psychology was known as *behaviourism*. It largely replaced introspectionism, and advocated that people should be regarded as complex animals, and studied using the same scientific methods as used by chemistry and physics. For Watson, the only way psychology could make any claims to be scientific was to emulate the natural sciences, and adopt its own objective methods. Watson (1919) defined psychology as:

> ' ... that division of Natural Science which takes human behaviour – the doings and sayings, both learned and unlearned – as its subject matter'.

The study of inaccessible, private, mental processes was to have no place in a truly scientific psychology.

Figure 1.3 *John Broadus Watson (1878–1958)*

Behaviourism (in one form or another) remained the dominant force in psychology for the next 40 years or so especially in America. The emphasis on the role of learning (in the form of *conditioning*) was to make that topic one of the central areas of psychological research as a whole (see Box 1.4, pages 5–6).

Box 1.1   Psychoanalytic theory and Gestalt psychology

In 1900, Sigmund Freud, a neurologist living in Vienna, published his *psychoanalytic theory* of personality in which the *unconscious* mind played a crucial role. In parallel with this theory, he developed a form of psychotherapy called psychoanalysis. Freud's theory (which forms the basis of the psychodynamic approach) represented a challenge and a major alternative to behaviourism (see pages 6–7).

A reaction against both structuralism and behaviourism came from the Gestalt school of psychology, which emerged in the 1920s in Austria and Germany. Gestalt psychologists were mainly interested in perception, and believed that perceptions could not be broken down in the way that Wundt proposed and behaviourists advocated for behaviour. Gestalt psychologists identified several 'laws' or principles of perceptual organisation (such as 'the whole is greater than the sum of its parts'), which have made a lasting contribution to our understanding of the perceptual process.

In the late 1950s, many British and American psychologists began looking to the work of computer scientists to try to understand more complex behaviours which, they felt, had been either neglected altogether or greatly oversimplified by learning theory (conditioning). These complex behaviours were what Wundt, James and other early scientific psychologists had called '*mind*' or mental processes. They were now called *cognition* or *cognitive processes*, and refer to all the ways in which we come to know the world around us, (such as perception, attention, memory, problem-solving, language and thinking in general).

Cognitive psychologists see people as *information processors*, and cognitive psychology has been heavily influenced by computer science. Human cognitive processes are compared with the operation of computer programs (the *computer analogy*). Cognitive psychology now forms part of *cognitive science*, which emerged in the late 1970s (see Figure 1.4, page 3).

The influence of both behaviourism and cognitive psychology is reflected in Clark & Miller's (1970) definition of psychology as:

' ... the scientific study of behaviour. Its subject matter includes behavioural processes that are observable, such as gestures, speech and physiological changes, and processes that can only be inferred, such as thoughts and dreams'.

Similarly, Zimbardo (1992) states that:

'*Psychology* is formally defined as the scientific study of the behaviour of individuals and their mental processes ... '.

CLASSIFYING THE WORK OF PSYCHOLOGISTS

Despite behaviourist and cognitive psychology's influence on psychology's general direction in the last 80 years or so, much more goes on within psychology than has been outlined so far. There are other theoretical approaches or orientations, other aspects of human (and non-human) activity that constitute the special focus of study, and different kinds of work that different psychologists do.

A useful, but not hard and fast, distinction is that between the *academic* and *applied* branches of psychology. Academic psychologists carry out research in a particular area, and are attached to a university or research establishment where they will also teach undergraduates and supervise the research of postgraduates. Research is *pure* (done for its own sake and intended, primarily, to increase our knowledge and understanding) and *applied* (aimed at solving a particular problem). Applied research is usually funded by a government institution like the Home Office or the Department of Education and Employment, or by some commercial or industrial institution. The range of topics that may be investigated is as wide as psychology itself, but they can be classified as focusing either on the *processes* or *mechanisms* underlying various aspects of behaviour, or more directly on the *person* (Legge, 1975).

The process approach

This divides into four main areas: *physiological psychology*, *learning*, *cognitive processes* and *comparative psychology* (the study of the behaviour of non-humans).

Physiological psychology

Physiological psychologists are interested in the physical basis of behaviour, how the functions of the nervous system (in particular the brain) and the endocrine (hormonal) system are related to and influence behaviour *and* mental processes. One important area of research in physiological psychology is *stress*. This is discussed in Chapter 4.

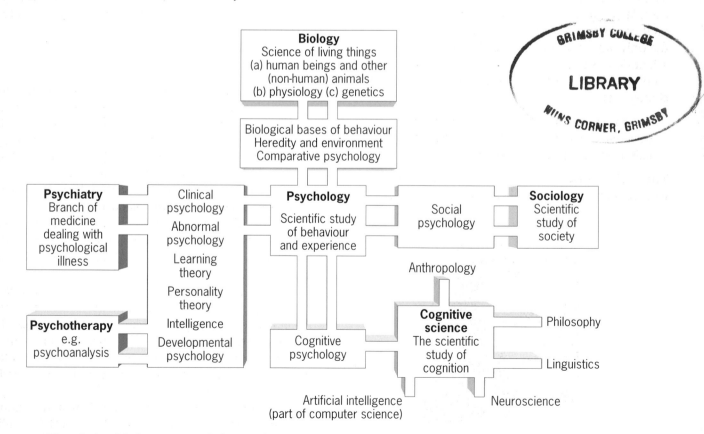

Figure 1.4 *The relationship between psychology and other scientific disciplines*

Cognitive psychology

As was seen on page 2, cognitive (or mental) processes include *attention, memory, perception, language, thinking, problem-solving, reasoning* and *concept-formation* ('higher-order' mental activities). Although these are often studied for their own sake, they may have important practical implications too, such as understanding the memory processes involved in eyewitness testimony. These are discussed in Chapter 2.

The person approach

Developmental psychology

Developmental psychologists study the biological, cognitive, social and emotional changes that occur in people over time. One significant change within developmental psychology during the past 25 years or so is the recognition that development is not confined to childhood and adolescence, but is a lifelong process (the *lifespan approach*). It is now generally accepted that adulthood is a developmental stage, distinct from childhood, adolescence and old age. A major research area in developmental psychology is attachment and, related to this, the impact of early experience. These are discussed in Chapter 3.

Social psychology

Some psychologists would claim that 'all psychology is social psychology' because all behaviour takes place within a social context and, even when we are alone, our behaviour continues to be influenced by others. However, other people usually have a more immediate and direct influence upon us when we are actually in their presence, as in *conformity* and *obedience* which are examined in Chapter 6.

Individual differences

This covers a wide range of topics and issues, including psychological abnormality. There have been many attempts to define abnormality, and each major theoretical approach offers its own explanation of *mental disorders*. In Chapter 5, these explanations are applied to the eating disorders anorexia nervosa and bulimia nervosa. Abnormal psychology is closely linked with clinical psychology, one of the major applied areas of psychology (see below).

Comparing the process and person approaches

In practice, it is very difficult to separate the two approaches, even if it can be done theoretically. However, there are important *relative* differences between them.

Box 1.2   Some important differences between the process and person approaches

- The *process approach* is typically confined to the laboratory (where experiments are the method of choice: see Chapter 7, pages 134–135). It makes far greater experimental use of non-humans, and assumes that psychological processes (particularly learning) are essentially the same in *all* species and that any differences between species are only *quantitative* (differences of degree).

- The *person approach* makes much greater use of field studies (such as observing behaviour in its natural environment) and of non-experimental methods (e.g. correlational studies: see Chapter 7, pages 136–137). Typically, human participants are studied, and it is assumed that there are *qualitative* differences (differences in kind) between humans and non-humans.

Areas of applied psychology

Discussion of the person/process approaches has been largely concerned with the *academic* branch of psychology. Since the various areas of *applied* psychology are all concerned with people, they can be thought of as the applied aspects of the person approach. According to Hartley & Branthwaite (1997), most applied psychologists work in four main areas: *clinical, educational, occupational* and *government* service (such as prison psychologists). Additionally, Coolican (1996) identifies *criminological* (or *forensic*), *sports, health* and *environmental* psychologists. Hartley and Branthwaite argue that the work psychologists do in these different areas has much in common: it is the *subject matter* of their jobs which differs, rather than the skills they employ. Consequently, they consider an applied psychologist to be a person who can deploy specialised skills appropriately in different situations.

Box 1.3   Seven major skills (or roles) used by applied psychologists

- The *psychologist as counsellor*: helping people to talk openly, express their feelings, explore problems more deeply and see these problems from different perspectives. Problems may include school phobia, marriage crises and traumatic experiences (such as being the victim of a hijacking), and the counsellor can adopt a more or less *directive* approach.

- The *psychologist as colleague*: working as a member of a team and bringing a particular perspective to a task, namely drawing attention to the human issues, such as the point of view of the individual end-user (be it a product or a service of some kind).

- The *psychologist as expert*: drawing upon psychologists' specialised knowledge, ideas, theories and practical knowledge to advise on issues ranging from incentive schemes in industry to appearing as an 'expert witness' in a court case.

- The *psychologist as toolmaker*: using and developing appropriate measures and techniques to help in the analysis and assessment of problems. These include questionnaire and interview schedules, computer-based ability and aptitude tests and other *psychometric* tests.

- The *psychologist as detached investigator*: many applied psychologists carry out evaluation studies to assess the evidence for and against a particular point of view. This reflects the view of psychology as an objective science, which should use controlled experimentation whenever possible. The validity of this view is a recurrent theme throughout psychology.

- The *psychologist as theoretician*: theories try to explain observed phenomena, suggesting possible underlying mechanisms or processes. They can suggest where to look for causes and how to design specific studies which will produce evidence for or against a particular point of view. Results from applied psychology can influence theoretical psychology and vice versa.

- The *psychologist as agent for change*: applied psychologists are involved in helping people, institutions and organisations, based on the belief that their work will change people and society for the better. However, some changes are much more controversial than others, such as the use of psychometric tests to determine educational and occupational opportunities and the use of behaviour therapy and modification techniques to change abnormal behaviour (see Gross *et al.*, 2000).

(Based on Hartley & Branthwaite, 2000)

MAJOR THEORETICAL APPROACHES IN PSYCHOLOGY

Different psychologists make different assumptions about what particular aspects of a person are worthy of study, and this helps to determine an underlying model or perspective of what people are like. In turn, this model or perspective determines a view of psychological normality, the nature of development, preferred methods of study, the major cause(s) of abnormality, and the preferred methods and goals of treatment.

As will be seen in the remainder of this chapter, the major approaches include two or more distinguishable theories, but within an approach, they share certain basic principles and assumptions which give them a distinct 'flavour' or identity. The focus here is on the *behaviourist* and *psychodynamic* approaches.

The behaviourist approach

Basic principles and assumptions

As seen on pages 1–2, Watson (1913) revolutionised psychology by rejecting the introspectionist approach and advocating the study of observable behaviour. Only by modelling itself on the natural sciences could psychology legitimately call itself a science. Watson was seeking to transform the very subject matter of psychology (from 'mind' to behaviour), and this is often called *methodological behaviourism*.

In this sense, what was revolutionary when Watson (1913) first delivered his 'behaviourist manifesto' has become almost taken-for-granted, 'orthodox' psychology. It could be argued that *all* psychologists are methodological behaviourists (Blackman, 1980). A central belief in mainstream psychology is the importance of empirical (scientific) methods, especially the experiment, for collecting data about humans (and non-humans), which can be quantified and statistically analysed. Even more influential than Watson, and more extreme in his views, was Skinner.

> **Box 1.4 Basic principles and assumptions made by the behaviourist approach**
>
> - Behaviourists emphasise the role of environmental factors in influencing behaviour, to the near exclusion of innate or inherited factors. This amounts essentially to a focus on learning. The key form of learning is *conditioning*, either *classical* (*Pavlovian* or *respondent*), which formed the basis of Watson's behaviourism, or *operant* (*instrumental*), which is at the centre of Skinner's.

Figure 1.5 *B.F. Skinner (1904–1990)*

- Both types of conditioning are forms of *associative learning*, whereby associations or connections are formed between stimuli and responses that did not exist before learning took place.

- The mechanisms proposed by a theory should be as simple as possible. Behaviourists stress the use of *operational definitions* (defining concepts in terms of observable, measurable events: see Chapter 7).

- The aim of a science of behaviour is to *predict* and *control* behaviour. This raises both *conceptual* questions (about the nature of science) and *ethical* questions (for example, about power and the role of psychologists as agents of change: see Chapter 6).

Theoretical and practical contributions

Behaviourism made a massive contribution to psychology, at least up to the 1950s, and explanations of behaviour in conditioning terms recur throughout the discipline. For example, the interference theory of forgetting (see Chapter 2) is largely couched in stimulus–response terms, and a major theory of attachment formation is based on conditioning principles (see Chapter 3). The behaviourist approach also offers one of the major models of abnormal behaviour (see Chapter 5).

Methodological behaviourism (see page 5) may be regarded as a major influence on the practice of scientific psychology in general. Other, more 'tangible' contributions include:

- *behaviour therapy* and *behaviour modification* (based on *classical* and *operant conditioning* respectively) as major approaches to the treatment of abnormal behaviour and one of the main tools in the clinical psychologist's 'kit bag' (see Box 1.3);

- *biofeedback* as a non-medical treatment for stress-related symptoms, derived from attempts to change rats' autonomic physiological functions through the use of operant techniques (see Chapter 4).

The psychodynamic approach

The term 'psychodynamic' refers to the active forces within the personality that motivate behaviour, in particular, the unconscious conflict between the different structures that compose the whole personality. Whilst Freud's *psychoanalytic theory* was the original psychodynamic theory, the approach includes all those theories based on his ideas, such as those of Jung (1964), Adler (1927) and Erikson (1950).

Basic principles and assumptions

Freud stressed certain key principles as essential to the practice of *psychoanalysis*, the form of psychotherapy he pioneered and from which most others are derived (see below).

Box 1.5	The major principles and assumptions of psychoanalytic theory

- Much of our behaviour is determined by unconscious thoughts, wishes, memories and so on. What we are consciously aware of at any one time represents the tip of an iceberg: most of our thoughts and ideas are either not accessible at that moment (*pre-conscious*) or are totally inaccessible (*unconscious*). These unconscious thoughts and ideas can become conscious through the use of special techniques, such as free association, dream interpretation and transference, the cornerstones of psychoanalysis (see text below and Gross *et al.*, 2000).

- Much of what is unconscious has been made so through repression, whereby threatening or unpleasant experiences are 'forgotten' (see Chapter 2, pages 25–26). They become inaccessible, locked away from our conscious awareness. This is a major form of ego defence (see Chapter 4, page 82, and Chapter 5, page 94).

- According to the *theory of infantile sexuality*, the sexual instinct or drive is active from birth and develops through a series of five psychosexual stages (see Chapter 5, page 94). The most important of these is the *phallic stage* (spanning the ages 3 to 5 or 6), during which all children experience the *Oedipus complex*.

- Related to infantile sexuality is the general impact of early experience on later personality (see Chapter 3). According to Freud (1949):

'It seems that the neuroses are only acquired during early childhood (up to the age of six), even though their symptoms may not make their appearance until much later ... the child is psychologically father of the man and ... the events of its first years are of paramount importance for its whole subsequent life'.

Theoretical and practical contributions

As with behaviourist accounts of conditioning, many of Freud's ideas and concepts have become part of mainstream psychology's vocabulary. You do not have to be a 'Freudian' to use concepts such as 'repression', 'unconscious' and so on, and many of the vast number of studies of different aspects of the theory have been conducted by critics hoping to discredit it (such as Eysenck, 1985; Eysenck & Wilson, 1973, see Box 2.12, pages 25–26).

Like behaviourist theories, Freud's can also be found throughout psychology as a whole. Examples include forgetting (see Chapter 2), attachment (see Chapter 3), and abnormality (see Chapter 5). As noted earlier, Freud's theories have stimulated the development of alternative theories, often resulting from the rejection of some of his fundamental principles and assumptions, but reflecting his influence enough for them to be described as psychodynamic.

The current *psychotherapy* scene is highly diverse, with only a minority using Freudian techniques. However, as Fancher (1996) points out:

> 'Most modern therapists use techniques that were developed either by Freud and his followers or by dissidents in explicit reaction against his theories. Freud remains a dominating figure, for or against whom virtually all therapists feel compelled to take a stand'.

Even Freud's fiercest critics concede his influence, not just within world of psychiatry but in philosophy, literary criticism, history, theology, sociology and art and literature generally. Freudian terminology is commonly used in conversations between therapists well beyond Freudian circles, and his influence is brought daily to therapy sessions as part of the cultural background and experience of nearly every client (see Box 5.7, pages 94–95). As Fancher (1996) notes:

> 'Although always controversial, Freud struck a responsive chord with his basic image of human beings as creatures in conflict, beset by irreconcilable and often unconscious demands from within as well as without. His ideas about repression, the importance of early experience and sexuality, and the inaccessibility of much of human nature to ordinary conscious introspection have become part of the standard Western intellectual currency'.

CONCLUSIONS

Psychology is a diverse discipline. Psychologists investigate a huge range of behaviours and mental or cognitive processes. There is a growing number of applied areas, in which theory and research findings are brought to bear in trying to improve people's lives in various ways. During the course of its life as a separate discipline, definitions of psychology have changed quite fundamentally, reflecting the influence of different theoretical approaches. This chapter has considered the basic principles and assumptions of the behaviourist and psychodynamic approaches, together with their theoretical and practical contributions to the discipline of psychology as a whole.

Summary

- Early psychologists, such as Wundt, attempted to study the mind through **introspection** under controlled conditions, aiming to analyse conscious thought into its basic elements (**structuralism**).

- Watson rejected introspectionism's subjectivity and replaced it with **behaviourism**. Only by regarding people as complex animals, using the methods of natural science and studying observable behaviour, could psychology become a true science.

- **Gestalt** psychologists criticised both structuralism and behaviourism, advocating that 'the whole is greater than the sum of its parts'. Freud's **psychoanalytic theory** was another major alternative to behaviourism.

- Following the **cognitive revolution**, people came to be seen as **information processors**, based on the computer analogy. Cognitive processes, such as perception and memory, became an acceptable part of psychology's subject matter, even though they can only be inferred from behaviour.

- **Academic** psychologists are mainly concerned with conducting either **pure** or **applied research**, which may focus on underlying processes/mechanisms or on the person.

- The **process approach** includes physiological psychology, learning, cognitive processes and comparative psychology, whilst the **person approach** covers developmental and social psychology, and individual differences.

- Whilst the process approach is largely confined to laboratory experiments using non-humans, the person approach makes greater use of field studies and non-experimental methods using humans. The two approaches see species differences as **quantitative** or **qualitative** respectively.

- Most **applied** psychologists work in clinical, educational, occupational or government service, with newer fields including criminological/forensic, sports, health and environmental psychology. Common skills or roles shared by all these practitioners include counsellor, expert, toolmaker, detached investigator, theoretician and agent for change.

- Different theoretical **approaches/perspectives** are based on different models/images of the nature of human beings.

- Watson's **methodological behaviourism** removes mental processes from the science of psychology and focuses on what can be quantified and observed by different researchers.

- The behaviourist approach stresses the role of environmental influences (learning), especially **classical** and **operant conditioning**. Behaviourists also advocate the use of **operational definitions**. Psychology's aim is to **predict** and **control** behaviour.

- Methodological behaviourism has influenced the practice of scientific psychology in general. Other practical contributions include behaviour therapy and modification, and biofeedback.

- The **psychodynamic approach** is based on Freud's **psychoanalytic theory**. Central aspects of Freud's theory are the **unconscious** (especially **repression**), **infantile sexuality** and the **impact of early experience** on later personality. The cornerstones of psychoanalysis are **free association**, **dream interpretation** and **transference**.

- Freud identified five stages of **psychosexual development**, the most important being the **phallic stage**, during which all children experience the **Oedipus complex**. Freud's ideas have become part of mainstream psychology, contributing to our understanding of forgetting, attachment, and abnormality.

- All forms of **psychotherapy** stem directly or indirectly from psychoanalysis. Freud's influence on a wide range of disciplines outside psychology and psychotherapy is undeniable, as is his more general impact on Western culture.

Cognitive
and Developmental
Psychology

2 Human Memory

Reber (1985) identifies three meanings of the word 'memory'. First, it is the mental function of retaining information about events, images, ideas and so on after the original stimuli are no longer present. Second, memory is a hypothesised 'storage system' that holds such information. Third, it is the actual information that has been retained. Whatever meaning we consider, memory clearly plays a central role in all cognitive processes.

This chapter looks at theories and research studies of human memory, particularly those concerned with memory as a 'storage system'. The first part of this chapter examines research into the nature and structure of memory, including the *encoding, capacity* and *duration* of short-term memory (STM) and long-term memory (LTM). It also examines Atkinson & Shiffrin's (1968) *multi-store model* of memory, and Baddeley & Hitch's (1974) *working-memory model* and Craik & Lockhart's (1972) *levels-of-processing approach*, as alternatives to it.

The second part of this chapter is concerned with *forgetting* from STM and LTM, and examines various theories of forgetting, such as *decay, displacement, retrieval failure* and *interference*. It also looks at research into the role of *emotional factors* in forgetting, in particular the nature of *repression* and *flashbulb memories*.

The role of stereotypes and schemas in *reconstructive memory* is also a popular area of theory and research, and has been applied to *eyewitness testimony*. The final part of this chapter examines research into eyewitness testimony and face recognition.

Short-term and Long-term Memory

How is memory measured?

The systematic scientific investigation of memory began with Ebbinghaus (1885). To study memory in its 'purest' form, Ebbinghaus invented three-letter *nonsense syllables* (a consonant followed by a vowel followed by another consonant, such as XUT and JEQ). Ebbinghaus spent several years using only himself as the subject of his research. He read lists of nonsense syllables out loud, and when he felt that he had recited a list sufficiently to retain it, he tested himself.

If Ebbinghaus could recite a list correctly twice in succession, he considered it to be learnt. After recording the time taken to learn a list, he then began another one. After specific periods of time, Ebbinghaus would return to a particular list and try to memorise it again. He calculated the number of attempts (or *trials*) it took him to *relearn* the list, as a percentage of the number of trials it had *originally* taken to learn it. He found that memory declines sharply at first, but then levels off. This finding has been subsequently replicated many times. Ebbinghaus carried out many experiments of

this sort and showed that memory *could* be scientifically investigated under carefully controlled conditions.

PAUSE FOR THOUGHT

In studies conducted between 1883 and 1884, Ebbinghaus *always* tested himself between 1 p.m. and 3 p.m. Why do you think he did this?

By always testing himself during these times, he was trying to rule out time of day as a variable affecting his memory performance.

Other techniques for measuring memory include:

- **Recognition**: This involves deciding whether or not a particular piece of information has been encountered before (as in a multiple-choice test, where the correct answer is presented along with incorrect ones).

- **Recall**: This involves participants actively searching their memory stores in order to retrieve particular information (as in timed essays). This can either be in the order in which it was presented (*serial recall*) or in any order at all (*free recall*).

- **Memory-span procedure**: This is a version of serial recall, in which a person is given a list of unrelated digits or letters and then required to repeat them back immediately in the order in which they were heard. The number of items on the list is successively increased until an error is made. The maximum number of items that can be consistently recalled correctly is a measure of *immediate memory span*.

- **Paired-associates recall**: In this, participants are required to learn a list of paired items (such as 'chair' and 'elephant'). When one of the words (e.g. 'chair') is re-presented, the participant must recall the paired word ('elephant').

Memory as information processing

For some researchers, the best way of understanding memory is in terms of the three basic operations involved in information processing by modern computers: *registration* (or *encoding*), *storage* and *retrieval*. Although researchers do not see human memory operating in *exactly* the same way as a computer, they believe that this approach can help to understand an extremely complex phenomenon.

Box 2.1 The three basic information-processing operations involved in memory

- **Registration** (or **encoding**) involves the transformation of sensory input (such as a sound or visual image) into a form which allows it to be entered into (or registered in) memory. With a computer, for example, information can only be encoded if it is presented in a format the computer recognises.

- **Storage** is the operation of holding or retaining information in memory. Computers store information by means of changes in the system's electrical circuitry. With people, the changes occurring in the brain allow information to be stored, though exactly what these changes involve is unclear.

- **Retrieval** is the process by which stored information is extracted from memory.

Another process is *forgetting*, the inability to recall accurately what was presented. This can occur at the encoding, storage or retrieval stage.

Availability, accessibility and forgetting

Registration is a *necessary* condition for storage. However, it is not *sufficient* (since not everything which registers on the senses is stored). Similarly, storage is a necessary but not sufficient condition for retrieval. So, we can only recover information that has been stored, but the fact that something has been stored is no guarantee that it will be remembered on any particular occasion.

This suggests a distinction between *availability* (whether or not the information is actually stored) and *accessibility* (whether or not it can be retrieved). This distinction is especially relevant to theories of forgetting (see pages 21–27).

THE NATURE OF MEMORY AND THE MULTI-STORE MODEL

James (1890) observed that whilst memory appears to store some information for a lifetime, other information is lost very quickly. James distinguished between two structures or types of memory, which he called *primary* and *secondary memory*. These relate to the psychological *present* and *past* respectively (Eysenck, 1993). Today, what James called primary memory is referred to as *short-term memory*, whilst secondary memory is called *long-term memory*. To these can be added a third, which is known as *sensory memory*.

Box 2.2 Sensory memory

Sights, sounds, and so on are constantly stimulating our senses, but not all this information is important. An efficient memory system would only retain information which was 'significant' in some way. The function of sensory memory (the *sensory register*) is to retain information long enough to enable us to decide whether it is worthy of further processing.

Most of the time we are unaware of sensory memory. However, if someone waves a lighted cigarette in a darkened room, a streak rather than a series of points will be seen. This indicates that an image persists (there is a memory of it) after the stimulus has disappeared.

Since humans have several sensory systems, it is likely that there is a sensory memory for each. Two important examples are:

- **Visual sensory memory** (or *iconic memory*): excitation on the retina of the eye lasts for a few tenths of a second after the stimulus has gone.

- **Auditory sensory memory** (or *echoic memory*): persists for about four seconds and plays a crucial role in speech perception.

Short-term memory (STM)

Probably less than one-hundredth of all the sensory information that strikes the human senses every second reaches consciousness. Of this, only about five per cent is stored permanently (Lloyd *et al.*, 1984). Clearly, if we possessed only sensory memory, our capacity for retaining information would be extremely limited. Information that has not been lost from sensory memory is passed on to *short-term memory*.

The capacity of STM

Miller (1956) showed that most people could store only about seven unrelated *independent* items (numbers, letters, words) or *chunks* of information. However, STM's capacity can be enlarged if separate items of information are *combined* to form a larger piece (or smaller chunks combined to form a larger one).

For example, the sequence 246813579 can be 'chunked' by applying a rule concerning odd and even numbers. Therefore, the amount that can be held in STM depends on the *rules* used to organise the information. For Miller, the capacity of STM is seven plus or minus two *chunks*, rather than individual pieces of information.

Box 2.3   Miller and the concept of chunking

According to Miller, chunking is central to human thought. Our capacity to read and understand is largely based on the chunking of:

- letters into words;
- words into phrases;
- phrases into sentences.

So, STM's ability to deal with vast amounts of information is aided by the chunking of information. However, we cannot do this until certain information in *long-term memory* (LTM) has been activated, and a match made between incoming information and its representation in LTM.

Miller & Selfridge (1950) gave participants 'sentences' of varying lengths which resembled (or approximated to) true English to different degrees, and asked them to recall the words in the order they were presented. The closer a 'sentence' approximated to true English, the better it was

---

recalled. This suggests that knowledge of semantic and grammatical structure (presumably stored in LTM) is used to aid recall from STM.

In a similar study, Bower & Springston (1970) presented one group of American college students with letters that formed familiar acronyms (e.g. fbi, phd, twa, ibm). A second group was presented with the same letters, but in a way that did not form those acronyms (e.g. fb, iph, dtw, aib, m). The first group recalled many more letters than the second group. The pause after 'fbi' and so on allowed the students to 'look up' the material in their mental dictionaries and so encode the letters in one chunk.

Coding in STM

Conrad (1964) presented participants with a list of six consonants (such as BKSJLR), each of which was *seen* for about three-quarters of a second. They were then instructed to *write down* the consonants. Mistakes tended to be related to a letter's *sound*. For example, there were 62 instances of B being mistaken for P, 83 instances of V being mistaken for P, but only two instances of S being mistaken for P. These *acoustic confusion errors* suggested to Conrad that STM must code information according to its sound. When information is presented visually, it must somehow be *transformed* into its acoustic code (see also Baddeley's, 1966, study on page 13.)

Other forms of coding in STM

Shulman (1970) showed participants lists of ten words. Recognition of the words was then tested using a visually presented 'probe word', which was either:

- a *homonym* of one of the words on the list (such as 'bawl' for 'ball'),
- a *synonym* (such as 'talk' for 'speak'), or
- identical to it.

PAUSE FOR THOUGHT

Shulman found that homonym and synonym probes produced *similar* error rates. What does this tell us about the types of coding used in STM?

Shulman's results imply that some *semantic coding* (coding for meaning) had taken place in STM. If an error was made on a synonym probe, some matching for meaning *must* have taken place.

Visual images (such as abstract pictures, which would be difficult to store using an acoustic code) can also be maintained in STM, if only briefly.

The duration of STM

A way of studying 'pure' STM was devised by Brown (1958) and Peterson & Peterson (1959), and is called the Brown–Peterson technique. By repeating something that has to be remembered (*maintenance rehearsal*), information can be held in STM almost indefinitely. The Brown–Peterson technique overcomes this problem.

Box 2.4   The Brown–Peterson technique

In the *Brown–Peterson technique*, participants hear various *trigrams* (such as XPJ). Immediately afterwards, they are instructed to recall what they heard or to count backwards in threes out loud from some specified number for a pre-determined period of time (the *retention interval*). The function of this *distractor task* is to prevent rehearsal. At the end of the time period, participants try to recall the trigram.

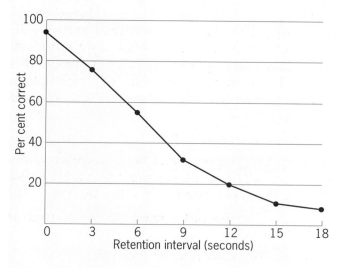

Figure 2.1 *The data reported by Peterson and Peterson in their experiment on the duration of STM*

Peterson and Peterson found that the average percentage of correctly recalled trigrams was high with short delays, but decreased as the delay interval lengthened. It dropped to a mere six per cent after only 18 seconds. In the absence of rehearsal, then, STM's duration is very short and it can be made even shorter if a more difficult distractor task is used.

Long-term memory (LTM)

In discussing STM, two important points have already been made about LTM:

- it forms part of James's (1890) distinction between *primary* and *secondary* memory (see page 11);

- *chunking* can increase STM's capacity by drawing on knowledge already stored in LTM to give meaning to incoming information.

The capacity and duration of LTM

LTM has been depicted as a vast storehouse of information, in which memories are stored in a relatively permanent way. Exactly how much information can be stored in LTM is not known, but most psychologists agree that there is no evidence of any limit to LTM's capacity. In contrast with STM, then, the *capacity* of LTM is far greater, and its *duration* is also considerably longer.

Coding in LTM

With verbal material, coding in LTM appears to be mainly *semantic*. For example, Baddeley (1966) presented participants with words which were either:

- *acoustically similar* (such as 'mad', 'man' and 'mat'),

- *semantically similar* (such as 'big', 'broad' and 'long'),

- *acoustically dissimilar* (such as 'foul', 'old' and 'deep'), or

- *semantically dissimilar* (such as 'pen', 'day' and 'ring').

When recall from STM was tested, acoustically similar words were recalled less well than acoustically dissimilar words. This supports the claim that acoustic coding occurs in STM (see above, page 12) There was a small difference between the number of semantically similar and semantically dissimilar words recalled (64 and 71 per cent respectively). This suggests that whilst *some* semantic coding occurs in STM, it is not dominant.

When an equivalent study was conducted on LTM, fewer semantically similar words were recalled, whilst acoustically similar words had no effect on LTM recall. This suggests that LTM's dominant code is semantic.

Does LTM only use semantic coding?

Findings such as Baddeley's do not imply that LTM *only* uses a semantic code (Baddeley, 1976). Our ability to picture a place we visited on holiday indicates that at least some information is stored or coded *visually*. Also, some types of information in LTM (such as songs) are coded *acoustically*. Smells and tastes are also stored in LTM, suggesting that it is a very *flexible* system, as well as being large and long-lasting.

Table 2.1 *Summary of main differences between STM and LTM*

	Capacity	Duration	Coding
STM	Seven bits of (unrelated) information. Can be increased through *chunking*.	15–30 seconds (unaided). Can be increased by (maintenance) *rehearsal*.	Mainly *acoustic*. Some *semantic*. *Visual* is also possible.
LTM	Unlimited.	From a few seconds to several years (perhaps permanently).	*Semantic, visual, acoustic*, and also *olfactory* (smells) and *gustatory* (tastes). *Very* flexible.

The multi-store model

Atkinson & Shiffrin's (1968, 1971) *multi-store model* of memory (sometimes called the *dual-memory model* because it emphasises STM and LTM) was an attempt to explain

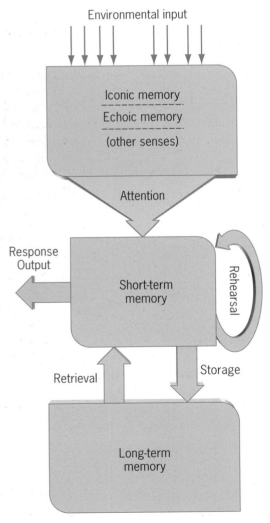

Figure 2.2 *The multi-store/dual-memory model of memory proposed by Atkinson and Shiffrin*

how information flows from one storage system to another. The model sees sensory memory, STM, and LTM as *permanent structural components* of the memory system and built-in features of human information processing. In addition to these structural components, the memory system comprises less permanent *control processes*.

Rehearsal is a key control process with two major functions:

- it acts as a *buffer* between sensory memory and LTM by maintaining incoming information within STM;

- it enables information to be transferred to LTM.

Experimental studies of STM and LTM

Murdock (1962) presented participants with a list of words at a rate of about one per second. They were required to free-recall as many of these as they could. Murdock found that those words at the beginning and end of the list were much more likely to be recalled than those in the middle (the *serial position effect*). The superior recall of the words at the *beginning* is called the *primacy effect*, and the superior recall of the words at the *end* is called the *recency effect*.

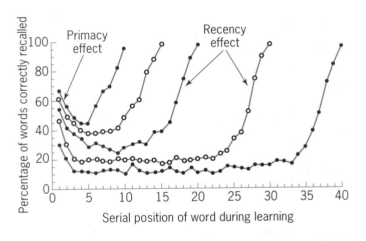

Figure 2.3 *Serial position curves for word lists of different lengths*

PAUSE FOR THOUGHT

Using what you already know about STM, LTM and rehearsal, try to explain:

- the primacy and recency effects;

- why words in the middle of the list are the least well remembered.

The *primacy effect* occurs because the items at the beginning of the list have (presumably) been rehearsed and transferred to LTM, from where they are recalled. The *recency effect* presumably occurs because items currently in STM are recalled from there. Because STM's capacity is limited and can only hold items for a brief period of time, words in the middle are either lost from the system completely or are otherwise unavailable for recall.

In a variation of Murdock's study, Glanzer & Cunitz (1966) delayed recall of a list of words for 30 seconds *and* prevented rehearsal (by using the Brown–Peterson counting task). This resulted in the recency effect disappearing, but the primacy effect remained (see Figure 2.4).

PAUSE FOR THOUGHT

Try to account for Glanzer and Cunitz's findings.

It is likely that the earlier words had been transferred to LTM (from where they were recalled), whilst the most recent words were 'vulnerable' to the counting task (Eysenck, 1993).

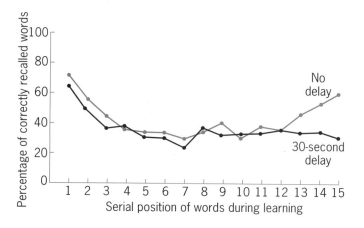

Figure 2.4 *Data from Glanzer and Cunitz's study showing serial position curves after no delay and after a delay of 30 seconds*

Clinical studies of amnesics

Amnesics suffer from memory loss, usually as a result of brain damage. If STM and LTM are distinct and separate storage systems, then certain types of damage should affect only one system whilst leaving the other one intact. For example, chronic alcoholics suffering from *Korsakoff's syndrome* appear to have an intact STM, can hold a normal conversation, and are capable of reading a newspaper. However, the transfer of information to LTM is seriously impaired, and they may have no memory of a conversation taking place or of having read a particular newspaper.

Shallice & Warrington (1970) reported the case of K.F., brain damaged as a result of a motorbike accident. His STM was severely impaired and he could often recall only one or two digits on a digit span test. However, his LTM for events occurring after the accident was normal.

This supports the view that STM and LTM are separate and distinct, and also suggests that information can find its way *directly* into LTM.

The working-memory (WM) model: rethinking STM

In their multi-store model, Atkinson and Shiffrin saw STM as a system for temporarily holding and manipulating information. However, Baddeley & Hitch (1974) criticised the model's concept of a *unitary* STM. Whilst accepting that STM rehearses incoming information for transfer to LTM, they argued that it was much more complex and versatile than a mere 'stopping-off station' for information.

PAUSE FOR THOUGHT

How does Miller & Selfridge's (1950) experiment (described in Box 2.3, see page 12) demonstrate the two-way flow of information between STM and LTM?

Box 2.5   The two-way flow of information between STM and LTM

It is highly unlikely that STM contains only *new* information. It is more likely that information is retrieved from LTM for use in STM. For example, the string of numbers 18561939 may appear to be unrelated. However, they can be 'chunked' into one unit according to the rule 'the years in which Sigmund Freud was born and died'. If we can impose meaning on a string of digits, we must have learned this meaning *previously*, the previously learned rule presumably being stored in LTM. Information has flowed not only from STM to LTM, but also in the opposite direction.

A vivid illustration of this comes from studies of people who are experts in some particular field. De Groot (1966), for example, showed that expert chess players had a phenomenal STM for the positions of chess pieces on a board *provided* they were organised according to the rules of chess. When the pieces were arranged randomly, recall was no better than that of non-chess players. Chess experts use information about the rules of chess, stored in LTM, to aid recall from STM.

Other examples of how 'expertise' can increase STM capacity for information include the observations that:

• avid football supporters can remember match scores more accurately than more casual fans (Morris *et al.*, 1985);

- experienced burglars can remember details of houses seen a few moments before in photographs better than police officers or householders can (Logie *et al.*, 1992).

These examples show that STM is an *active store* used to hold information which is being manipulated. According to Groome *et al.* (1999), working memory (WM) is like the computer screen, a kind of mental workspace where various operations are performed on current data. By contrast, LTM resembles the computer's memory ('storage memory'), which holds large amounts of information in a fairly passive state for possible future retrieval. WM is a cognitive function that:

- helps us keep track of what we are doing or where we are from moment to moment;
- holds information long enough to make a decision, dial a telephone number, or repeat a strange foreign word that we have just heard.

Instead of a single, simple STM, Baddeley & Hitch (1974) proposed a more complex, multi-component WM. This comprises a *central executive*, which is in overall charge, plus sub- or *slave systems*, whose activities are controlled by the central executive. These are the *articulatory* (or *phonological*) *loop* and the *visuo-spatial scratch* (or *sketch*) *pad*.

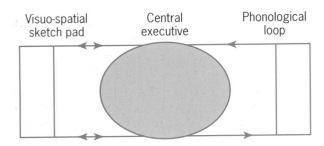

Figure 2.5 *A simplified representation of the working-memory model (from Baddeley, 1997)*

The central executive

This is thought to be involved in many higher mental processes, such as decision-making, problem-solving and making plans. More specifically, it may co-ordinate performance on two separate tasks, and attend selectively to one input whilst inhibiting others (Baddeley, 1996). Although capacity-limited, it is very flexible and can process information in any sense modality (it is *modality-free*). It resembles a *pure attentional system* (Baddeley, 1981).

The articulatory (or phonological) loop

This is probably the most extensively studied component of the model. It was intended to explain the extensive evidence for acoustic coding in STM (Baddeley, 1997). It can be thought of as a verbal rehearsal loop used when, for example, we try to remember a telephone number for a few seconds by saying it silently to ourselves. It is also used to hold words we are preparing to speak aloud. It uses an *articulatory/phonological code*, in which information is represented as it would be *spoken*. For this reason it has been called the *inner voice*.

Its name derives from the finding that its capacity is *not* limited by the number of items it can hold, but by the *length of time* taken to recite them (Baddeley *et al.*, 1975). The faster you recite something into a microphone, the more words you can record on a short loop of recording tape (Groome *et al.*, 1999).

The articulatory loop has two components:

- a *phonological store* capable of holding speech-based information
- an *articulatory control process* based on inner speech.

Whilst memory traces within the store fade after about two seconds, the control process feeds it back into the store (the process underlying silent rehearsal). The control process is also able to convert *written* material into a phonological code, which is then transferred to the phonological store (Baddeley, 1997).

The visuo-spatial scratch (or sketch) pad

This can also rehearse information, but deals with visual and/or spatial information as, for example, when we

Figure 2.6 *The visuo-spatial scratch pad is where we store information about familiar roads, so we know what is round the bend*

drive along a familiar road, approach a bend, and think about the road's spatial layout beyond the bend (Eysenck, 1986). It uses a *visual code*, representing information in the form of its visual features such as size, shape and colour. For this reason, it has been called the *inner eye*.

The scratch pad appears to contain separate visual and spatial components. The *more active spatial component* is involved in movement perception and control of physical actions, whilst the *more passive visual component* is involved in visual pattern recognition (Logie, 1995).

PAUSE FOR THOUGHT

One way of understanding how WM operates can be gained from trying to calculate the number of windows in your house (Baddeley, 1995). Most of us do this by forming a visual image and then either 'looking' at the house from the outside, or taking a 'mental journey' through its various rooms. Complete the following sentences:

To set up and manipulate the image, we need the ____-____ ____ ____, and to sub-vocally count the number of windows we need the ____ ____. The whole operation is organised and run by the ____ ____.

(Answers can be found on page 34.)

Research into WM has often used the *concurrent (interference- or dual-) task method*, in which participants perform two tasks at the same time. Assuming that each slave system's capacity is limited:

- with two tasks making use of the *same* slave system(s), performance on one or both should be *worse* when they are performed together than when they are performed separately (Baddeley *et al.*, 1975);

- if two tasks require *different* slave systems, it should be possible to perform them as well *together* as *separately*.

PAUSE FOR THOUGHT

Some researchers have used *articulatory suppression*, in which the participant rapidly repeats out loud something meaningless (such as 'hi-ya' or 'the').

Explain the reasoning behind the use of articulatory suppression. If this method produces *poorer* performance on another simultaneous task, what can we infer about the slave system involved in the first task?

Articulatory suppression uses up the articulatory loop's resources, so it cannot be used for anything else. If articulatory suppression produces poorer performance on another simultaneous task, then we can infer that this task *also* uses the articulatory loop (Eysenck & Keane, 1995).

An evaluation of the WM model

- It is generally accepted that STM is better seen as a number of relatively independent processing mechanisms than as the multi-store model's single unitary store.

- It is also generally accepted that attentional processes and STM are part of the *same* system, mainly because they are probably used together much of the time in everyday life.

- The idea that any one slave system (such as the phonological loop) may be involved in the performance of apparently very different tasks (such as memory span, mental arithmetic, verbal reasoning and reading) is a valuable insight.

- It has *practical applications* which extend beyond its theoretical importance (Gilhooly, 1996; Logie, 1999: see Box 2.6).

- One weakness of the WM model is that *least* is known about the *most* important component, namely the central executive (Hampson & Morris, 1996). It can apparently carry out an enormous variety of processing activities in different conditions. This makes it difficult to describe its *precise* function, and the idea of a single central executive might be as inappropriate as that of a unitary STM (Eysenck, 1986).

Box 2.6   Working memory and learning to read

One of the most striking features of children with specific problems in learning to read (despite normal intelligence and a supportive family) is their impaired memory span (Gathercole & Baddeley, 1990). They also tend to do rather poorly on tasks which do not test memory directly, such as judging whether words rhyme. These children show some form of phonological deficit that seems to prevent them from learning to read (and which is detectable before they have started to learn). This deficit might be related to the phonological loop.

The levels of processing (LOP) model

Rehearsal and the multi-store model

As noted above (page 14), the multi-store model sees rehearsal as a key control process which helps to transfer information from STM to LTM. Some psychologists have challenged the role of rehearsal in the multi-store model.

Key STUDY
Box 2.7 Craik & Watkins' (1973) experiment

Craik and Watkins asked participants to remember only certain 'critical' words (those beginning with a particular letter) from lists presented either rapidly or slowly. The position of the critical words relative to the others determined the amount of time a particular word spent in STM and the number of potential rehearsals it could receive.

Craik and Watkins found that long-term remembering was unrelated to *either* how long a word had spent in STM *or* the number of explicit or implicit rehearsals it received.

Based on this and later findings, Craik and Watkins distinguished between:

- *maintenance rehearsal*, in which material is rehearsed in the form in which it was presented ('rote'), and
- *elaborative rehearsal* (or *elaboration of encoding*), which elaborates the material in some way (such as by giving it a meaning or linking it with pre-existing knowledge stored in LTM).

Is the amount of rehearsal all that matters?

According to the multi-store model, there is only one kind of rehearsal (what Craik and Watkins call *maintenance* rehearsal), so that what matters is *how much* rehearsal occurs. However, according to Craik & Lockhart (1972), it is the *kind* of rehearsal or processing that is important. Craik and Lockhart also considered that the multi-store model's view of the relationship between *structural components* and *control processes* was, essentially, the wrong way round.

PAUSE FOR THOUGHT

Explain how the multi-store model sees the relationship between structural components and control processes.

The multi-store model sees the structural components (sensory memory, STM and LTM) as fixed, whilst control processes (such as rehearsal) are less permanent. Craik and Lockhart's *levels of processing* (LOP) model *begins* with the proposed control processes. The structural components (the memory system) are what results from the operation of these processes. In other words, memory is a *by-product of perceptual analysis*. This is controlled by the *central processor*, which can analyse a stimulus (such as a word) on various levels:

- at a superficial (or *shallow*) level, the surface features of a stimulus (such as whether the word is in small or capital letters) are processed;
- at an intermediate (*phonemic* or *phonetic*) level, the word is analysed for its sound;
- at a deep (or *semantic*) level, the word's meaning is analysed.

The level at which a stimulus is processed depends on both its nature and the processing time available. The more deeply information is processed, the more likely it is to be retained.

Key STUDY
Box 2.8 Craik & Tulving's (1975) experiment

Craik & Tulving (1975) presented participants with a list of words via a tachistoscope (a device which allows visual stimuli to be flashed onto a screen for very short time intervals). Following each word, participants were asked one of four questions, to which they had to answer 'yes' or 'no'. The four questions were:

1 Is the word (e.g. TABLE/table) in capital letters? (This corresponds to **shallow processing**.)

2 Does the word (e.g. hate/chicken) rhyme with 'wait'? (This corresponds to **phonemic processing**.)

3 Is the word (e.g. cheese/steel) a type of food? (This corresponds to **semantic processing**.)

4 Would the word (e.g. ball/rain) fit in the sentence 'He kicked the ... into the tree'? (This also corresponds to **semantic processing**.)

Later, participants were unexpectedly given a recognition test, in which they had to identify the previously presented words which appeared amongst words they had not seen. There was significantly better recognition of words that had been processed at the deepest (semantic) level (questions 3 and 4). Also, recognition was superior when the answer was 'yes' rather than 'no'.

It has also been found that *elaboration* (the *amount* of processing of a particular kind at a particular level) is important in determining whether material is stored or not. For example, Craik & Tulving (1975) asked participants to decide if a particular (target) word would be appropriate in *simple* sentences (such as 'She cooked the ...') or *complex* sentences (such as 'The great bird swooped down and carried off the struggling ...'). When participants were later given a *cued recall* test, in which the original sentences were again presented but without the target words, recall was much better for those that fitted into the *complex* sentences.

More important than elaboration is *distinctiveness*, which relates to the *nature* of processing. For example, 'A mosquito is like a doctor because they both draw blood' is more distinctive than 'A mosquito is like a racoon because they both have hands, legs and jaws'. Although the former involves less elaboration, it was *more* likely to be remembered (Bransford *et al.*, 1979). However, because level of processing, elaboration and distinctiveness can occur together, it is often difficult to choose between them, and all three may contribute to remembering.

Evaluation of the LOP model

- The model was proposed as a new way of intepreting existing data and to provide a conceptual framework for memory research. Prior to 1972, it was assumed that the same stimulus would typically be processed in a very similar way by all participants on all occasions. The LOP model proposed that perception, attention and memory are *interrelated* processes.

- It is mainly descriptive rather than explanatory (Eysenck & Keane, 1995). In particular, it fails to explain *why* deeper processing leads to better recall.

- It is difficult to define/measure depth *independently* of a person's actual retention score. So, if 'depth' is defined as 'the number of words remembered', and 'the number of words remembered' is taken as a measure of 'depth', this definition of depth is *circular* (what is being defined is part of the definition!). There is no *generally accepted* way of independently assessing depth, which 'places major limits on the power of the levels-of-processing approach' (Baddeley, 1990).

- Some studies have directly contradicted the model. For example, Morris *et al.* (1977) predicted that stored information (deep or shallow) would be remembered only to the extent that it was *relevant* to the memory test used. So, deep or semantic information would be of little use if the memory test involved learning a list of words and later selecting those that *rhymed* with the stored words, whilst shallow rhyme information would be very relevant. The prediction was supported.

Section Summary

- Ebbinghaus began the systematic study of memory, using nonsense syllables. He showed that memory declined very rapidly at first, then levelled off.

- Other techniques for measuring memory include **recognition**, **recall** (serial or free), **memory-span procedure**, and **paired associates** recall.

- According to the **information-processing approach**, memory is best understood in terms of **registration/encoding**, **storage** and **retrieval**. These represent basic operations used by modern computers.

- Registration is necessary (but not sufficient) for storage, which in turn is necessary (but not sufficient) for retrieval. This suggests a distinction between **availability** and **accessibility**.

- James's distinction between **primary** and **secondary memory** corresponds to that between **short-term memory** (STM) and **long-term memory** (LTM). Initially, environmental stimulation is retained by **sensory memory** (the **sensory register**) before being passed on to STM for further processing.

- The limited **capacity** of STM can be increased through **chunking**. However, chunking depends on matching incoming information and its representation in LTM, as demonstrated in Miller and Selfridge's study using approximations to true English.

- **Coding** in STM is mainly **acoustic**, as indicated by **acoustic confusion errors**. However, **semantic** and **visual** coding are also used.

- The **Brown–Peterson technique** shows that STM's **duration** is very short in the absence of rehearsal. However, information can be held in STM almost indefinitely through **maintenance rehearsal**.

- LTM probably has an **unlimited capacity**. It has a much **longer duration** than STM, with memories being stored in a relatively permanent way.

- **Coding** in LTM is mainly **semantic**, but information may also be coded **visually** and **acoustically**. Smells and tastes are also stored in LTM, making it a very **flexible** system.

- Atkinson and Shiffrin's **multi-store/dual-memory model** sees sensory memory, STM and LTM as **permanent structural components** of the memory system. Rehearsal is a **control process**, which acts as a **buffer** between sensory memory and LTM, and helps the **transfer** of information to LTM.

- The **primacy effect** reflects recall from LTM, whilst the **recency effect** reflects recall from STM. Together they comprise the **serial position effect**.

- Clinical studies of **amnesics** suggest that STM and LTM are separate storage systems, as when a patient with an intact STM is unable to transfer information to LTM.

- Baddeley and Hitch's **working-memory (WM) model** rejected the multi-store model's view of STM as unitary. Instead, STM is seen as comprising a **central executive**, which controls the activities of independent **slave systems**, namely the **phonological loop** (inner voice), and **visuo-spatial scratch pad** (inner eye).

- The **concurrent/interference-task method** and **articulatory suppression** can reveal whether different tasks use the same or different slave systems.

- **Practical applications** of the WM model include mental arithmetic and reading. Children who have difficulty learning to read may show some deficit in their phonological loops.

- Craik and Watkins' distinction between **maintenance** and **elaborative rehearsal** implies that it is not the amount but the **kind** of rehearsal or processing that matters.

- According to Craik and Lockhart's **levels of processing (LOP) model**, memory is a **by-product of perceptual analysis**, such that STM and LTM are the **consequences** of the operation of control processes.

- In the LOP model, the **central processor** is capable of analysing information at shallow, phonemic/phonetic, or deep levels. The more deeply information is processed, the more likely it is to be retained. **Semantic processing** represents the **deepest** level.

- **Elaboration** may also influence whether material is stored or not, but this is only a measure of the **amount** of processing. **Distinctiveness**, which relates to the **nature** of processing, is probably more important than elaboration.

- LOP was the first model to propose that perception, attention and memory are **interrelated** processes. However, it cannot explain **why** deeper processing produces better recall, or define/measure depth **independently** of people's actual retention scores (and so is **circular**).

Self-Assessment Questions

1 a Explain what is meant by the terms 'encoding' and 'chunking' in relation to human memory.
(3 marks + 3 marks)

   b Describe **one** research study of memory in amnesics and **one** research study that has investigated coding in STM and/or LTM. *(6 marks + 6 marks)*

   c 'Rehearsal is the key to understanding human memory.'
   To what extent does psychological research support Atkinson and Shiffrin's multi-store model of memory? *(12 marks)*

2 a Explain what is meant by the terms 'maintenance rehearsal' and 'elaborative rehearsal'.
(3 marks + 3 marks)

   b Describe **two** research studies that have investigated the capacity of STM and/or LTM. *(6 marks + 6 marks)*

   c 'Unlike the multi-store model's view of STM as unitary, STM should be seen as comprising several components, which together act like a computer screen or mental workspace.'
   Critically consider Baddeley and Hitch's model of working memory. *(12 marks)*

Forgetting

THEORIES OF FORGETTING FROM STM AND LTM

Forgetting can occur at the encoding, storage or retrieval stages. A crucial distinction was made earlier between *availability* and *accessibility* (see page 11). In terms of the multi-store model, since information must be transferred from STM to LTM for permanent storage, availability mainly concerns STM and the transfer of information from it into LTM. Accessibility (retrievability), however, mainly concerns LTM.

Decay theory

Decay (or *trace decay*) theory tries to explain why forgetting increases with time. Clearly, memories must be stored somewhere, the most obvious place being the brain. Presumably, some sort of structural change (the *engram*) occurs when learning takes place. According to decay theory, metabolic processes occur over time which cause the engram to degrade/break down, unless it is maintained by repetition and rehearsal. This results in the memory contained within it becoming unavailable.

Hebb (1949) argued that whilst learning is taking place, the engram which will eventually be formed is very delicate and liable to disruption (the *active trace*). With learning, it grows stronger until a permanent engram is formed (the *structural trace*) through neuro-chemical and neuroanatomical changes.

Decay in STM and LTM

The active trace corresponds roughly to STM, and, according to decay theory, forgetting from STM is due to disruption of the active trace. Although Hebb did not apply the idea of decay to LTM, other researchers have argued that it can explain LTM forgetting if it is assumed that decay occurs through disuse (hence, *decay through disuse*). So, if certain knowledge or skills are not used or practised for long periods of time, the corresponding engram will eventually decay away (Loftus & Loftus, 1980).

PAUSE FOR THOUGHT

Try to think of examples of skills/knowledge which, contrary to *decay-through-disuse* theory, are *not* lost even after long periods of not being used/practised.

Is forgetting just a matter of time?

Peterson & Peterson's (1959) experiment (see Figure 2.1, page 13) has been taken as evidence for the role of decay in STM forgetting. If decay did occur, then we would expect poorer recall of information with the passage of time, which is exactly what the Petersons reported.

The difficulty with the Petersons' study in particular, and decay theory in general, is that other possible effects need to be excluded before a decay-based account can be accepted. The ideal way to study decay's role in forgetting would be to have people receive information and then do *nothing*, physical or mental, for a period of time. If recall was poorer with the passage of time, it would be reasonable to suggest that decay had occurred. Such an experiment is, of course, impossible. However, Jenkins & Dallenbach (1924) were the first to attempt an *approximation* to it.

Key STUDY

Box 2.9 Jenkins & Dallenbach's (1924) experiment

Participants learnt a list of ten nonsense syllables. Some then went to sleep immediately (approximating the ideal 'do nothing' state), whilst the others continued with their normal activities.

As Figure 2.7 indicates, after intervals of one, two, four or eight hours, all participants were tested for their recall of the syllables. Whilst there was a fairly steady increase in forgetting as the retention interval increased for the 'waking' participants, this was not true for the sleeping participants.

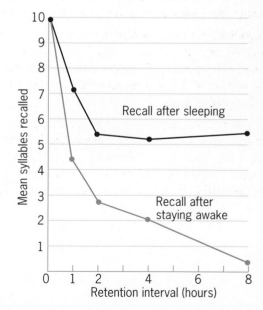

Figure 2.7 *Mean number of syllables recalled by participants in Jenkins and Dallenbach's experiment*

This led Jenkins and Dallenbach to conclude that:

'forgetting is not so much a matter of decay of old impressions and associations as it is a matter of interference, inhibition or obliteration of the old by the new'.

Interference theory is discussed in the text below.

Displacement theory

In a *limited-capacity* STM system, forgetting might occur through displacement. When the system is 'full', the oldest material in it would be displaced ('pushed out') by incoming new material. This possibility was explored by Waugh & Norman (1965) using the *serial probe task*. Participants were presented with 16 digits at the rate of either one or four per second. One of the digits (the 'probe') was then repeated and participants had to say which digit *followed* the probe. Presumably:

- if the probe was one of the digits at the *beginning* of the list, the probability of recalling the digit that followed would be *small*, because later digits would have displaced earlier ones from the system;

- if the probe was presented towards the *end* of the list, the probability of recalling the digit that followed would be *high*, since the last digits to be presented would still be available in STM.

When the number of digits following the probe was small, recall was good, but when it was large, recall was poor. This is consistent with the idea that the earlier digits are replaced by later ones.

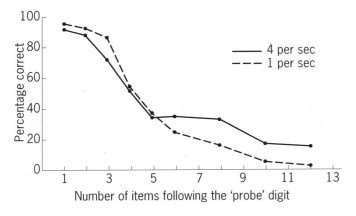

Figure 2.8 *Data from Waugh and Norman's serial probe experiment*

PAUSE FOR THOUGHT

Waugh and Norman also found that recall was generally better with the faster (4 per sec) presentation rate. How does this support decay theory?

Since *less* time had elapsed between presentation of the digits and the probe in the four-per-second condition, there would have been *less* opportunity for those digits to have decayed away. This makes it unclear whether displacement is a process distinct from decay.

Retrieval-failure theory

According to *retrieval-failure theory*, memories cannot be recalled because the correct *retrieval cues* are not being used. The role of retrieval cues is demonstrated by the *tip-of-the-tongue phenomenon*, in which we know that we know something but cannot retrieve it at that particular moment in time (Brown & McNeill, 1966).

Key STUDY

Box 2.10 Brown & McNeill's (1966) 'tip-of-the-tongue' experiment

Brown and McNeill gave participants dictionary definitions of unfamiliar words and asked them to provide the words themselves. Most participants either knew the word or knew that they did not know it.

Some, however, were sure they knew the word but could not recall it (it was on the tip of their tongue). About half could give the word's first letter and the number of syllables, and often offered words which sounded like the word or had a similar meaning. This suggests that the required words were in memory, but the absence of a correct retrieval cue prevented them from being recalled.

Examples of definitions used by Brown and McNeill

1 A small boat used in the harbours and rivers of Japan and China, rowed with a scull from the stern, and often having a sail.

2 Favouritism, especially governmental patronage extended to relatives.

3 The common cavity into which the various ducts of the body open in certain fish, reptiles, birds and mammals.

Answers

1 sampan; 2 nepotism; 3 cloaca.

Tulving & Pearlstone (1966) read participants lists of varying numbers of words (12, 24 or 48) consisting of categories (e.g. animals) of one, two, or four exemplars (e.g. dog) per list, plus the category name. Participants were instructed to try to remember only the exemplars. Half the participants (group 1) free-recalled the words and wrote them down on blank pieces of paper. The other half (group 2) was given the category names.

Group 2 recalled significantly *more* words, especially on the 48-item list. However, when group 1 was given the category names, recall improved.

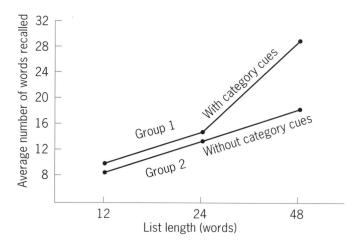

Figure 2.9 *Average number of words recalled with and without cues in Tulving & Pearlstone's (1966) experiment*

Tulving (1968) showed participants a list of words and then asked them to write down as many as they could remember in any order. Later, and without being presented with the list again or seeing the words they had written down previously, participants were asked to recall them. Later still, they were asked a third time to recall the words on the original list.

Table 2.2 *Typical results from Tulving's experiment*

Trial 1	Trial 2	Trial 3
Table	Table	Table
Driver	Escalator	Driver
Escalator	Apple	Escalator
Apple	Railway	Apple
Railway	Pen	Pen
Pen		Fountain

PAUSE FOR THOUGHT

As Table 2.2 shows, the same words were *not* recalled across the three trials. Why is this finding difficult for decay theory to explain?

Decay theory would not predict the recall of a word on trial 3 if it was not recalled on trials 1 or 2. For it to be recalled on a later trial, it could not have decayed away on the earlier trials. However, retrieval-failure theory can explain these findings by arguing that different *retrieval cues* were involved in the three trials.

According to Tulving & Thompson's (1973) *encoding-specificity principle*, recall improves if the same cues are present during recall as during the original learning. Tulving (1974) used the term *cue-dependent forgetting* to refer jointly to *context-dependent* and *state-dependent forgetting*.

Table 2.3 *Cue-dependent forgetting*

Context-dependent forgetting	State-dependent forgetting
Occurs in absence of relevant environmental or contextual variables. These represent *external cues*.	Occurs in absence of relevant psychological or physiological variables. These represent *internal cues*.
• Abernathy (1940): One group had to learn and then recall material in the *same* room, whilst a second group learned and recalled in *different* rooms. The first group's recall was superior.	• Clark *et al.* (1987): Victims' inabilities to recall details of a violent crime may be due at least partly to the fact that recall occurs in a less emotionally aroused state. (See **Critical issue** section on eyewitness testimony.)
• Godden & Baddeley (1975): Divers learned lists of words *either* on land *or* 15 ft under water. Recall was then tested in the same or a different context. Those who learned and recalled in *different* contexts showed a 30 per cent deficit compared with those who learned and recalled in the *same* context.	• McCormick & Mayer (1991): The important link may be between mood and the sort of material being remembered. So, we are more likely to remember happy events when we are feeling happy rather than sad.

According to Baddeley (1995), large effects of context on memory are only found when the contexts in which encoding and retrieval occur are *very different*. Although less marked changes can produce *some* effects, studies (other then Abernathy's) looking at the effects of context on examination performance have *tended* to show few effects. This may be because when we are learning, our surroundings are not a particularly *salient* feature of the situation, unlike our *internal* state (such as our emotional state: see Table 2.3 above).

Interference theory

According to *interference theory*, forgetting is influenced more by what we do before or after learning than by the mere passage of time (see Box 2.9, pages 21–22).

• In *retroactive interference/inhibition* (RI), later learning interferes with the recall of earlier learning. Suppose someone originally learned to drive in a manual car, then learned to drive an automatic car. When returning to a manual, the person might try to drive it as though it was an automatic.

• In *proactive interference/inhibition* (PI), earlier learning interferes with the recall of later learning. Suppose someone learned to drive a car in which the indicator lights are turned on using the stalk on the left of the steering wheel, and the windscreen wipers by the stalk on the right. After passing the driving test, the person then buys a car in which this arrangement is reversed. PI would be shown by the windscreen wipers being activated when the person was about to turn left or right!

Interference theory has been extensively studied in the laboratory using *paired associate lists* (see page 11). The usual procedure for studying interference effects is shown in Figure 2.10.

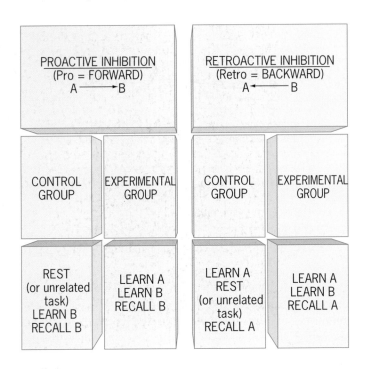

Figure 2.10 *Experimental procedure for investigating retroactive and proactive interference*

Usually, the first member of each pair in list A is the same as in list B, but the second member of each pair is different in the two lists.

• In RI, the learning of the second list interferes with recall of the first list (the interference works *backwards* in time).

• In PI, the learning of the first list interferes with recall of the second list (the interference works *forwards* in time).

Interference theory offers an alternative explanation of Peterson & Peterson's (1959) data (see Box 2.4, page 13). Keppel & Underwood (1962) noted that the Petersons gave two *practice trials*, and were interested in how these practice trials affected those in the actual experiment. Whilst there was no evidence of forgetting on the first trial, there was some on the second and even more on the third.

Although forgetting *can* occur on the first trial (supporting decay theory), Keppel and Underwood's finding that performance did not decline until the second trial suggests that PI was occurring in the Petersons' experiment.

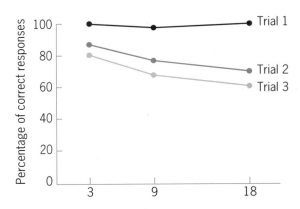

Figure 2.11 *Mean percentage of items correctly recalled on trials 1, 2 and 3 for various delay times (Based on Keppel & Underwoood, 1962)*

Like Keppel and Underwood, Wickens (1972) found that participants became increasingly poor at retaining information in STM on successive trials. However, when the *category* of information was changed, they performed as well as on the first list. So, performance with lists of numbers became poorer over trials, but if the task was changed to lists of letters, it improved. This is called *release from proactive inhibition*.

Limitations of laboratory studies of interference theory

The strongest support for interference theory comes from laboratory studies. However:

• learning in such studies does not occur in the same way as it does in the real world, where learning of potentially interfering material is spaced out over time. In the laboratory, learning is artificially compressed in time, which maximises the likelihood that interference will occur (Baddeley, 1990). Such studies therefore lack *ecological validity*;

• laboratory studies tend to use *nonsense syllables* as the stimulus material. When meaningful material is used, interference is more difficult to demonstrate (Solso, 1995);

• when people have to learn, say, the response 'bell' to the stimulus 'woj', the word 'bell' is not actually learned in the laboratory, since it is already part of people's *semantic memory*. What is being learned (a specific response to a specific stimulus in a specific laboratory situation) is stored in a different type of LTM, namely *episodic memory* (see Box 2.14, page 30). Semantic memory is much more stable and structured than episodic, and so is much more resistant to interference effects (Solso, 1995).

However, in support of interference theory, it is generally agreed that if students have to study more than one subject in the same time frame, they should be as *dissimilar* as possible.

PAUSE FOR THOUGHT

Think of examples of subjects that (a) should definitely *not* be studied together in the same time frame, and (b) *could* be studied together without much risk of interference.

THE ROLE OF EMOTIONAL FACTORS IN FORGETTING

Clearly, memory for past events is affected by their *emotional* significance (Groome *et al.*, 1999), making them either *very difficult to remember* (as in Freud's motivated-forgetting theory) or *'unforgettable'* (as in flashbulb memories).

Motivated-forgetting theory

According to Freud (1901), forgetting is a motivated process rather than a failure of learning or other processes. *Repression* refers to an unconscious process in which certain memories are made inaccessible. Memories which are likely to induce guilt, embarrassment, shame or anxiety are repressed from consciousness as a form of *defence mechanism* (see Chapter 5, page 94).

Box 2.11 A case of repression

Freud (1901) reported the case of a man who continually forgot the line that followed 'with a white sheet', even though he was familiar with the poem it came from. Freud found that the man associated 'white sheet' with the linen sheet that is placed over a corpse. An overweight friend of the man's had recently died from a heart attack, and the man was worried that

---

because he was a little overweight, and his grandfather had died of heart disease, so would he. For Freud, the apparently innocent forgetting of a line of poetry involved the repression of unconscious conflicts over the fear of death.

Traumatic experiences can undoubtedly produce memory disturbances, but there is greater doubt as to whether Freud's explanation is the best one (Anderson, 1995). Evidence based on people receiving treatment for psychological problems provides some support for Freud's theory. For example, *psychogenic amnesia* (amnesia which does *not* have a physiological cause) commonly takes the form of memory loss for events occurring over some specific time-frame (*event-specific amnesia*). It may last for hours or years, although it can disappear as suddenly as it appeared. This is difficult for motivated-forgetting theory to explain.

Figure 2.12 *This shell-shocked World War I soldier illustrates Freud's view of how memory disturbances can be caused by traumatic experiences*

Key STUDY

Box 2.12 Levinger & Clark's (1961) experimental test of Freud's repression hypothesis

Levinger & Clark (1961) looked at the retention of associations to negatively-charged words (such as 'quarrel', 'angry', 'fear') compared with those for neutral words (such as 'window', 'cow', 'tree'). When participants were asked to give immediate free associations to the words (to say exactly what came into their minds), it took them longer to respond to the emotional words. These words also produced higher *galvanic skin responses* (GSR – a measure of emotional arousal).

Immediately after the word association tests had been completed, participants were given the cue words again and asked to try to recall their associations.

They had particular trouble remembering the associations to the *emotionally charged* words. This is exactly what Freud's repression hypothesis predicted, and for some years the study stood as the best experimental demonstration of repression (Parkin, 1993).

However, there are other studies which show that, whilst highly arousing words tend to be poorly recalled when tested immediately, the effect reverses after a delay (Eysenck & Wilson, 1973). If the words are being repressed, this should not happen (they should *stay* repressed), suggesting that *arousal* was the cause of the reversal.

PAUSE FOR THOUGHT

If you were to repeat the Levinger and Clark experiment, what change would you introduce in order to test the 'arousal hypothesis'?

Parkin *et al.* (1982) replicated the original study but added a *delayed recall* condition, in which participants were asked to recall their associations seven days after the original test. The results supported Eysenck and Wilson's interpretation – higher arousal levels inhibit immediate recall but increase longer-term recall. However, later research has not always supported the arousal interpretation and the question of emotional inhibition remains open (Parkin, 1993).

According to Parkin (1993), repressive mechanisms may be beneficial in enabling people with *post-traumatic stress disorder* to adjust. For example, Kaminer & Lavie (1991) found that Holocaust survivors judged to be better adjusted to their experiences were less able to recall their dreams when deliberately woken from rapid eye movement (REM) sleep than those judged to be less well adjusted.

However, when the term 'repression' is used, it does not necessarily imply a strict Freudian interpretation. Instead, Parkin sees the use of the word as simply acknowledging that memory can make part of its contents inaccessible as a means of coping with distressing experiences. Exactly how this happens is unclear.

Recovered memories and false-memory syndrome

One difficulty with accepting *recovered memories* as literal interpretations of past events (such as child sexual abuse) is that they might (supposedly) have happened at a very early age, when experience is not verbalised as it is later on in life (British Psychological Society (BPS), 1995). Very early memories are *implicit* rather than explicit, and are not usually part of our conscious awareness. Therefore, repression is not *necessary* for explaining the 'forgetting' of childhood experiences.

According to Loftus (1997), *false memories* can be constructed by combining actual memories with the content of suggestions from others. This may result in *source confusion*, in which the content and the source become dissociated. However, the fact that false memories *can* be created does not mean that all recovered memories are false. Reconstructive memory and Loftus's research into eye witness testimony are both discussed in the final part of this chapter.

Flashbulb memories

Brown & Kulik (1977) coined the term *flashbulb memory* (FM) to refer to a special kind of *episodic memory* (see Box 2.14, page 30), in which we can supply a vivid and detailed recollection of where we were and what we were doing when we heard about or saw some major public event.

PAUSE FOR THOUGHT

Where were you and what were you doing when you heard of the death of Diana, Princess of Wales?

Key STUDY

Box 2.13 Flashbulb memories (FMs)

Brown & Kulik (1977) asked participants about their memories of various actual or attempted assassinations which had occurred in the previous 15 years, including those of John F. Kennedy, Martin Luther King and Robert Kennedy. They were also asked if they had FMs for more personal shocking events.

Of 80 participants, 73 reported FMs associated with personal shocks, commonly the sudden death of a relative. John F. Kennedy's assassination was recalled most vividly, although other successful or unsuccessful assassinations also produced detailed memories.

Brown and Kulik also found that an FM was more likely if an event was unexpected and of personal relevance. For example, whilst 75 per cent of black participants reported a FM for Martin Luther King's assassination, only 33 per cent of white participants did so.

The FM phenomenon is so called because it as though the brain has recorded an event like the scene caught in the glare of a camera's flashlight. Indeed, Brown & Kulik (1982) have argued that there is a special mechanism in the brain which is triggered by events that are emotionally arousing, unexpected or extremely important. This results in the whole scene becoming 'printed' on the memory.

Figure 2.13 *Eighty-six per cent of British people surveyed had a FM for the resignation of the then Prime Minster Margaret Thatcher 11 months later*

FMs are durable because they are frequently rehearsed and reconsidered after the event. However, the detail of people's memories and their vividness are not necessarily signs of their accuracy. An example of this is a study of recall of the 1989 Hillsborough football disaster when 95 Liverpool supporters were crushed to death at a FA Cup semi-final. Wright (1993) found that five months later participants could remember little and, over time, they were more likely to say they were watching television when the event occurred. According to Wright, people reconstruct events after they have occurred, and such memories may not require a 'special' flashbulb mechanism.

Studies which have failed to find evidence of FMs may have concerned events which lacked personal consequences for the participants. For example, the resignation in 1990 of the then British Prime Minister Margaret Thatcher was likely to have been of some personal consequence for most British people. So, it is not surprising that 86 per cent of a British sample had a FM of this event after 11 months, compared with only 26 per cent of samples from other countries.

Section Summary

- **Decay/trace decay theory** attempts to explain why forgetting increases over time. STM forgetting is due to disruption of the **active trace**, and **decay through disuse** explains LTM forgetting.

- As a test of decay theory, Jenkins and Dallenbach's experiment comes close to the ideal of having people do nothing following learning. However, they concluded that **interference** is more important than the mere passage of time.

- **Displacement theory** is supported by data from Waugh and Norman's **serial probe task**. However, displacement may not be distinct from decay.

- According to **retrieval-failure theory**, memories cannot be recalled because the correct **retrieval cues** are missing. This is demonstrated by the **tip-of-the-tongue phenomenon** and the provision of **category names**. Unlike decay theory, retrieval-failure theory can explain why we are able to recall different items on different occasions.

- **Cue-dependent forgetting** comprises **context-dependent** and **state-dependent forgetting**, which refer to **external** and **internal cues** respectively. Context may have less influence on examination performance than was once thought.

- According to **interference theory**, forgetting is influenced more by what we do before/after learning than by the mere passage of time. **Retroactive interference/inhibition** (RI) works **backwards in time** (later learning affects recall of earlier learning), whilst **proactive interference/inhibition** (RI) works **forwards in time** (earlier learning affects recall of later learning).

- Laboratory studies of interference lack **ecological validity**, and interference is more difficult to demonstrate when material other than nonsense syllables is used. Some types of LTM (such as **episodic**) are more vulnerable to interference effects than others (such as **semantic**).

- According to Freud's **motivated-forgetting theory**, unacceptable memories are made inaccessible through the defence mechanism of **repression**.

- Whilst cases of **psychogenic amnesia** are consistent with Freud's theory, a strictly Freudian interpretation may not be necessary, and experimental support for the repression hypothesis is inconclusive.

- The vividness of **flashbulb memories** (FMs) is no guarantee of their accuracy, and we only have FMs of events which have personal relevance and consequences.

Self-Assessment Questions

3 a Explain what is meant by the terms 'retroactive inhibition/interference' and 'proactive inhibition/interference'. *(3 marks + 3 marks)*

b Describe **one** research study that has investigated decay theory. *(6 marks)*

c Give **two** criticisms of this study. *(6 marks)*

d 'All forgetting can be explained in terms of the effects of later learning on earlier learning or vice versa.'

To what extent does psychological research support the claims of interference theory? *(12 marks)*

4 a Explain what is meant by the terms 'tip-of-the-tongue phenomenon' and 'cue-dependent forgetting'. *(3 marks + 3 marks)*

b Describe **two** research studies that have investigated retrieval-failure theory. *(6 marks + 6 marks)*

c 'All forgetting is motivated forgetting.'

To what extent does psychological research support Freud's theory of repression? *(12 marks)*

Figure 2.14

Critical ISSUE

Eyewitness Testimony

EYEWITNESS TESTIMONY AND RECONSTRUCTIVE MEMORY

The Bartlett 'approach'

As noted earlier (see page 10), Ebbinghaus was the first to study memory systematically, using nonsense syllables. Although this 'tradition' is still popular with today's memory researchers, Ebbinghaus had his critics, notably Bartlett (1932), who argued that:

- Ebbinghaus's use of nonsense syllables excluded 'all that is most central to human memory';

- the study of 'repetition habits' had very little to do with memory in everyday life;

- research should examine people's active search for *meaning*, rather than their passive responses to meaningless stimuli presented by an experimenter.

Although meaningful material is more complex than meaningless material, Bartlett argued that it too could be studied experimentally. One method Bartlett used was *serial reproduction*, in which one person reproduces some material, a second person has to reproduce the first reproduction, a third has to

reproduce the second reproduction and so on, until six or seven reproductions have been made. The method is meant to duplicate, to some extent, the process by which gossip or rumours are spread or legends passed from generation to generation (and may be more familiar as 'Chinese whispers').

One of the most famous pieces of material Bartlett used was *The War of the Ghosts*, a North American folk tale. When used with English participants, who were unfamiliar with its style and content, the story changed in certain characteristic ways as it was re-told.

- It became noticeably *shorter*. After six or seven reproductions, it shrank from 330 to 180 words.

- Despite becoming shorter and details being omitted, the story became *more coherent*. No matter how distorted it became, it remained a story: the participants were interpreting the story as a whole, both listening to it and retelling it.

- It became *more conventional*, retaining only those details which could be easily assimilated to the participants' shared past experiences and cultural backgrounds.

- It became *more clichéd* – any peculiar or individual interpretations tended to be dropped.

Critical ISSUE

Replications of Bartlett's findings

Hunter (1964) used *The War of the Ghosts* and the serial reproduction method. He found similar changes to those originally
reported by Bartlett. However, the use of this folk tale has been
criticised because it is written in an unusual style, making it difficult for Western participants to find connections between
different parts of the story.

Another method used by Bartlett, *repeated reproduction*,
involves the same participants recalling the story on different
occasions. This produced similar results to those obtained
with serial reproduction. Wynn & Logie (1998) used this
alternative method, but instead of *The War of the Ghosts*,
they used a real-life event, namely first-year undergraduates'
recollections of details of their first week at university. They
were asked to recall this information in November, January,
March and May (the students being unaware that this would
happen).

Contrary to Bartlett's findings, Wynn and Logie found that
the accuracy of the descriptions was maintained across the different intervals and regardless of the number of repeated
recalls. This suggests that memories for distinctive events can
be relatively resistant to change over time, even when repeatedly reproduced.

Schemas and reconstructive memory

Bartlett concluded from his findings that *interpretation* plays a
major role in the remembering of stories and past events.
Learning and remembering are both *active processes* involving
'effort after meaning', that is, trying to make the past more logical, coherent and generally 'sensible'. This involves making
inferences or deductions about what *could or should have happened*. We *reconstruct* the past by trying to fit it into our
existing understanding of the world. Unlike a computer's memory, where the output exactly matches the input, human
memory is an 'imaginative reconstruction' of experience.

Bartlett called this existing understanding of the world a
schema. Schemas (or schemata):

- provide us with ready-made expectations which help to
  interpret the flow of information reaching the senses;

- help to make the world more predictable;

- allow us to 'fill in the gaps' when our memories are incom-
  plete;

- can produce significant distortions in memory processes,
  because they have a powerful effect on the way in which
  memories for events are encoded. This happens when new
  information conflicts with existing schemata.

For example, Allport & Postman (1947) showed white participants a picture of two men evidently engaged in an
argument.

Figure 2.15 *The stimulus material used by Allport &
Postman (1947). The two men are engaged in an argument.
The better-dressed man is black, and the white man has a cut-
throat razor in his hand*

After briefly looking at the picture, participants were asked to
describe the scene to someone who had not seen it. This person was then required to describe the scene to another person,
and so on. As this happened, details changed. The most significant change was that the cut-throat razor was reported as
being held by the black man.

PAUSE FOR THOUGHT

a What *method* was involved in Allport and Postman's
   experiment?

b What can you infer about the *schema* that the participants
   were using, which helps account for the distortion that
   took place?

c If the participants had been black, would you expect a similar distortion to have taken place?

d Are these results consistent with Bartlett's theory of
   reconstructive memory? Explain your answer.

Allport and Postman used serial reproduction, as Bartlett had
done in his study using the *War of the Ghosts* story.
Presumably, the white participants used a schema which
included the belief that black men are prone to violence. Black
participants would be expected to have a rather different
schema of black men, making them less likely to distort the
details in the picture. Allport and Postman's findings are consistent with Bartlett's theory of reconstructive memory.

Loftus's research

Bartlett's view of memory as reconstructive is also taken by
Loftus, who has investigated it mainly in relation to *eyewitness*

testimony. Loftus argues that the evidence given by witnesses in court cases is highly unreliable, and this is explained largely by the kind of misleading questions that witnesses are asked. Lawyers are skilled in deliberately asking such questions, as are the police when interrogating suspects and witnesses to a crime or accident.

Loftus has tried to answer questions such as:

- Is eyewitness testimony influenced by people's tendency to reconstruct their memories of events to fit their schemas?

- Can subtle differences in the wording of a question cause witnesses to remember events differently?

- Can witnesses be misled into remembering things that did not actually occur?

How useful are identification parades?

In 1973, the Devlin Committee was established to look at legal cases in England and Wales that had involved an identification parade (or line-up). Of those people prosecuted after being picked out from an identification parade, 82 per cent were convicted. Of the 347 cases in which prosecution occurred when eyewitness testimony was the *only* evidence against the defendant, 74 per cent were convicted (Devlin, 1976).

Figure 2.16 *An identity parade with a difference*

Although eyewitness testimony is regarded as important evidence in legal cases, the reconstructive nature of memory has led some researchers to question its usefulness (e.g. Wells, 1993). The Devlin Committee recommended that the trial judge

be required to instruct the jury that it is not safe to convict on a single eyewitness's testimony *alone*, except in exceptional circumstances (such as where the witness is a close friend or relative, or there is substantial corroborative evidence).

This recommendation is underlined by a famous case of misidentification involving an Australian psychologist. The psychologist in question had appeared in a TV discussion on eyewitness testimony, and was later picked out in an identity parade by a very distraught woman who claimed that he had raped her. The rape had in fact occurred whilst the victim was watching the psychologist on TV. She correctly recognised his face, but not the circumstances!

Eyewitness testimony, episodic memory and semantic memory

Two very different kinds of LTM, which are relevant to understanding eyewitness testimony, are *episodic* memory and *semantic* memory.

Box 2.14 Episodic and semantic memory

Episodic memory (EM) is responsible for storing a record of the events, people, objects and so on which we have personally encountered. This typically includes details about times and places in which things were experienced (for example, knowing that we learned to ride a bike at the age of three). Although EMs have a subjective or 'self-focused' reality, most of them (such as knowing what we had for breakfast) can, at least in theory, be verified by others.

Semantic memory (SM) is our store of general factual knowledge about the world, including concepts, rules and language. It is a 'mental thesaurus', that is, a mental dictionary or encyclopaedia (Tulving, 1972). SM can be used without reference to where and when the knowledge was originally acquired. For example, most people do not remember 'learning to speak'; we 'just know' our native language.

SM can, however, also store information about ourselves, such as the number of sisters and brothers we have. With memories like this, we do not have to remember specific past experiences to retrieve this information. Similarly, much of our SM is built up through past experiences. For example, a 'general knowledge' about computers is built up from past experiences with particular computers (through abstraction and generalisation).

According to Fiske & Taylor (1991), it is easy to see how a witness could confuse the mention of something in a question with its actual presence at the scene of the crime, if that something is commonly found in such situations. For example, a 'leading' question might refer to things that were not actually present at the scene of the crime (stored in EM), but which might well have been (based on our schemas and stereotyped beliefs about the world stored in SM).

Similarly, a witness who examines a preliminary identification parade may later remember having seen one of the suspects before, but fail to distinguish between the identification parade and the scene of the crime – the innocent suspect may be misidentified as the criminal because he/she is *familiar*. This can be taken one stage further back. Several studies have shown that when witnesses view a line-up after having looked at mugshots, they are more likely to identify one of those depicted (regardless of whether that person actually committed the crime) than people who are not shown the mugshot (Memon & Wright, 1999).

These (and the case of the Australian psychologist above) are examples of *source confusion* (or *source misattribution*: see page 32) – you recognise someone but are mistaken about where you know them from! This can have very serious consequences for the person who is misidentified.

Is a mistaken eyewitness better than none?

Using a fictitious case, Loftus (1974) asked students to judge the guilt or innocence of a man accused of robbing a grocer's and murdering the owner and his five-year-old granddaughter. On the evidence presented, only nine of the 50 students considered the man to be guilty.

Other students were presented with the same case, but were also told that one of the shop assistants had testified that the accused was the man who had committed the crimes. Thirty-six of these 50 students judged him to be guilty.

A third group of 50 students was presented with the original evidence and the assistant's eyewitness testimony. However, they were also told that the defence lawyer had *discredited* the assistant: he was shortsighted, had not been wearing his glasses when the crime occurred and so could not possibly have seen the accused's face from where he was standing at the time.

PAUSE FOR THOUGHT

How many students in the third group do you think judged the accused to be guilty?
Explain your answer and say what this tells us about the importance of eyewitness testimony.

In fact, 34 out of 50 thought he was guilty! So, a mistaken witness does seem to be 'better' than no witness. Moreover, *confident* witnesses are more likely to be seen as credible (i.e. accurate) compared with anxious witnesses, even though actual accuracy may not differ (Nolan & Markham, 1998).

Factors influencing eyewitness testimony

- **Race**: Errors are more likely to occur when the suspect and witness are racially different (Brigham & Malpass, 1985). So, we are much better at recognising members of our own racial groups than members of other racial groups. This is reflected in the comment that 'They all look the same to me' when referring to members of different races (*the illusion of outgroup homogeneity*).

- **Clothing**: Witnesses pay more attention to a suspect's clothing than to more stable characteristics, such as height and facial features. It seems that criminals are aware of this, since they change what they wear prior to appearing in a line-up (Brigham & Malpass, 1985).

- **Social influence:** One source of social influence (see Chapter 6) is contact and exchange of information among witnesses. For example, Memon & Wright (1999) describe a study in which participants were asked in pairs whether they had seen several cars in a previous phase of the study. When responding second, people were influenced by the first person's answers. If the first person said s/he did see the car previously, the second person was more likely to say the same, irrespective of whether the car really was previously seen.

- **Misleading questions and suggestibility:** It seems that both adults and children are subject to *reconstructive errors* in recall, particularly when presented with misleading information. In other words, a witness can be highly suggestible. Different types of misleading question include:

  - *leading questions*, as illustrated by Loftus & Palmer's (1974) experiment (see Box 2.15);
  - questions which introduce *after-the-fact information*, as illustrated by Loftus (1975: see Box 2.16).

Key STUDY

Box 2.15 The effect of leading questions (Loftus & Palmer, 1974)

Loftus & Palmer (1974) tested the effect of changing single words in certain critical questions on the judgement of speed. Participants were shown a 30-second videotape of two cars colliding, and were then asked several questions about the collision.

One group was asked 'About how fast were the cars going when they *hit*?' For others, the word 'hit' was replaced by '*smashed*', '*collided*', '*bumped*' or '*contacted*'. These words have very different connotations regarding the speed and force of impact, and this was reflected in the judgements given.

Those who heard the word 'hit' produced an average speed estimate of 34.0 mph. For 'smashed', 'collided', 'bumped' and 'contacted', the average estimates were 40.8, 39.3, 38.1 and 31.8 mph respectively.

Figure 2.17 *Assessments of speeds of crashing vehicles can be influenced by the verb used to describe the impact. Whilst (a) represents 'two cars hitting', (b) represents 'two cars smashing'. Which word is used in a question can influence people's estimates of how fast the cars were travelling at the time of impact.*

What do leading questions actually do?

Loftus and Palmer wanted to know if memory for events actually *changes* as a result of misleading questions, or whether the existing memory is merely *supplemented*. *Memory as reconstruction* implies that memory itself is transformed at the point of retrieval, so that what was originally encoded changes when it is recalled.

To test this, Loftus & Palmer's (1974) study included a follow-up experiment. A week after the original experiment, those participants who had heard the word 'smashed' or 'hit' were asked further questions, one of which was whether they remembered seeing *any broken glass* (even though there was none in the film). If 'smashed' really had influenced participants' memory of the accident as being more serious than it was, then they might also 'remember' details they did not actually see, but which are *consistent with* an accident occurring at high speed (such as broken glass).

Of the 50 'smashed' participants, 16 (32 per cent) reported seeing broken glass. Only seven (14 per cent) of the 50 'hit' participants did so. These results appear to support the *memory-as-reconstruction* explanation.

Similarly, Loftus & Zanni (1975) showed participants a short film of a car accident, after which they answered questions about what they had witnessed. Some were asked if they had seen *a* broken headlight, whilst others were asked if they had seen *the* broken headlight. Those asked about *the* headlight were far more likely to say 'yes' than those asked about *a* headlight.

As with leading questions, *memory as reconstruction* sees questions which provide *misleading new information* about an event becoming integrated with how the event is already represented in memory.

Box 2.16 The effect of 'after-the-event' information (Loftus, 1975)

Participants watched a short film of a car travelling through the countryside. They were all asked the same ten questions about the film, except for one critical question.

- Group A was asked 'How fast was the white sports car going when it passed the 'Stop' sign while travelling along the country road?' (There *was* a 'Stop' sign in the film)

- Group B was asked 'How fast was the white sports car going when it passed the barn while travelling along the country road?' (There was *no* barn)

'The' barn implies that there actually was a barn in the film, which is what makes it misleading.

A week later, all the participants were asked ten new questions about the film. The final question was ''Did you see a barn?''. Of Group A participants, only 2.7 per cent said 'yes', whilst 17.3 per cent of Group B participants said 'yes'.

Suggestibility and source misattribution

As the Loftus studies show, witnesses may come to believe that they actually remember seeing items in an event that in fact have been (falsely) suggested to them. Currently, the most popular explanation for suggestibility effects is *source misattribution*. Witnesses are confusing information obtained *outside* of the context of the witnessed event (*post-event information*) with the witnessed event itself (Memon & Wright, 1999). Memories of details from various sources can be combined with memories of that event ('*memory blending*').

Video-witness testimony: a special case of eyewitness testimony

Now that closed-circuit television (CCTV) is commonplace in shops, banks, and so on, there is an increased chance that an image of a criminal will be captured on videotape. This *seems* to neatly side-step the problems with human face memory. Once a suspect has been apprehended (using some combination of eyewitness and other forensic evidence), the person's identity can readily be confirmed by comparison with the videotape.

According to Bruce (1998), however, things are rather more complicated than this. She cites the case of a prosecution based entirely on the evidence of a CCTV image which showed a young black man robbing a building society. The defence used an expert witness, who helped get the evidence thrown out. Clearly, a CCTV image *alone* might prove very little about a suspect's precise identity.

Face recognition via CCTV is trickier than it looks

Bruce (1998) has investigated face recognition and memory for over 25 years. She had always assumed that people's difficulties in matching two different views, expressions or lightings were due to major changes along these dimensions. Evidence now suggests that rather subtle pictorial differences are difficult for human vision to deal with. Even the more successful computer systems for face recognition have the same difficulties.

The quality of CCTV images can vary considerably:

* Camera and lighting angles may only provide a poorly lit, messy image of the top or back of someone's head.

* Even when the image quality is reasonably high, judging different images as being of the same individual may be remarkably prone to error.

* CCTV images may be most helpful in identifying criminals when the faces captured on tape are of someone known to a witness. People who are highly familiar are easily identified from CCTV images of a quality that would make identification of an unfamiliar face extremely difficult.

Figure 2.18 *Could you identify this person caught on CCTV if asked to pick him out at an identity parade? Research suggests that the answer is 'No', unless you already knew him*

PAUSE FOR THOUGHT

According to Harrower (1998), research clearly shows that most people remember faces poorly and recall details *not* from memory but in terms of what they believe criminals *should* look like. How can this finding be explained?

This is another example of how *schemas* are used to fill in the gaps in memory. It represents another demonstration of reconstructive memory.

An evaluation of Loftus's research

Whilst the evidence described above suggests that eyewitnesses are unreliable, not everyone accepts this conclusion:

* Bekerian & Bowers (1983) have argued that Loftus questions her witnesses in a rather unstructured way. If questions follow the order of events in strict sequence, then witnesses are *not* influenced by the biasing effect of subsequent questions.

* Contrary to the *memory-as-reconstruction* interpretation, Baddeley (1995) believes that the 'Loftus effect' is *not* due to the destruction of the original memory of the event. Rather, it is due to interference with its *retrieval.*

* Loftus herself has acknowledged that when misleading information is 'blatantly incorrect', it has no effects on a witness's memory. For example, Loftus (1979) showed participants colour slides of a man stealing a red purse from a woman's bag. Ninety-eight per cent correctly identified the purse's colour, and when they read a description of the event which referred to a 'brown purse', whilst just two per cent continued to remember it as red.

Loftus's (1979) study suggests that our memory for obviously important information accurately perceived at the time is not easily distorted. This finding has been confirmed by studies involving real (and violent) crimes, such as Yuille & Cutshall's (1986) study of a shooting that occurred outside a gun shop in Canada. Witnesses were interviewed by both the police and the researchers, and a large amount of accurate detail was obtained in both cases. Yuille and Cutshall asked two misleading questions (based on Loftus's '*a* broken headlight'/'*the* broken headlight' technique), but these had no effect on witnesses' recall.

According to Cohen (1993), people are more likely to be misled if:

* the false information they are given concerns *insignificant* details that are not central to the main event;

* the false information is given after a *delay* (when the memory of the event has had time to fade);

* they have no reason to distrust it.

PAUSE FOR THOUGHT

Without looking back at the photograph on page 28 of two men involved in a violent incident, try to answer the following questions:

a What are the two men doing?
b In which hand is one of the men holding a knife?
c Are both men clean-shaven?
d Is there anone else in the picture?
e How would you describe the man who is not holding the knife?

Now look back at the photograph and check your answers.

Section Summary

■ Bartlett was concerned with memory for stories and other meaningful material. He used **serial reproduction** to study **reconstructive memory**, which uses **schemata** to interpret new information. Whilst schemata help to make the world more predictable, they can also distort our memories.

■ Loftus has applied Bartlett's view of memory as reconstructive to the study of **eyewitness testimony**. The unreliability of such testimony has led some to doubt its value as evidence in trials. The Devlin Committee recommended that convictions should not be based on a single eyewitness testimony alone (except in exceptional circumstances).

■ Whilst actual events are stored in **episodic memory** (EM), we may infer additional details from **semantic memory** (SM), thus confusing the mention of something at the scene of a crime in a question with its actual presence at that scene.

■ **Source confusion/misattribution** can account for why suspects may be mistakenly selected from identification parades. A suspect may be familiar from an earlier identification parade or mugshots, rather than from the scene of a crime.

■ Eyewitness testimony appears to be a persuasive source of evidence, even if the witness is **discredited** by the defence lawyer.

■ Eyewitnesses are more likely to misidentify the suspect if their **racial backgrounds** are different, consistent with the **illusion of outgroup homogeneity**.

■ Witnesses pay more attention to a suspect's **clothing** than to more stable characteristics, such as height or facial features. Eyewitness testimony can also be affected by **social influence**, as when hearing what others remember about an event.

■ **Misleading questions** can take the form of either **leading questions** or those which introduce **after-the-fact information**. Both types can induce **reconstructive errors**.

■ Loftus believes that leading questions actually **change** the memory for events, rather than merely **supplementing** the existing memory. Similarly, after-the-fact questions provide misleading new information which becomes integrated with the original memory. This can be explained in terms of **source misattribution/memory blending**.

■ The use of CCTV has not removed the problem of misidentification of suspects. Both humans and computer systems have difficulty dealing with subtle pictorial differences, and the quality of CCTV images can vary considerably. Highly familiar faces are identified most reliably.

■ The influence of misleading questions may be reduced if witnesses are interviewed in a structured way, and the 'Loftus effect' may relate to the **retrieval** of the original memory (rather than to its destruction).

■ Blatantly incorrect information has no effect on a witness's memory, and accurately perceived information is not easily distorted. People are more likely to be misled if the false information is **insignificant**, presented after a **delay**, and **believable**.

Self-Assessment Questions

5 a Explain what is meant by the terms 'serial reproduction' and 'schema'. *(3 marks + 3 marks)*

 b Describe **two** research studies that have investigated eyewitness testimony. *(6 marks + 6 marks)*

 c 'All remembering is reconstruction.'
   To what extent does psychological research support Bartlett's theory of reconstructive memory? *(12 marks)*

6 a Explain what is meant by the terms 'source confusion' and 'episodic memory'. *(3 marks + 3 marks)*

 b Describe **two** research studies that have investigated the influence of misleading questions on eyewitness testimony. *(6 marks + 6 marks)*

 c 'Eyewitness accounts are inherently unreliable and should never be taken at face value.'
   To what extent does psychological research into eyewitness testimony support this claim? *(12 marks)*

Answers to questions on page 17

visuo-spatial scratchpad, articulatory loop, central executive

CONCLUSIONS

This chapter has considered theories and research relating to human memory, especially in the sense of a storage system for holding information. An important theory of the structure of memory is the *multi-store model*, which makes a fundamental distinction between short-term memory (STM) and long-term memory (LTM).

The first part of this chapter examined the *encoding*, *capacity* and *duration* of these two storage systems. It also examined two important alternatives to the multi-store model, namely Baddeley & Hitch's (1974) *working-memory* model and Craik & Lockhart's (1972) *levels-of-processing approach*.

The chapter then discussed theories of *forgetting* from STM and LTM, namely *decay*, *displacement*, *retrieval-failure*, and *interference* theories. Emotional factors in forgetting were also considered, in particular *repression* and *flashbulb memories*.

The final part of this chapter examined research into *eyewitness testimony* and *face recognition*. Much of this research has been conducted from the perspective of *reconstructive memory*.

WEB ADDRESSES

http://www.brainresearch.com/
http://www.yorku.ca/faculty/academic/ecorcos/psy3390/eyem.htm
http://www.psy.jhu.edu/~nightfly/
http://www.memory.uva.nl/
http://www.wm.edu/PSYC/psy201efr/intro_70.htm
http://cogsci.umn.edu/millenium/home.html
http://members.xoom.com/tweety74/memory/index.html
http://www.exploratorium.edu/memory/index.html
http://www.usu.edu/~acaserv/center/pages/mnemonics.html
http://olias.arc.nasa.gov/cognition/tutorials/index.html

Attachments in Development

One important challenge faced by human beings is learning to relate to other people. Normally, the first people with whom the new-born interacts are its parents. In early childhood, relationships are formed with brothers and/or sisters, and other children beyond the immediate family. As social development continues, so the child's network of relationships increases to include teachers, class-mates, neighbours and so on.

This chapter looks at theories and research studies of the development of *attachments* in infancy and early childhood. It also considers the impact of this early experience on later development.

The first part of this chapter describes stages in the development of attachments in infancy. It also examines *individual differences*, including *secure* and *insecure* attachments, and *cross-cultural variations* in attachments. Theories of attachment are then discussed, including Bowlby's influential theory.

The second part of this chapter considers research into both the short-term and long-term effects of *deprivation* (or separation) and *privation*. Bowlby's *maternal-deprivation hypothesis* is discussed, together with challenges and alternatives to it.

The effects of *day care* are a hotly debated issue, both within and outside psychology. The final part of this chapter examines research into the effects of day care on children's *cognitive* (intellectual) and *social* development (their attachments).

The Development and Variety of Attachments

What is sociability?

Sociability refers to one of three dimensions of temperament (the others being *emotionality* and *activity*), which are taken to be present at birth and inherited (Buss & Plomin, 1984). Specifically, sociability is:

- seeking and being especially satisfied by rewards from social interaction;

- preferring to be with others;

- sharing activities with others;

- being responsive to and seeking responsiveness *from* others.

Whilst babies differ in their degree of sociability, it is a general human tendency to want and seek the company of others. As such, sociability can be regarded as a pre-requisite for attachment development: the attraction to *people in general* is necessary for attraction to *particular individuals* (attachment figures). It corresponds to the *pre-attachment* and *indiscriminate attachment* phases of the attachment process (see page 37).

What is attachment?

According to Kagan *et al.* (1978), an attachment is:

'an intense emotional relationship that is specific to two people, that endures over time, and in which prolonged separation from the partner is accompanied by stress and sorrow'.

Whilst this definition applies to attachment formation at any point in the life cycle, our first attachment is crucial for healthy development, since it acts as a *prototype* (or model) for all later relationships. Similarly, although the definition applies to any attachment, the crucial first attachment is usually taken to be the mother–child *relationship*.

Figure 3.1 *This baby is still in the indiscriminate attachment phase and will accept care from strangers*

PHASES IN THE DEVELOPMENT OF ATTACHMENTS

The attachment process can be divided into several *phases* (Schaffer, 1996a):

1 The first (*pre-attachment phase*) lasts until about three months of age. From about six weeks, babies develop an attraction to other human beings in preference to physical aspects of the environment. This is shown through behaviours such as nestling, gurgling and smiling, which are directed to just about anyone (the *social smile*).

2 At about three months, infants begin to discriminate between familiar and unfamiliar people, smiling much more at the former (the social smile has now disappeared). However, they will allow strangers to handle and look after them without becoming noticeably distressed, provided the stranger gives adequate care. This *indiscriminate attachment phase* lasts until around seven months.

3 From about seven or eight months, infants begin to develop specific attachments. This is demonstrated through actively trying to stay close to certain people (particularly the mother) and becoming distressed when separated from them (*separation anxiety*). This *discriminate attachment phase* occurs when an infant can consistently tell the difference between the mother and other people, and has developed *object permanence* (the awareness that things – in this case, the mother – continue to exist even when they cannot be seen).

Also at this time, infants avoid closeness with unfamiliar people and some, though not all, display the *fear-of-strangers response*, which includes crying and/or trying to move away. This response will usually only be triggered when a stranger tries to make direct contact with the baby (rather than when the stranger is just 'there').

4 In the *multiple attachment phase* (from about nine months onwards), strong additional ties are formed with other major caregivers (such as the father, grandparents and siblings) and with non-caregivers (such as other children). Although the fear of strangers response typically weakens, the strongest attachment continues to be with the mother.

THEORIES OF THE ATTACHMENT PROCESS

'Cupboard love' theories

According to *psychoanalytic* accounts, infants become attached to their caregivers (usually the mother) because of the caregiver's ability to satisfy *instinctual needs*. For Freud (1926):

'the reason why the infant in arms wants to perceive the presence of its mother is only because it already knows that she satisfies all its needs without delay'.

Freud believed that healthy attachments are formed when feeding practices satisfy the infant's needs for food, security and oral sexual gratification. Unhealthy attachments occur when infants are *deprived* of food and oral pleasure, or are *overindulged*. Thus, psychoanalytic accounts stress the importance of feeding, especially breast-feeding, and of the *maternal figure*.

The *behaviourist* view of attachment also sees infants as becoming attached to those who satisfy their physiological needs. Infants associate their caregivers (who act as *conditioned* or *secondary reinforcers*) with gratification/satisfaction (food being an *unconditioned* or *primary reinforcer*), and they learn to approach them to have their needs satisfied. This eventually *generalises* into a feeling of security whenever the caregiver is present.

However, both behaviourist and psychoanalytic accounts of attachment as '*cupboard love*' were challenged by Harlow's studies involving rhesus monkeys (e.g. Harlow, 1959; Harlow & Zimmerman, 1959). In the course of studying learning, Harlow separated newborn monkeys from their mothers and raised them in individual cages. Each cage contained a 'baby blanket', and the monkeys became intensely attached to them, showing great distress when they were removed for any reason. This apparent attachment to their blankets, and the display of behaviours comparable to those of infant monkeys actually separated from their mothers, seemed to contradict the view that attachment comes from an association with nourishment.

Box 3.1 The need for contact comfort in rhesus monkeys

To determine whether food or the close comfort of a blanket was more important, Harlow placed infant rhesus monkeys in cages with two 'surrogate (substitute) mothers'. In one experiment, one of the surrogate mothers was made from wire and had a baby bottle attached to 'her'. The other was made from soft and cuddly terry cloth but did not have a bottle attached.

The infants spent most of their time clinging to the cloth mother, even though 'she' provided no nourishment. Harlow concluded from this that monkeys have an unlearned need for *contact comfort*, which is as basic as the need for food.

PAUSE FOR THOUGHT

If the cloth mother had been fitted with a bottle but the wire mother had not, would the baby's preference for the cloth mother still have indicated an unlearned need for contact comfort?

By fitting only the wire mother with a bottle, Harlow was trying to *separate* the two variables (the need for food and the need for something soft and cuddly), so as to assess their relative importance. If the cloth mother had been fitted with a bottle, it would have been impossible to interpret the infants' clinging: was it due to the food or to her being soft and cuddly?

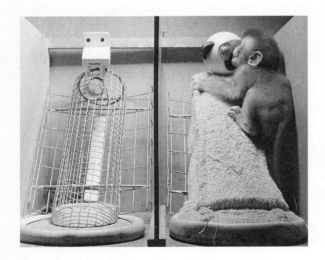

Figure 3.2 *Even when the wire monkey is the sole source of nourishment, infant monkeys show a marked preference for the terry-cloth 'mother'.*

The cloth surrogate also served as a 'secure base' from which the infant could explore its environment. When novel stimuli were placed in the cage, the infant would gradually move away from the 'mother' for initial exploration, often returning to 'her' before exploring further. When 'fear stimuli' (such as an oversized wooden insect or a toy bear loudly beating a drum) were placed in the cage, the infant would cling to the cloth mother for security before exploring the stimuli. However, when they were alone or with the wire surrogate, they would either 'freeze' and cower in fear or run aimlessly around the cage.

Figure 3.3 *Infant monkeys frightened by a novel stimulus (in this case a toy teddy bear banging a drum) retreat to the terry cloth-covered 'mother' rather than to the wire 'mother'.*

Is there more to attachment than contact comfort?

Later research showed that when the cloth 'mother' had other qualities, such as rocking, being warm and feeding, the attachment was even stronger (Harlow & Suomi, 1970). This is similar to what happens when human infants have contact with parents who rock, cuddle and feed them.

Although attachment clearly does not depend on feeding alone, the rhesus monkeys reared exclusively with their cloth 'mothers' failed to develop normally. They became extremely aggressive adults, rarely interacted with other monkeys, made inappropriate sexual responses, and were difficult (if not impossible) to breed. So, in monkeys at least, normal development seems to depend on factors other than having something soft and cuddly to provide comfort. Harlow and

Suomi's research indicates that one of these is *interaction with other members of the species* during the first six months of life. Research on attachment in humans also casts doubt on 'cupboard love' theories.

Figure 3.4 *Lorenz being followed by goslings which had imprinted on him soon after hatching*

Key STUDY

Box 3.2 Schaffer & Emerson's (1964) study of Scottish infants

Sixty infants were followed up at four-weekly intervals throughout their first year, and then again at 18 months. Mothers reported on their infants' behaviour in seven everyday situations involving separations, such as being left alone in a room, with a babysitter, and put to bed at night. For each situation, information was obtained regarding whether the infant protested or not, how much and how regularly it protested, and whose departure elicited it.

Infants were clearly attached to people who did not perform caretaking activities (notably the father). Also, in 39 per cent of cases, the person who usually fed, bathed and changed the infant (typically the mother) was *not* the infant's primary attachment figure.

Schaffer & Emerson (1964) concluded that the two features of a person's behaviour which best predicted whether s/he would become an attachment figure for the infant were:

- responsiveness to the infant's behaviour;
- the total amount of stimulation s/he provided (e.g. talking, touching and playing).

For Schaffer (1971), 'cupboard love' theories of attachment put things the wrong way round. Instead of infants being passive recipients of nutrition (they 'live to eat'), he prefers to see them as active seekers of stimulation (they 'eat to live').

Ethological theories

The term attachment was actually introduced to psychology by *ethologists*. Lorenz (1935) showed that some non-humans form strong bonds with the first moving objects they encounter (usually, but not always, the mother). In *precocial species* (in which the new-born is able to move around and possesses well-developed sense organs), the mobile young animal needs to learn rapidly to recognise its caregivers and to stay close to them. Lorenz called this *imprinting*. Since imprinting occurs simply through perceiving the caregiver without any feeding taking place, it too makes a 'cupboard love' account of attachment seem less valid, at least in goslings.

Box 3.3 Some characteristics of imprinting

- The response of following a moving object indicates that a bond has been formed between the infant and the individual or object on which it has been imprinted.

- Ethologists see imprinting as an example of a *fixed-action pattern*, which occurs in the presence of a species-specific releasing stimulus (or *sign stimulus*).

- Lorenz saw imprinting as unique, because he believed it only occurred during a brief *critical period* of life and, once it had occurred, was irreversible. This is supported by the finding that when animals imprinted on members of other species reach sexual maturity, they may show a sexual preference for members of that species.

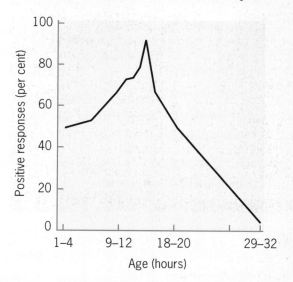

Figure 3.5 *The graph represents the relationship between imprinting and the age (hours after hatching) at which a duckling was exposed to a moving model of a male duck.*

A *critical period* is a restricted time period during which certain events must take place if normal development is to occur (Bornstein, 1989). Lorenz saw imprinting as being genetically 'switched on' and then 'switched off' again at the end of the critical period. However, studies have shown that the critical period can be extended by changing the environment in certain ways. This has led some researchers (e.g. Sluckin, 1965) to propose the existence of a *sensitive period* instead: learning is *most likely* to happen at this time, and will occur most easily, but it *may still occur* at other times. Also, imprinting *can* be reversed (at least in the laboratory).

How relevant are Harlow's and Lorenz's findings with rhesus monkeys and goslings respectively to understanding human attachments?

Most psychologists would agree that the only way to be sure about a particular species is to study *that* species. To *generalise* the findings from rhesus monkeys and goslings to human infants is dangerous (although *less* so in the case of rhesus monkeys). However, Harlow's and Lorenz's findings can *suggest* how attachments are formed in humans. Indeed, Bowlby, whose theory is discussed below, was greatly influenced by ethological theory, especially by Lorenz's concept of imprinting.

Bowlby's theory

This represents the most comprehensive theory of human attachment formation. Bowlby (1969, 1973) argued that because new-born human infants are entirely helpless, they are *genetically programmed* to behave towards their mothers in ways that ensure their survival.

Box 3.4   Species-specific behaviours used by infants to shape and control their caregivers' behaviour

Sucking: Whilst sucking is important for nourishment, not all sucking is nutritive (and so is called *non-nutritive sucking*). Non-nutritive sucking, also seen in non-humans, seems to be an innate tendency which inhibits a new-born's distress. In Western societies, babies are often given 'dummies' (or 'pacifiers') to calm them when they are upset.
Cuddling: Human infants adjust their postures to mould themselves to the contours of the parent's body. The reflexive response that encourages front-to-front contact with the mother plays an important part in reinforcing the caregiver's behaviour (see page 38).
Looking: When parents do not respond to an infant's eye contact, the infant usually shows signs of distress. An infant's looking behaviour, therefore, acts as an invitation to its mother to respond. If she fails to do so, the infant is upset and avoids further visual contact. By contrast, mutual gazing is rewarding for the infant.
Smiling: This seems to be an innate behaviour, since babies can produce smiles shortly after birth. Although the first 'social smile' does not usually occur before six weeks (see page 37), adults view the smiling infant as a 'real person', which they find very rewarding.
Crying: Young infants usually cry only when they are hungry, cold, or in pain, and crying is most effectively ended by picking up and cuddling them. Caregivers who respond quickly during the first three months tend to have babies that cry *less* during the last four months of their first year than infants with unresponsive caregivers (Bell & Ainsworth, 1972).

Bowlby argued that the mother also inherits a genetic blueprint which programmes her to respond to the baby. There is a critical period during which the *synchrony* of action between mother and infant produces an attachment. In Bowlby's (1951) view, mothering is useless for all children if delayed until after two-and-a-half to three years, and for most children if delayed until after twelve months.

Strictly speaking, it is only the child who is attached to the mother, whilst she is *bonded* to the baby. The child's attachment to the mother helps to regulate how far away from the mother the child will move and the amount of fear it will show towards strangers. Generally, attachment behaviours (see Box 3.4) are more evident when the child is distressed, unwell, afraid, in unfamiliar surroundings and so on.

Bowlby believed that infants display a strong innate tendency to become attached to to one particular adult female (not necessarily the natural mother), a tendency he called *monotropy*. This attachment to the mother-figure is *qualitatively* different (different in kind) from any later attachments. For Bowlby (1951):

'mother love in infancy is as important for mental health as are vitamins and proteins for physical health'.

Do you agree with Bowlby that the infant's relationship with the mother is unique, or are men just as capable as women of providing adequate parenting and becoming attachment figures for their young children?

An evaluation of Bowlby's theory

Bowlby's views on monotropy have been criticised. For example, infants and young children display a whole range of attachment behaviours towards a variety of attachment figures other than the mother, that is, the mother is not special in the way the infant shows its attachment to her (Rutter, 1981). Although Bowlby did not deny that children form *multiple attachments*, he saw attachment to the mother as being unique: it is the first to develop and is the strongest of all. However, Schaffer & Emerson's (1964) study (see Box 3.2, page 39) showed that multiple attachments seem to be the rule rather than the exception:

- At about seven months, 29 per cent of infants had already formed several attachments simultaneously (10 per cent had formed five or more).

- At 10 months, 59 per cent had developed more than one attachment.

- By 18 months, 87 per cent had done so (a third had formed five or more).

Although there was usually one particularly strong attachment, most infants showed multiple attachments of varying intensity.

- Only half the 18-month-olds were most strongly attached to the mother.

- Almost a third were most strongly attached to the father.

- About 17 per cent were equally attached to both parents.

What about fathers?

For Bowlby, the father is of no direct emotional significance to the young infant, but only of *indirect* value as an emotional and economic support for the mother. *Evolutionary psychologists* see mothers as having a greater *parental investment* in their offspring, and hence are better prepared for child rearing and attachment (Kenrick, 1994). However, Bowlby's views on fathers as attachment figures are disputed by findings such as those of Schaffer & Emerson (1964).

According to Parke (1981):

'both mother and father are important attachment objects for their infants, but the circumstances that lead to selecting mum or dad may differ'.

Rather than being a poor substitute for a mother, fathers make their own unique contribution to the care and development of infants and young children (at least in two-parent families).

INDIVIDUAL AND CULTURAL VARIATIONS IN ATTACHMENT

A pioneering study of individual differences in children's attachment to their mothers was conducted by Ainsworth (1967) in Uganda.

Key STUDY

Box 3.5 Ainsworth's (1967) Ganda project

Ainsworth studied 28 unweaned babies from several villages near Kampala, Uganda. At the beginning of the study, the babies ranged from 15 weeks to two years and they were observed every two weeks, for two hours at a time, over a nine-month period. Visits took place in the family living-room, where Ugandan women generally entertain in the afternoon. The mothers were interviewed (with the help of an interpreter), and naturalistic observations (see chapter 7) were made of the occurrence of specific attachment-related behaviours.

Ainsworth was particularly interested in *individual differences* between mother–child pairs regarding the quality of their attachment relationships. To tap into these differences, she devised various rating scales. The most important of these in terms of her future research was a scale for evaluating *maternal sensitivity* to the baby's signals.

Individual differences among babies were assessed by classifying them into three groups: securely attached, insecurely attached, and the not-yet-attached. These infant classifications were significantly correlated with ratings of the mothers' sensitivity (based purely on interview data) and the amount of holding by the mother (based on observation).

Ainsworth replicated her Ugandan study in Baltimore, USA (Ainsworth *et al.*, 1971; 1978). Van Ijzendoorn & Schuengel (1999) describe the Baltimore study as the most important study in the history of attachment research. Like the earlier study, both interviews and naturalistic observation were used, but the latter now played a much greater role.

Also like the Ganda project, the Baltimore study was *longitudinal*: 26 mother–infant pairs were visited at home every three to four weeks, each visit lasting three to four hours, for the first year of the baby's life. In order to make sense of the enormous amount of data collected for each pair (72 hours worth), there needed to be an external criterion measure (some standard against which to compare the observations), and what was chosen was the *Strange Situation*.

The Strange Situation had been devised earlier by Ainsworth & Wittig (1969). They wanted to study how the baby's tendencies towards attachment and exploration interact under conditions of low and high stress. They believed that the balance between these two systems could be observed more easily in an *unfamiliar* environment. In the Baltimore study, the Strange

Mother   Stranger   **Figure 3.6**

Table 3.1 *The eight episodes in the 'Strange Situation'*

Episode	Persons present	Duration	Brief description
1	Mother, baby and observer	30 seconds	Observer introduces mother and baby to experimental room, then leaves.
2	Mother and baby	3 minutes	Mother is non-participant while baby explores; if necessary, play is stimulated after two minutes.
3	Stranger, mother and baby	3 minutes	Stranger enters. First minute: stranger silent. Second minute: stranger converses with mother. Third minute: stranger approaches baby. After three minutes, mother leaves unobtrusively.
4	Stranger and baby	3 minutes or less*	First separation episode. Stranger's behaviour is geared to that of baby.
5	Mother and baby	3 minutes or more**	First reunion episode. Stranger leaves. Mother greets and/or comforts baby, then tries to settle the baby again in play. Mother then leaves, saying 'bye-bye'.
6	Baby alone	3 minutes or less	Second separation episode.
7	Stranger and baby	3 minutes or less	Continuation of second separation. Stranger enters and gears her behaviour to that of baby.
8	Mother and baby	3 minutes	Second reunion episode. Mother enters, greets baby, then picks up baby. Meanwhile, stranger leaves unobtrusively.

* Episode is ended early if the baby is unduly distressed.
** Episode is prolonged if more time is required for the baby to become reinvolved in play.
(Based on Ainsworth *et al.*, 1978, and Krebs & Blackman, 1988)

Situation was modified to enable infant and maternal *behaviour patterns* to be classified.

Group data confirmed that babies explored the playroom and toys more vigorously in the mothers' presence than after the stranger entered or while the mothers were absent. However, Ainsworth was particularly fascinated by the unexpected variety of infants' *reunion behaviours* (how they reacted to the mothers' return). Both the expected and unexpected behaviour are built into the classification system (see Table 3.2, page 43).

Although every aspect of the participants' reactions is observed and videotaped, what is most carefully attended to is the child's response to the mother's return. This provides a clearer picture of the state of attachment than even the response to separation itself (Marrone, 1998).

The crucial feature determining the quality of attachment is the mother's *sensitivity*. The sensitive mother sees things from her baby's perspective, correctly interprets its signals, responds to its needs, and is accepting, co-operative and accessible. By contrast, the insensitive mother interacts almost exclusively in terms of her own wishes, moods and activities. According to Ainsworth *et al.*, sensitive mothers tend to have babies who are *securely attached*, whereas insensitive mothers have *insecurely attached* babies (either *anxious–avoidant/detached* or *anxious–resistant/ambivalent*).

Although both the Uganda and Baltimore studies provided support for the idea that parental sensitivity is the key factor in attachment development, both used rather small samples and were promising explorations into the roots of early differences in attachment. During the past 20 years or so, several studies with larger samples have tested, and supported, the original claim that parental sensitivity actually *causes* attachment security (van Ijzendoorn & Schuengel, 1999).

Table 3.2 *Behaviour associated with three types of attachment in one-year-olds using the 'Strange Situation'*

Category	Name	Sample (%)
Type A	Anxious–avoidant	15

Typical behaviour: Baby largely ignores mother, because of *indifference* towards her. Play is little affected by whether she is present or absent. No or few signs of distress when mother leaves, and actively ignores or avoids her on her return. *Distress is caused by being alone*, rather than being left by the mother. Can be as easily comforted by the stranger as by the mother. In fact, *both adults are treated in a very similar way.*

Type B	Securely attached	70

Typical behaviour: Baby plays happily whilst the mother is present, whether the stranger is present or not. Mother is largely 'ignored', because she can be trusted to be there if needed. Clearly distressed when the mother leaves, and play is considerably reduced. Seeks immediate contact with mother on her return, is quickly calmed down in her arms, and resumes play. The *distress is caused by the mother's absence*, not being alone. Although the stranger can provide some comfort, *she and the mother are treated very differently.*

Type C	Anxious–resistant	15

Typical behaviour: Baby is fussy and wary whilst the mother is present. Cries a lot more than types A and B and *has difficulty using mother as a safe base.* Very distressed when mother leaves, seeks contact with her on her return, but simultaneously shows anger and resists contact (may approach her and reach out to be picked up, then struggles to get down again). This demonstrates the baby's *ambivalence* towards her. Does not return readily to play. *Actively resists stranger's efforts to make contact.*

Evaluating the Strange Situation

When the family's living conditions do not change, the children's attachment patterns also remain fairly constant, both in the short-term (six months: Waters, 1978) and the long-term (up to five years: Main *et al.*, 1985). This is commonly interpreted as reflecting a fixed characteristic of the child, such as temperament (see page 36). However:

• Vaughn *et al.* (1980) showed that attachment type may change depending on variations in the family's circumstances. Children of single parents living in poverty were studied at 12 and 18 months. Significantly, 38 per cent were classified differently on the two occasions, reflecting changes in the families' circumstances, par-

ticularly changes in accommodation and the mothers' degree of stress. This suggests that attachment types are *not* necessarily permanent characteristics.

• Patterns of attachment to mothers and fathers are *independent*, so that the same child might be securely attached to the mother, but insecurely attached to the father (Main & Weston, 1981). This shows that attachment patterns derived from the Strange Situation reflect *qualities of distinct relationships*, rather than characteristics of the child. If temperament, for example, were the main cause of attachment classification, the same child should develop the same kind of attachment pattern to both parents (van Ijzendoorn & De Wolff, 1997).

• According to Main (1991), there is a fourth attachment type, namely *insecure–disorganised/disoriented* (Type D). This refers to a baby that acts as if afraid of the attachment figure (as well as the environment). Fear usually *increases* attachment behaviour, which includes seeking closer proximity to the attachment figure. However, since the attachment figure is itself a source of fear, the infant faces a conflict between seeking and avoiding closeness to the attachment figure.

Key **STUDY**

Box 3.6 Cross-cultural studies of attachment using the Strange Situation

Cross-cultural studies have also revealed important differences, both within and between cultures. van Ijzendoorn & Kroonenberg (1988) carried out a major review of 32 worldwide studies involving eight countries and over 2000 infants, and reached three main conclusions:

1 There are marked differences *within* cultures in the distribution of types A, B and C. For example, in one of two Japanese studies, there was a complete absence of type A but a high proportion of type C, whilst the other study was much more consistent with Ainsworth *et al.*'s findings.

2 The overall worldwide pattern, and that for the USA, was similar to the Ainsworth *et al.* 'standard' pattern. However, within the USA there was considerable variation between samples.

3 There seems to be a pattern of cross-cultural differences, such that whilst type B is the most common, type A is relatively more common in Western European countries and type C is relatively more common in Israel and Japan.

How can we account for these differences? As far as 3 is concerned, Japanese children are rarely separated from their mothers, so that the departure of the mother is the most upsetting episode in the Strange Situation. For children raised on Israeli kibbutzim (small, close-knit groups), the entrance of a stranger was the main source of distress.

Whilst the Strange Situation is the most widely used method for assessing infant attachment to a caregiver (Melhuish, 1993), Lamb *et al.* (1985) have criticised it for:

- being highly artificial;
- being extremely limited in terms of the amount of information that is actually gathered;
- failing to take account of the mother's behaviour.

PAUSE FOR THOUGHT

How could the Strange Situation be criticised on *ethical* grounds?

As noted previously (see page 41), the Strange Situation is designed to see how young children react to stress, with the stranger becoming more intrusive over the course of the eight episodes. According to Marrone (1998), although the Strange Situation has been criticised for being stressful, it has also been argued that it is modelled on common, everyday experiences: mothers do leave their children for brief periods of time in different settings, and often with strangers, such as baby-sitters. However, *deliberately* exposing children to stress as part of a psychological study is very different from what happens in the course of normal, everyday life (see Chapter 6, pages 128–132).

Section Summary

- **Sociability**, the general human tendency to seek the company of others, is necessary for the development of **attachments**, which are intense, enduring emotional ties to specific people. The crucial first attachment usually involves the mother–child relationship, which is taken as a model for all later relationships.

- The attachment process can be divided into several phases: **pre-attachment**, **indiscriminate attachment**, **discriminate attachment**, and **multiple attachment**.

- The development of specific attachments is shown through **separation anxiety**, and depends on the baby's ability to distinguish between the mother and other people, and the development of **object permanence**. Some babies also display the **fear of strangers response**.

- According to **cupboard love theories**, such as Freud's **psychoanalytic** theory and **behaviourist** accounts, attachments are learned through satisfaction of the baby's need for food.

- Harlow's studies of isolated baby rhesus monkeys showed that they have an unlearned need for **contact comfort**. Even when the cloth mother provided no food, the baby used her as a 'secure base' from which to explore unfamiliar and frightening stimuli.

- Although attachment is not entirely dependent on feeding, the social and sexual behaviour of isolated rhesus monkeys failed to develop normally. **Interaction with other members of the species** during the first six months is essential.

- Schaffer and Emerson found that not only were infants attached to people who did not perform caretaking activities, but those who did were not always their primary attachment figures. Important predictors of attachment are **responsiveness** to the infant and total amount of **stimulation** provided.

- According to **ethologists** such as Lorenz, **imprinting** is a **fixed-action pattern**, which only occurs during a brief **critical period** and is **irreversible**. However, 'sensitive period' may be a more accurate term, and imprinting can be reversed.

- According to Bowlby, new-born humans are **genetically programmed** to behave towards their mothers in ways that ensure their survival, such as **sucking**, **cuddling**, **looking**, **smiling** and **crying**.

- There is a critical period for attachment development, and attachment to the mother-figure is **qualitatively** different from other attachments. It is based on **monotropy**.

- **Multiple attachments** seem to be the rule rather than the exception, with fathers being of more direct emotional significance to the infant than Bowlby believed.

- The **Strange Situation** is used to classify the baby's basic attachment to the mother: **anxious–avoidant (type A)**, **securely attached (type B)**, or **anxious–resistant (type C)**.

- The **anxious–avoidant** baby is indifferent towards the mother, treating her and the stranger in a very similar way. The *securely attached* baby is distressed by the mother's absence and treats the two adults very differently. The **anxious–resistant** baby has difficulty using the mother as a safe base and shows ambivalence towards her.

- The crucial feature determining the quality of attachment is the mother's **sensitivity**. Sensitive mothers tend to have **securely attached** babies, whereas insensitive mothers have **insecurely attached** babies (either anxious–avoidant or anxious–resistant).

■ Patterns of attachment to mothers and fathers are **independent**, showing that attachment patterns are not characteristics of the child but reflect **qualities of distinct relationships**. Attachment type may change depending on variations in the family's circumstances. Main identified **disorganised/disoriented** attachment (**type D**).

■ van Ijzendoorn and Kroonenberg's review of **cross-cultural studies** found that whilst type B is the most common across a wide range of cultures, type A is relatively more common in Western Europe, and type C in Israel and Japan.

■ The Strange Situation has been criticised for its artificiality, the limited amount of information actually gathered (especially regarding the mother's behaviour), and the increasing stress the infants are exposed to.

Self-Assessment Questions

1 a Explain what is meant by the terms 'sociability' and 'attachment'. *(3 marks + 3 marks)*

  b Describe **two** research studies that appear to contradict *cupboard love* theories of attachment.
(6 marks + 6 marks)

  c 'Mother love in infancy is as important for mental health as are vitamins and proteins for physical health.' (Bowlby, 1951)

  To what extent has research supported Bowlby's claim that the child's attachment to the mother is unique? *(12 marks)*

2 a Explain what is meant by the terms 'securely attached' and 'anxious–avoidant'. *(3 marks + 3 marks)*

  b Describe **two** research studies that have investigated **either** individual differences **or** cross-cultural differences in the development of attachments. *(6 marks + 6 marks)*

  c 'The best way to investigate young children's attachment patterns is to observe how they react to reunion with their mother in an unfamiliar situation.'

  Critically consider the use of the Strange Situation as a method for studying young children's attachments. *(12 marks)*

Deprivation and Privation

BOWLBY'S MATERNAL-DEPRIVATION HYPOTHESIS

As noted earlier, Bowlby argued for the existence of a *critical period* in attachment formation. This, along with his theory of *monotropy* (see page 40), led him to claim that mother–infant attachment could not be broken in the first few years of life without serious and permanent damage to social, emotional and intellectual development. For Bowlby (1951):

'an infant and young child should experience a warm, intimate and continuous relationship with his mother (or permanent mother figure) in which both find satisfaction and enjoyment'.

Bowlby's *maternal-deprivation hypothesis* was based largely on studies conducted in the 1930s and 1940s of children brought up in residential nurseries and other large institutions (such as orphanages).

Key STUDY

Box 3.7 Some early research findings on the effects of institutionalisation

Goldfarb (1943): Fifteen children raised in institutions from about six months until three-and-a-half years of age were matched with 15 children who had gone straight from their mothers to foster homes. The institutionalised children lived in almost complete social isolation during their first year. The matching was based on genetic factors and mothers' education and occupational status.

At age three, the institutionalised group was behind the fostered group on measures of abstract thinking, social maturity, rule-following and sociability. Between ten and 14, the institutionalised group continued to perform more poorly on the various tests, and their average IQs (intelligence quotients) were 72 and 95 respectively.

PAUSE FOR THOUGHT

Note that the children were *not* assigned randomly to the two 'conditions' (as would happen in a true experiment). So, how was the decision made? Try to identifiy characteristics of the children which might have determined whether they were fostered or kept in the institution, and how this might have accounted for the results.

Those who appeared to be brighter or more easygoing, more sociable and healthy, were more likely to have been fostered. In this case, the differences in development of the two groups might have been due to these initial characteristics. However, Goldfarb concluded that *all* the institutionalised children's poorer abilities were due to the time spent in the institutions.

Spitz (1945, 1946) and **Spitz & Wolf (1946)**: Spitz found that in some very poor South American orphanages, overworked and untrained staff rarely talked to the infants, hardly ever picked them up even for feeding, gave them no affection and provided no toys. The orphans displayed *anaclitic depression* (a reaction to the loss of a love object). This involves symptoms such as apprehension, sadness, weepiness, withdrawal, loss of appetite, refusal to eat, loss of weight, inability to sleep, and developmental retardation. It is similar to *hospitalism*.

After three months of unbroken deprivation, recovery was rarely, if ever, complete. In their study of 91 orphanage infants in the USA and Canada, Spitz and Wolf found that over one-third died before their first birthday, despite good nutrition and medical care.

Interpreting the findings from studies of institutions

Bowlby, Goldfarb, Spitz and Wolf explained the harmful effects of growing up in an institution in terms of what Bowlby called *maternal deprivation*. In doing so, they failed to:

- recognise that the *understimulating nature* of the institutional environment, as well as (or instead of) the absence of maternal care, could be responsible for the effects they observed;
- disentangle the different *types* of deprivation and the different kinds of retardation produced (Rutter, 1981);
- distinguish between the effects of deprivation and privation. Strictly, *deprivation* ('de-privation') refers to the *loss*, through separation, of the maternal attachment figure (which assumes that an attachment with her has already taken place). Privation refers to the *absence* of an attachment figure (there has been no opportunity to form an attachment in the first place: Rutter, 1981).

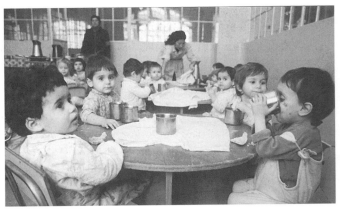

Figure 3.7 *Children raised in large institutions are not only denied the opportunity of forming attachments with mother-figures but also experience poor, unstimulating environments that are associated with learning difficulties and retarded linguistic development*

Poor, unstimulating environments are generally associated with learning difficulties and retarded language development. Language development is crucial for overall intellectual development. Hence, a crucial variable in intellectual development is the amount of *intellectual stimulation* a child receives, *not* the amount of mothering.

Deprivation *vs* privation

The studies described in Box 3.7 (on which Bowlby originally based his maternal deprivation hypothesis) are most accurately thought of as demonstrating the effects of *privation*. However, Bowlby's own theory and research were mainly concerned with *deprivation*. By only using the one term (deprivation), he confused two very different types of *early experience*, which have very different types of effect (both short- and long-term).

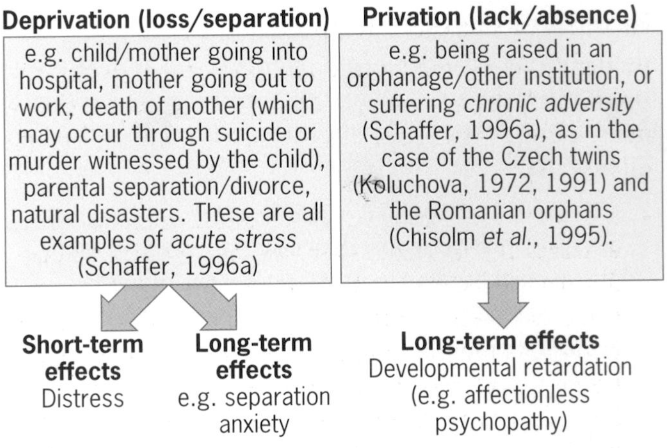

Deprivation (loss/separation)
e.g. child/mother going into hospital, mother going out to work, death of mother (which may occur through suicide or murder witnessed by the child), parental separation/divorce, natural disasters. These are all examples of acute stress (Schaffer, 1996a)
Privation (lack/absence)
e.g. being raised in an orphanage/other institution, or suffering chronic adversity (Schaffer, 1996a), as in the case of the Czech twins (Koluchova, 1972, 1991) and the Romanian orphans (Chisolm et al., 1995).
Short-term effects
Distress
Long-term effects
e.g. separation anxiety
Long-term effects
Developmental retardation (e.g. affectionless psychopathy)

Figure 3.8 *Examples of the difference between deprivation and privation, including their effects*

DEPRIVATION (SEPARATION OR LOSS)

Short-term deprivation and its effects

One example of short-term deprivation (days or weeks, rather than months or years) is a child going into a nursery whilst its mother goes into hospital. Another is the child itself going into hospital. Bowlby showed that when young children go into hospital, they display *distress*, which typically involves three components or stages.

Box 3.8   The components or stages of distress

Protest: The initial, immediate reaction takes the form of crying, screaming, kicking and generally struggling to escape, or clinging to the mother to prevent her from leaving. This is an outward and direct expression of the child's anger, fear, bitterness, bewilderment and so on.

Despair: The struggling and protest eventually give way to calmer behaviour. The child may appear apathetic, but internally still feels all the anger and fear previously displayed. It keeps such feelings 'locked up' and wants nothing to do with other people. The child may no longer anticipate the mother's return, and barely reacts to others' offers of comfort, preferring to comfort itself by rocking, thumb-sucking and so on.

Detachment: If the separation continues, the child begins to respond to people again, but tends to treat everyone alike and rather superficially. However, if reunited with the mother at this stage, the child may well have to 'relearn' its relationship with her and may even 'reject' her (as she 'rejected' her child).

Factors influencing distress

Evidence suggests that not all children go through the stages of distress, and that they differ as to how much distress they experience. Separation is likely to be most distressing:

- between the ages of seven/eight months (when attachments are just beginning to develop: see page 37) and three years, with a peak at 12–18 months (Maccoby, 1980). This is related to the child's inability to retain a mental image of the absent mother and its limited understanding of language. For example, because young children cannot understand phrases like 'in a few days' time' or 'next week', it is difficult to explain to them that the separation is only temporary. They might believe that they have been abandoned totally and that they are in some way to blame for what has happened ('Mummy is going away because I've been naughty');

- for boys (although there are also wide differences *within* each gender);

- if there have been any behaviour problems, such as aggressiveness, that existed before the separation. Such problems are likely to be accentuated if separation occurs;

- if the mother and child have an extremely close and protective relationship, in which they are rarely apart and the child is unused to meeting new people. Children appear to cope best if their relationship with her is stable and relaxed, but not too close, and if they have other attachment figures (such as the father) who can provide love and care. Many institutions used to be run in a way which made the development of substitute attachments very difficult. High staff turnover, a large number of children competing for the attention of a small number of staff, and the sometimes deliberate policy of no special relationships being formed, could all have worked against the provision of high-quality substitute attachments (Tizard & Rees, 1974).

One *long-term* effect of short-term separation is *separation anxiety*. This is also associated with long-term deprivation and is discussed below.

Figure 3.9 *John (17 months) experienced extreme distress while spending nine days in a residential nursery when his mother was in hospital having a second baby. According to Bowlby, he was grieving for the absent mother. Robertson & Robertson (1969) (who made a series of films called* Young Children in Brief Separation*) found that the extreme distress was caused by a combination of factors: loss of the mother, strange environment and routines, multiple caretakers and lack of a mother substitute.*

Long-term deprivation and its effects

Long-term deprivation includes the permanent separation resulting from parental *death* and the increasingly common separation caused by *divorce*. Perhaps the most common effect of long-term deprivation is what Bowlby called *separation anxiety* (the fear that separation will occur again in the future).

Box 3.9   Characteristics associated with separation anxiety

- Increased aggressive behaviour and greater demands towards the mother;

- Clinging behaviour: the child will not let the mother out of its sight. This may generalise to other relationships, so that a man who experienced 'bad' childhood separations may be very dependent on, and demanding of, his wife;

- Detachment: the child becomes apparently self-sufficient, because it cannot afford to be let down again;

- Some fluctuation between clinging and detachment;

- Psychosomatic (psychophysiological) reactions (physical symptoms that are associated with/caused by stress, anxiety or other psychological factors).

The effects of divorce

According to Schaffer (1996a), nearly all children (especially boys), regardless of their age, are adversely affected by parental divorce, at least in the short-term. However, despite the stresses involved, most children are resilient enough to adapt to their parents' divorce eventually (Hetherington & Stanley-Hagan, 1999). The nature, severity and duration of the effects vary greatly between children. These are influenced by many factors, including:

- continuity of contact with the non-custodial parent;

- the financial status/lifestyle of the single-parent family;

- whether the custodial parent remarries and the nature of the resulting step-family.

Box 3.10   Some of the major effects on children of parental divorce

Compared with children of similar social backgrounds whose parents remain married, those whose parents divorce show small but consistent differences throughout childhood. They also have different life courses as they move into adulthood. The differences include:

- lower levels of academic achievement and self-esteem;

- higher incidence of antisocial and delinquent behaviour, and other problems of psychological adjustment during childhood and adolescence;

- earlier social maturity, with certain transitions to adulthood (such as leaving home, beginning sexual relationships, cohabiting or getting married, and becoming pregnant) typically occurring younger;

- a tendency in young adulthood to more frequent changes of job, lower socioeconomic status, and indications of a higher frequency of depression and lower scores on measures of psychological well-being;

- more distant relationships in adulthood with parents and other relatives.

(Based on Hetherington & Stanley-Hagan, 1999; Richards, 1995)

Interpreting the findings from studies of the effects of divorce

The findings summarised in Box 3.10 are *correlational*, so we cannot be sure that it is divorce (or divorce alone) that is responsible for the differences that have been reported. For example, *divorce-prone* couples (those most likely to divorce) might have particular child-rearing styles which account for the differences. This possibility is supported by the finding that some of the effects associated with divorce can be seen *before* couples separate (Elliott & Richards, 1991). However, this hypothesis cannot account for all the effects seen *later* (Booth & Amato, 1994).

According to Schaffer (1996a), *inter-parental conflict* before, during and after the separation/formal divorce, is the single most damaging factor. Amato (1993), for example, showed that conflict between parents who live together is associated with low self-esteem in children. In turn, low self-esteem may lead to other problems, including lower school achievement and difficulties in forming relationships.

However, Hetherington & Stanley-Hagan (1999) argue that we cannot just assume (as is often done) that conflict declines following divorce. In fact, conflict often *increases* in the first few years after divorce, due to financial arrangements, visitation/access, co-parenting, parents' rights and responsibilities and so on. Under these conditions, it is better for children to remain in an unhappy two-parent household than to suffer the effects of divorce. If there is a shift to a more harmonious household, then a divorce is advantageous to both boys and girls. However, even in low-conflict divorced families, boys (but not girls) are *worse off* than those in low-conflict non-divorced families (Hetherington & Stanley-Hagan, 1999).

Figure 3.10 *It is not divorce as such that makes children maladjusted, but inter-parental conflict, especially when the child becomes the focus of the conflict, as in* Kramer vs Kramer, *starring Dustin Hoffman and Meryl Streep*

PRIVATION

As noted earlier (see page 46), *privation* is the failure to develop an attachment to any individual. Given the importance of the child's first relationship as a model or *prototype* of relationships in general, failure to develop an attachment of any kind is likely to adversely affect all subsequent relationships.

Harlow's research (see pages 37–39) showed that monkeys brought up with only surrogate mothers were very disturbed in their later sexual behaviour. For example, females had to be artificially inseminated, because they would not mate naturally. The unmothered females also became very inadequate mothers, rejecting their infants whenever they tried to cling to their bellies and, literally, walking all over them.

Affectionless psychopathy

According to Bowlby, maternal deprivation in early childhood causes *affectionless psychopathy*. This is the inability to care and have deep feelings for other people

and the consequent lack of meaningful interpersonal relationships, together with the inability to experience guilt.

Key STUDY

Box 3.11 Bowlby's (1946) study of 44 juvenile thieves

Bowlby compared a group of 44 juvenile thieves with a control group of emotionally disturbed juveniles not guilty of any crime. They all attended child guidance clinics where Bowlby worked. Fourteen of the thieves showed many characteristics of *affectionless psychopathy*, compared with none in the control group.

Of the two groups as a whole, about 43 per cent of the thieves had suffered complete and prolonged separation (six months or more) from their mothers, or established foster mothers, during their first five years of life. This compared with just five per cent of the control group. Twelve of the affectionless thieves (86 per cent) had experienced such separations, but only five of the non-affectionless thieves (17 per cent) had done so.

Bowlby interpreted his findings in terms of *maternal deprivation*: antisocial behaviour was specifically linked to loss of the mother-figure. However, Rutter (1981) believes that it is more likely that *privation* was the major cause of the affectionless character. The juveniles concerned had experienced multiple changes of mother-figure and home during their early years, making the *formation* of attachments very difficult.

PAUSE FOR THOUGHT

Bowlby's study was *retrospective*. What does this mean and why does it make Bowlby's conclusions even more doubtful?

The data were based on the *histories* of the children and adolescents, which required them and their mothers to *remember* past events. Human memory is known to be less than perfectly reliable (see Chapter 2).

An additional criticism is that Bowlby offered no explanation as to why the 30 non-affectionless thieves (68 per cent of the whole group), most of whom (83 per cent) had not suffered maternal deprivation, had got involved in juvenile delinquency.

Later, Bowlby *et al.* (1956) studied 60 children aged seven to 13, who had spent between five months and two years in a tuberculosis sanitorium (which provided no substitute mothering) at various ages up to four. About half had been separated from their parents before they were two years old. When compared with a group of non-separated 'control' children from the same school classes, the *overall* picture was that the two groups were more similar than different. The separated children were more prone to 'daydreaming', showed less initiative, were more over-excited, rougher in play, concentrated less well and were less competitive. However, they were not more likely to show affectionless psychopathy, regardless of when their separation had occurred (before or after two).

Bowlby *et al.* admitted that 'part of the emotional disturbance can be attributed to factors other than separation', such as the common occurrence of illness and death in the sanitorium children's families. So, there was very little evidence for the link between affectionless psychopathy and *separation* (or bond disruption). However, Bowlby may have provided evidence for an association with *privation* instead (a failure to form bonds in early life). According to Rutter (1981), privation is likely to lead to:

- an initial phase of clinging, dependent behaviour;
- attention-seeking, and for uninhibited, indiscriminate friendliness;
- a personality characterised by lack of guilt, an inability to keep rules and an inability to form lasting relationships.

Are the effects of privation reversible?

Suomi & Harlow (1977) found that the effects on rhesus monkeys of being reared in isolation from other monkeys (their mother or siblings) *could* be reversed, or at least moderated. This was achieved by allowing them to have extensive contact with 'monkey therapists'. In humans, there are (at least) three kinds of study which demonstrate that it is possible to undo the effects of early privation:

1 *Case studies* of children who have endured *extreme* early privation, often in near complete isolation. One example is the Czech twins studied by Koluchova, (1972, 1991: see Box 3.12).

2 Studies of *late adoption*: children raised in institutions are adopted *after* Bowlby's *critical period* for attachment development (12 months for most children, up to two-and-a-half/three years for the rest). Studies include those of Tizard and her colleagues (e.g. Hodges & Tizard, 1989), and Chisolm *et al.* (1995).

3 Studies of *developmental pathways* (see pages 51–52).

Studies of extreme privation

As with other similar studies, the case of the Czech twins highlights the importance of having somebody (not necessarily a mother-figure) with whom it is possible to form an emotional bond: the twins at least had *each other* as attachment figures during their early years of extreme privation.

Key (STUDY)

Box 3.12 The case of PM and JM (Koluchova, 1972, 1991)

Identical twin boys, born in 1960 in the former Czechoslovakia, lost their mother shortly after birth and were cared for by a social agency for a year, and then fostered by a maternal aunt for a further six months. Their father remarried but his new wife proved to be excessively cruel to the twins, banishing them to the cellar for the next five-and-a-half years, during which time they also received harsh beatings.

When discovered in 1967, they were very short in stature, had rickets, no spontaneous speech (communicating largely by gestures), and were terrified of many aspects of their new environment.

Legally removed from their parents, they first underwent a programme of physical rehabilitation and entered a school for children with severe learning difficulties. They were subsequently legally adopted by two exceptionally dedicated women. Academically, they caught up with their peers and achieved emotional and intellectual normality. At follow-up in 1974 (at age 14), they showed no signs of psychological abnormality or unusual behaviour. They had gone on to technical school, training as typewriter mechanics, but later went on to further education, specialising in electronics.

They both had very good relationships with their adoptive mothers, their adopted sisters, and the women's relatives. Both were drafted for national service, and later married and had children. At age 29, they are said to be entirely stable, lacking abnormalities and enjoying warm relationships. One is a computer technician and the other a technical training instructor (Koluchova, 1991).

Studies of late adoption

Tizard (1977) and Hodges & Tizard (1989) studied children who, on leaving care between the ages of two and seven, were either adopted or returned to their own families. The institutions they grew up in provided good physical care and appeared to provide adequate intellectual stimulation. However, staff turnover was high, and they operated a policy against allowing strong attachments to develop between the staff and children (see *Critical issue*, pages 53–56). As a result, the children had little opportunity to form close, continuous relationships with adults. Indeed, by age two, they had been looked after for at least a week by an average of 24 different caregivers. By age four, this had risen to 50. The children's attachment behaviour was very unusual and, in general, the first opportunity to form long-term attachments came when they left the institutions and were placed in families.

By age eight, the majority of the adopted children had formed close attachments to their adoptive parents (who very much wanted a child), despite the lack of early attachments in the institutions (Tizard & Hodges, 1978). However, only *some* of those children returned to their own families had formed close attachments. The biological parents often had mixed feelings about having the child back, and often had other children competing for their attention (as well as material hardship). As reported by their parents, the ex-institutional children as a whole did not display more problems than a comparison group who had never been in care. According to their teachers, however, they tended to display attention-seeking behaviour, restlessness, disobedience and poor peer relationships.

Key STUDY

Box 3.13 Ex-institution children at age 16 (Hodges & Tizard, 1989)

At age 16, the family relationships of most of the adopted children seemed satisfactory, both for them and their parents. They differed little from a non-adopted comparison group who had never been in care. Hence, early institutional care had not necessarily led to a later inability to form a close attachment to parents and become as much a part of the family as any other child (contrary to Bowlby's predictions). By contrast, those children returned to their families still suffered difficulties and poor family relationships. These included mutual difficulty in showing affection, and the parents reported feeling closer to the children's siblings than to the returned children.

Outside the family, however, *both* the adopted and returned children showed similar relationships with peers and adults. Compared with a control group, they were:

- still more likely to seek adult affection and approval;
- still more likely to have difficulties in their relationships with peers;
- less likely to have a special friend or to see peers as sources of emotional support;
- more likely to be friendly to *any* peer rather than choosing their friends.

These findings *are* consistent with Bowlby's maternal deprivation hypothesis.

Hodges and Tizard's research indicates that children who fail to enjoy close and lasting relationships with adults in the first years of life *can* make such attachments later on. However, these do not arise automatically, simply by being placed in a family. Rather, they depend on the adults concerned and how they nurture such attachments. Also, if these children experience difficulties in their relationships *outside* the family, they may have difficulties in future adult relationships and with their own children.

Another late-adoption study involved Romanian orphans (reared in extremely poor conditions in large-scale institutions) adopted by Canadian families between the ages of eight months and five years, six months (Chisolm *et al.*, 1995). It seems that some negative impact on the children's relationships with adoptive parents can result from their institutional experience. For example, their behaviour was often described as *ambivalent* (they both wanted contact and resisted it: see Box 3.2, page 39). They were also not easily comforted when distressed. Follow-up is needed to see if life in a loving family can eventually overcome this impairment. However, based on their intellectual recovery, there are good reasons for being optimistic (Schaffer, 1998).

Developmental pathways

Quinton & Rutter (1988) wanted to find out whether children deprived of parental care become depriving parents themselves. They observed one group of women, brought up in care, interacting with their own children, and compared them with a second group of non-institutionalised mothers. The women brought up in care were, as a whole, less sensitive, supportive and warm towards their children. This difference could be explained in terms of both:

- various subsequent experiences the women had as a result of their early upbringing (such as teenage pregnancy, marrying unsupportive spouses and marital breakdown);
- their actual deprived childhoods.

However, there was also considerable variability *within* the group brought up in care, with some women displaying good parenting skills. This could be explained in terms of *developmental pathways*. For example, some of the women had more positive school experiences than others. This made them three times more likely as adolescents or young adults to make proper career and marriage partner choices (Rutter, 1989). Such positive experience represents an escape route from the early hardships associated with being brought up in care. Similar adverse childhood experiences can have *multiple* outcomes (Schaffer, 1996b). *Starting off* at a disadvantage does not necessarily mean having to *finish up* at a disadvantage.

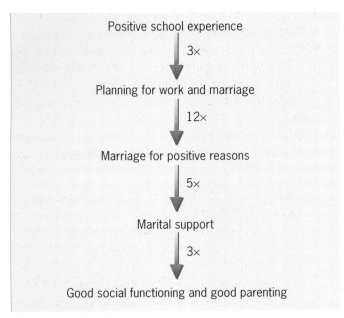

Figure 3.11 *A simplified adaptive chain of circumstances in institution-raised women (Based on Quinton & Rutter, 1988; Rutter, 1989)*

According to Schaffer (1996a):

'... Early experiences ... do not necessarily produce irreversible effects just because they are early ...'.

Similarly,

'The evidence is firm; while there is a range of outcomes, early social experience *by itself* does not predestine the future' (Clarke & Clarke, 1998).

Schaffer (1998) believes that psychological development is far more flexible than was previously thought. Our personalities are not fixed once and for all by events in the early years. Given the right circumstances, the effects of even quite severe and prolonged deprivation *can* be reversed.

Section Summary

- Bowlby's **maternal deprivation hypothesis** was based mainly on studies of children raised in large institutions. It was used to explain the harmful effects of growing up in such places, such as intellectual retardation, **anaclitic depression** and **hospitalism**.

- This explanation failed to recognise the understimulating nature of the institutional environment, and to disentangle the different kinds of retardation produced by different types of deprivation.

- The studies of institutions actually demonstrated the effects of **privation** (as opposed to **deprivation**), which refer to **absence** and **loss** respectively. Bowlby consequently confused two very different types of early experience, which have very different types of effect.

- Short-term deprivation produces short-term effects, notably **distress**. Privation produces long-term **developmental retardation** (such as affectionless psychopathy).

- Not all children go through all the stages of distress (**protest, despair** and **detachment**). Some children are more vulnerable than others, in particular 12–18-month-old boys who have had behaviour problems prior to the separation, or who have over-close relationships with their mothers.

- Parental **death** and **divorce** represent long-term deprivation, and are associated with long-term effects, particularly **separation anxiety**. This can take several forms, such as increased aggressiveness, clinging behaviour, detachment, and psychosomatic reactions.

- Children who experience parental divorce are more likely to display antisocial/delinquent behaviour, achieve earlier social maturity, become depressed, and have more distant relationships as adults with parents/other relatives. However, most children eventually adapt.

- According to Schaffer, **inter-parental conflict** is the single most damaging factor. However, conflict does not necessarily decline following divorce, and often actually increases.

- According to Bowlby, maternal deprivation in early childhood causes **affectionless psychopathy**. The main evidence for this claim came from his studies of juvenile thieves and of children in a tuberculosis sanitorium. However, both studies suggest that it is privation, not deprivation, which causes affectionless psychopathy.

- Case studies of children who have endured **extreme privation** (such as the Czech twins), studies of **late adoption** (such as Tizard's longitudinal study of institutionalised children), and Quinton and Rutter's study of **developmental pathways**, all indicate that the effects of early privation are reversible.

- There appears to be nothing special about early experiences, and our personalities are not determined once and for all by early events. The 'same' early experience may have many alternative outcomes.

Self-Assessment Questions

3 a Explain what is meant by the terms 'critical period' and 'monotropy'. *(3 marks + 3 marks)*

b Describe **one** research study that has investigated the effects of deprivation and **one** that has investigated the effects of privation. *(6 marks + 6 marks)*

c 'Early experiences … do not necessarily produce irreversible effects just because they are early … .' (Schaffer, 1996a)

To what extent does research evidence support this statement? *(12 marks)*

4 a Describe **two** differences between privation and deprivation. *(3 marks + 3 marks)*

b Describe **one** research study that has investigated the effects of institutionalisation on children's attachments. *(6 marks)*

c Give **two** criticisms of this study. *(3 marks + 3 marks)*

d 'If a child begins life at a disadvantage, it will remain disadvantaged throughout childhood and the rest of its life.'

Critically consider the impact of early experience on later development. *(12 marks)*

Critical ISSUE

The Effects of Day Care on Children's Development

What is day care?

According to Scarr (1998), day care includes all varieties of non-maternal care of children who reside with their parent(s) or close relatives, and so excludes foster care and institutional (residential) care. Examples of day care include:

- crèches, day nurseries, childminders and other 'out-of-home' facilities;

- nannies, non-resident grandparents and other 'in-the-home' arrangements. (What is called childminding in the UK is referred to as 'home-based day care' in the USA)

A deep-seated and widely held assumption is that child care provided by anyone other than the child's mother deserves special attention because it is *non-normative* (that is, it is not how most children are cared for). This partly reflects the continuing influence of Bowlby's theory of attachment (see page 40). However, shared childcare is actually a normative experience for contemporary American (and British) children, the

vast majority of whose mothers are employed. More than half the mothers of infants under 12 months of age, and three-quarters of those of school-age children, are in the labour force. According to Scarr (1998), non-maternal shared care is normative both historically and culturally (and so is universal):

'Exclusive maternal care of infants and young children is a cultural myth … not a reality anywhere in the world either now or in earlier times. Childcare has always been shared, usually among female relatives. What has changed over time and varies cross-nationally is the degree to which care is bought in the marketplace rather than shared among female relatives'.

In industrialised societies, such as Britain and the USA, mothers' employment outside the home has made non-maternal care of various kinds necessary. The demand for childcare is driven entirely by the economic need for women in the labour force. In 1997, women comprised 49.5 per cent of those in paid employment in the UK, and in 2000 they will outnumber

Figure 3.12 *Famous people, such as Cherie Blair, challenge the stereotype of women as born and bred to be mothers*

Figure 3.13 *These preschoolers are experiencing what appears to be high quality day care*

men (although with a far higher percentage in part-time work: Kremer, 1998).

Despite these changing patterns of female employment, the belief that women are born and reared to be, first and foremost, mothers (the *motherhood mystique/mandate*) remains an influence on our attitudes about working mothers (Kremer, 1998). Although attitudes to female employment in general have changed quite dramatically, whether or not working mothers have pre-school children is still a significant factor in shaping these attitudes.

Asking questions about the effects of day care

According to Scarr (1998), there have been three waves of research into day care:

- In the 1970s, maternal care was compared with any kind of non-maternal care, without assessing the quality of either. The implicit question being asked was: 'How much damage is done to infants and young children by working mothers?'. No consideration was given to whether variation in development depended on variation in kind or quality of care, either at home or in other settings.

- During the 1980s, research began to look at the quality and variety of care settings, introducing the idea that children's reactions to day care may differ.

- During the late 1980s/1990s, variation of day-care quality and type were looked at in relation to both family characteristics and individual differences among children.

How do we measure the quality of day care?

According to Scarr (1998), there is extraordinary international agreement among researchers and practitioners about what quality care is.

Box 3.14 Defining the quality of day care

Bredekamp (1989: cited in Scarr, 1998) defines quality care as:

'warm, supportive interactions with adults in a safe, healthy, and stimulating environment, where early education and trusting relationships combine to support individual children's physical, emotional, social and intellectual development'.

Although quality of care has many aspects, the most commonly used measures are remarkably similar in the dimensions of quality which they see as most important. The criteria most commonly agreed on (consistent with Bredekamp's definition above) are:

- health and safety requirements;

- responsive and warm interaction between staff and children;

- developmentally appropriate curricula;

- limited group size;

- age-appropriate caregiver–child ratios;

- adequate indoor and outdoor space;

- adequate staff training (in either early childhood education or child development);

- low staff turnover (as a measure of the *stability* of care).

(Based on Scarr, 1998)

In the USA, the quality of day care varies dramatically, whilst European studies show considerably less variation (Lamb *et al.*, 1992). Poor quality care has been reported to put children's development at risk for poorer language and cognitive scores and lower ratings of social and emotional adjustment.

However, interpreting these findings is difficult, because the quality of care selected by parents is correlated with their personal characteristics or circumstances. For example, children from families with single working mothers or low incomes are more likely to experience low quality care. What this means is that we cannot be sure whether it is quality of day care or parental characteristics which account for children's development. Scarr (1998) believes that this confusion between the two variables has resulted in an *overestimation* of the effects of day care.

The effects of day care on children's social development: attachments

PAUSE FOR THOUGHT

What would Bowlby's theory predict about the effects of working mothers on their child's attachment development?

According to Bowlby, a child whose mother goes out to work experiences maternal deprivation. If this happens during the child's first year (before an attachment has formed), an attachment may not develop at all (strictly, this is *privation*). If it happens *after* an attachment has developed, the child will be distressed, may experience separation anxiety and so on (see Boxes 3.8, page 47 and 3.9, page 48).

The results have tended to show that there is *no* weakening of the attachment to the mother resulting from the daily separations involved in day care. Provided certain conditions are met, especially the *stability* and *quality* of the care, children do not suffer any ill effects and will benefit from them in certain respects (Schaffer, 1996a).

One exception to this is a study by Belsky & Rovine (1988). They concluded that infants in day care were more likely to develop insecure attachments if they had been receiving day care for at least four months before their first birthday and for more than 20 hours per week. Although many children 'at risk' develop secure attachments, they are also more likely to develop insecure attachments than children who stay at home (see Table 3.2, page 43).

However, Belsky and Rovine's findings were obtained exclusively from one method of assessing attachment, namely the Strange Situation (see Table 3.1, page 42). Clarke-Stewart (1989) argues that this is an inappropriate technique for children in day care. As seen earlier, the Strange Situation is based on the assumption that repeated separations from the mother put children under stress and so highlights their attempts at security-seeking. However, day-care children are *used to* such separations and may, therefore, not experience stress. When they respond to the mother's return in the Strange Situation with (what looks like) indifference, they may be showing independence and self-reliance, *not* the 'avoidance' or 'resistance' that are used to classify children as insecurely attached. According to Schaffer (1996a):

'It is possible that the Strange Situation procedure is not psychologically equivalent for children of working and of non-working mothers. If that is so, it becomes even more important to ensure that any conclusions are based on a variety of assessment techniques ...'.

PAUSE FOR THOUGHT

If day care were harmful to young children's attachments, what kind of distribution of secure and insecure attachments would you expect among those whose mothers work compared with those who don't (e.g. what percentage of Type A and Type C attachments)?

- The observed distribution of insecure infants of working mothers in the USA (22 per cent Type A; 14 per cent Type C) is virtually identical to the overall distribution for studies around the world (21 per cent and 14 per cent, respectively, based on almost 2000 children of mainly non-working mothers: van Ijzendoorn & Kroonenberg, 1988).

- In theory, an attachment is a *relationship*, not a global personality trait (see page 43). If the children of working mothers are more insecure with them, this does not necessarily mean that they are emotionally insecure in general. We need to assess their emotional health in a range of situations, with a variety of attachment figures. Several studies have shown that children who were in day care as infants do as well as those who were not, using measures of security, anxiety, self-confidence and emotional adjustment (Clarke-Stewart, 1989).

The effects of day care on children's cognitive development

According to Scarr (1998), children from low-income families definitely *benefit* from high quality care. They show better school achievement and more socialised behaviour in later years than similar children without day-care experience or with lower quality care. High quality day-care provides learning opportunities and social and emotional supports that many would not enjoy at home. For middle class and upper-income families, the long-term picture is far less clear.

Clarke-Stewart (1991) found that 150 two- to four-year-olds who had experienced day-care centres had better intellectual (and social) development than those who had received home care (either with mothers or childminders). However, Baydar & Brooks-Gunn's (1991) study of 1181 children found that they were worse off, both cognitively and in behavioural terms, if their mothers went out to work before they were a year old, compared with those whose mothers started work later.

This latter finding supports the claim that day care before one year old, and for more than 20 hours per week, can be harmful (see page 55). However, Scarr & Thompson (1994) directly tested this claim in a study of 1100 children in Bermuda. Based on teacher ratings at ages five, six, seven and eight, there were *no* differences in cognitive (or socioemotional) development between those who had been placed in day care either before or after 12 months and for more or less than 20 hours per week.

A longitudinal study conducted in New Zealand of over 1200 children from the age of eight to 18 reached similar conclusions. Overall, children whose mothers worked tended to have slightly *higher* average test scores (on word recognition, reading comprehension, mathematical reasoning, overall academic ability, and success in the School Leaving examination) than those whose mothers did not work. However, when a number of related factors were taken into account (such as mother's education, socioeconomic status, ethnic background, early mother–child interaction, birth order, family composition, and the child's IQ), the differences largely disappeared (Horwood & Fergusson, 1999).

To work or not to work?

As Horwood & Fergusson (1999) point out, much of the research into the effects of day care has been carried out in the USA. The conclusions from these studies may not apply to other societies and cultures where patterns of maternal, and paternal, participation in the labour force and at home may differ from those in the USA.

In a review of 40 years' research, Mooney and Munton (cited in Judd, 1997) conclude that there is no evidence that working mothers stunt their children's emotional or social development. Even poor quality child care may make no difference to a child

from a stable family, whilst good quality care may provide positive benefits. Instead of debating the rights and wrongs of working mothers, we should focus on how to provide enough good childcare.

British families have changed fundamentally in the past 25 years. In more than 70 per cent of two-parent families with dependent children, both parents work, and the proportion of children living in single-parent families has risen from eight to 21 per cent. What is needed is a national strategy for childcare which ensures that all employees are properly trained and paid. Similarly (in relation to the American scene), Clarke-Stewart (1989) states that:

> 'Maternal employment is a reality. The issue today, therefore, is not whether infants should be in day care but how to make their experiences there and at home supportive of their development and of their parents' peace of mind'.

Section Summary

■ **Day care** includes all types of non-maternal care of children who live with their parent(s), such as crèches, day nurseries, childminders and nannies. This excludes foster and residential care.

■ It is widely assumed that childcare provided by anyone other than the child's mother is **non-normative**. However, non-maternal-shared care is normative, both historically and culturally.

■ Despite the changing patterns of female employment outside the home, the **motherhood mystique** continues to shape our attitudes about working mothers. In particular, those attitudes are influenced by whether or not they have pre-school children.

■ Research into day care initially compared maternal care with any kind of non-maternal care, without taking the kind or quality of care into account. Quality is now studied in relation to both family characteristics and individual differences among children.

■ There is widespread international agreement regarding the criteria used to assess the **quality** of day care. These include responsive and warm interactions between staff and children, limited group size, age-appropriate caregiver–child ratios, adequately trained staff, and low staff-turnover (a measure of **stability** of care).

■ Since there is a correlation between the quality of care parents choose and characteristics such as parental income, it is unclear which variable is influencing the child's development. This confusion has led to an **overestimation** of the effects of day care.

- Provided the stability and quality of day care are satisfactory, a child's attachment to its mother should not be weakened. However, Belsky and Rovine claimed that insecure attachments were more likely to develop if the child had been receiving care for at least four months before its first birthday and for more than 20 hours per week.

- This claim was based exclusively on studies using the Strange Situation, which assumes that repeated separations from the mother are stressful for the child. However, children in day care are used to such separations, making the Strange Situation an inappropriate method for assessing attachments in such children.

- Children from low-income families **benefit** from high quality care. Despite some evidence to the contrary, children in day care do not seem to be at a disadvantage in terms of cognitive or socioemotional development compared with those who stay at home.

Self-Assessment Questions

5 a Explain what is meant by the terms 'day care' and 'non-normative child care'. *(3 marks + 3 marks)*

b Describe **one** research study that has investigated the effects of day care on children's social **or** cognitive development. *(6 marks)*

c Give **two** criticisms of this study. *(3 marks + 3 marks)*

d 'Whilst going out to work may be beneficial to mothers of young children, the children themselves will suffer compared with those whose mothers do not work.'
To what extent does psychological research support this view of the effects of day care on children's social **and/or** cognitive development. *(12 marks)*

6 a Outline **two** factors that are likely to be taken into account when defining the quality of day care. *(3 marks + 3 marks)*

b Describe **two** research studies that have investigated the effects of day care on children's social **and/or** cognitive development. *(6 marks + 6 marks)*

c 'Working mothers will inevitably have young children whose attachments are insecure compared with those of non-working mothers.'
Critically consider the effects of day care on children's social development. *(12 marks)*

CONCLUSIONS

This chapter has considered theories and research relating to the development of attachments, both in infancy and early childhood, as well as later in life. Several influential theories of attachment have been discussed, which can be divided roughly into *cupboard-love* and *non-cupboard-love* theories. Whilst all babies appear to pass through the same *stages* in the development of attachments, there are important individual differences and cross-cultural variations.

The crucial distinction between *deprivation* and *privation* was then examined, and research relating to both kinds of early experience discussed. It was concluded that the harmful effects of even extreme and prolonged early (de-)privation can be reversed. Finally, the impact of day care on children's cognitive and social development was considered. It seems that it is not day care as such, but its *quality* and *stability*, which influence development.

WEB ADDRESSES

http://galton.psych.nwu/greatideas/attachment.html
http://samiam.colorado.edu/~mcclella/expersim/introimprint.html
http://www.bereavement.org.uk
http://www.geocities.com/Athens/Acropolis/3041/ARChrome.html
http://www.psychematters.com/
http://www./theamgroup.com/child/htm
http://blue.census.gov/population/www/socdemo/childcare.html
http://www.acf.dhhs.gov/programs/ccb/
http://www.psychology.sunysb.edu/ewaters/
http://www.johnbowlby.com

Physiological Psychology and Individual Differences

4 Stress

Many years ago, Selye (1936) conducted experiments whose aim was to discover a new sex hormone. In one, rats were injected with ovary tissue extracts. Various physiological changes occurred and, since no known hormone produced such effects, Selye believed he had discovered a new one. However, when he injected extracts from other tissues, or toxic fluids that did not come from ovary tissue extracts, the *same* physiological changes occurred.

Despite this setback, Selye did not abandon his research. Instead, he changed its direction:

'It suddenly struck me that one could look at [the experiments] from an entirely different angle. [Perhaps] there was such a thing as a non-specific reaction of the body to damage of any kind'. (Selye, 1976)

Later, Selye confirmed that when rats were exposed to adverse conditions like extreme cold, electric shocks, or surgical trauma, the same physiological changes occurred. Selye's research pioneered an interest in the study of *stress*, and its effects on *humans*. The first part of this chapter looks at what stress is, the effects that stress has on the body, and research into the relationship between stress and illness. The second part considers some sources of stress (*stressors*) in contemporary life, and the role of individual differences, such as personality, which modify the effects of stressors. The final part looks at some of the methods available to help manage the negative effects of stress, and assesses their strengths and weaknesses.

Stress as a Bodily Response

DEFINING STRESS

PAUSE FOR THOUGHT

What do you understand by the word '*stress*'? Is it used to mean different things in ordinary language?

Defining 'stress' is not easy. Physicists and engineers see stress as the pressure or force exerted on an object. Psychologists take a similar view, but look at stress in terms of the *demands* it makes on an organism, and the organism's efforts to adapt, cope or adjust to those demands. An adequate definition of stress must, therefore, recognise the *interaction* between external *stressors* and physiological and psychological responses to them. It must also acknowledge the role of *cognitive factors*, since how a stressor is *appraised* will influence its effects. Finally, whilst research interest has tended to concentrate on the harmful effects of stress (what Selye, 1980, calls *distress*), some stress (*eustress*) is beneficial and necessary

to keep us alert. So, an adequate definition must also appreciate that some stress can be healthy.

A generally accepted definition which meets these requirements is that of Lazarus & Folkman (1984), who define stress as:

'a pattern of negative physiological states and psychological responses occurring in situations where people perceive threats to their well-being which they may be unable to meet'.

THE GENERAL ADAPTATION SYNDROME (GAS)

As noted above, Selye's rats appeared to respond identically, irrespective of the adverse conditions to which they were exposed. Selye concluded that the body's response to a stressor is *non-specific*, and when an organism is confronted with an external *or* internal stressor, the body prepares for action to defend itself. If the stressor can be adequately managed, the body returns to its original state. However, if repeated or prolonged exposure to the stressor cannot be managed, the organism suffers tissue damage, increased susceptibility to disease and, in extreme cases, death.

Selye called the non-specific response to a stressor the *general adaptation syndrome* (GAS). It is also known as the *pituitary–adrenal stress syndrome*. The GAS consists of three distinct stages, and is an example of the interaction between the *central nervous system, autonomic nervous system,* and *endocrine system*. To understand the body's response to a stressor, we first need to consider these three systems.

The central nervous system

The central nervous system (CNS) consists of the *brain* and the *spinal cord*, whose primary function is to integrate and co-ordinate all body functions and behaviour. MacLean's (1982) *triune model* of the brain identifies three main components. These are the *central core* (the oldest part of the brain), the *limbic system* (which evolved more recently, and developed in early mammals about 100 million years ago), and the *cerebral cortex* (which developed about 2 million years ago, but only in some mammals). One structure in the central core, the *hypothalamus*, is especially important in understanding the effects of stress on the body.

Box 4.1   The hypothalamus

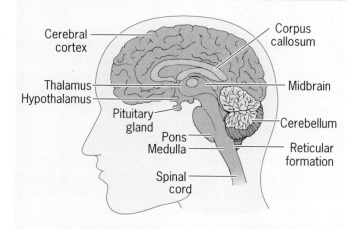

Figure 4.1 *A front-to-back cross-section of the brain showing some of its major structures. The hypothalamus is located just below the thalamus and is connected to the pituitary gland by the infundibulum (see Box 4.3, page 63)*

The hypothalamus consists of a mass of neural cell bodies (*nuclei*) located deep within the brain. The hypothalamus weighs about 4 g, and occupies less

than 1 cm³ of tissue. However, for its size, it is a remarkable and extremely important brain part, and is involved in many complex behaviours including:

- *species-typical behaviour* (those behaviours exhibited by most members of a species and which are important to survival);
- *homeostasis* (the maintenance of a proper balance of physiological variables such as body temperature and fluid concentration).

In relation to stress, the hypothalamus is important because it helps to regulate the *sympathetic branch* of the *autonomic nervous system*. It also controls the *pituitary gland*, which itself controls the rest of the body's *endocrine glands* (see text below).

The autonomic nervous system

As well as a CNS, we also have a *peripheral nervous system* (PNS). The PNS consists of nerves that connect the CNS with the sense organs, muscles and glands. The first of two essential PNS functions is to send information to the CNS from the outside world (which it achieves via the sense organs). The second is to transmit information from the CNS to produce a particular behaviour (which it achieves through the peripheral nerves to the muscles). The PNS is divided into two parts, the *somatic nervous system* (SNS) and the *autonomic nervous system* (ANS). The latter is of interest here.

The nerves of the ANS connect the CNS to the internal organs (or *viscera*), glands, and 'smooth' muscles over which we have no conscious control (such as the muscles of the digestive system). The ANS's primary function is to regulate internal bodily processes, and it is so called because it appears to operate as an independent and self-regulatory, or *autonomous*, control system. Although we learn to control some autonomic functions, such as urination and defecation, these would occur in the absence of control over them. So, many bodily processes are controlled by the ANS without requiring conscious effort.

As Figure 4.2 illustrates (see page 62), the ANS is divided into two *branches*, which are structurally different and operate in different ways. These are the *parasympathetic* and *sympathetic* branches. The parasympathetic branch stimulates processes that serve to *restore* or *conserve energy*. It also carries out the body's 'maintenance needs'. As well as promoting digestion, it provides for the elimination of waste products and directs tissue repair. Parasympathetic activity predominates when we are relaxed or inactive, or when an emergency necessitating sympathetic branch activity (which is the part of the ANS of most interest in the study of stress: see below) has passed.

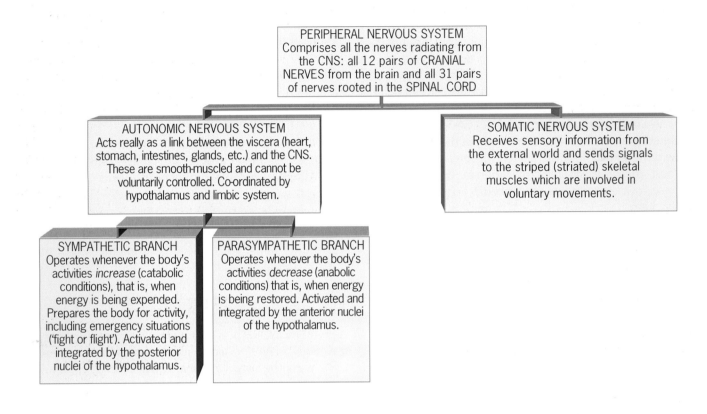

Figure 4.2 *The relationship between the PNS, SNS and ANS*

Box 4.2   The sympathetic branch of the ANS

The essential function of the sympathetic branch is to prepare the body to *expend energy* (or 'to mobilise the body for an emergency': Cannon, 1927). The bundles (or *ganglia*) of nerve cells comprising the branch are interconnected, and form a long vertical chain on each side of the spinal cord. The sympathetic branch originates in the two middle portions (the thoracic and lumbar regions) of the spinal cord. The interactions between the nerve cells allow the sympathetic branch to act as a *unit*. The fact that this branch seems to make the organs work 'in sympathy' led to its name, although it is now known that it can also act selectively on a single organ. Cannon (1927) called the activation of the sympathetic branch the *fight-or-flight response*, since the physiological changes that occur are designed to help us defend ourselves or flee from a threatening situation. Some of the ways in which the sympathetic branch prepares the body to expend energy are identified in Table 4.1 and Figure 4.4 (see page 64).

The endocrine system

The ANS exerts its effects by direct neural stimulation of body organs and by stimulating the release of *hormones* from the *endocrine glands*. These are ductless glands which secrete their products directly into the bloodstream, and are important because of their role in behaviour. Endocrine glands secrete *hormones*, powerful chemical messengers that have various effects on physical states and behaviour. They are poured into the bloodstream and circulate throughout the body, but act only on receptors in particular body locations. Because hormones are released into the blood, the endocrine system influences behaviour in a broad but slow way.

Many hormonal activities enable the body to maintain steady states. They achieve this by means of mechanisms that measure current levels, and signal glands to release appropriate regulatory chemicals whenever the steady state is disturbed. To maintain the steady state, information must then be fed back to the glands. Thus, whenever the required amount of a hormone has been secreted, the gland is instructed to stop (a *negative feedback loop*).

Essentially, the endocrine system is regulated by the *hypothalamus* (see Box 4.1, page 61), which exerts its influence through its effects on the *pituitary gland*. The pituitary is sometimes referred to as the 'master gland', because the hormones it releases control the secretion of the other endocrine glands. These include the *pancreas*, *gonads*, *thyroid*, *parathyroid* and *adrenal* glands. The last of these is particularly important in understanding the bodily effects of stress, and its role is described in detail below.

Box 4.3 The pituitary gland

The pituitary gland is located deep within the brain, slightly below the hypothalamus and is connected to it by means of a network of blood vessels called the *infundibulum* or *pituitary stalk* (see Figure 4.1, page 61). The pituitary gland consists of two parts, each with separate functions. The *anterior pituitary* (towards the *front* of the gland) is controlled *neurochemically*, by 'releasing factors' or 'releasing hormones'. These are produced by the hypothalamus, and transmitted via blood vessels in the infundibulum. The *posterior pituitary* (towards the *back* of the gland) is controlled *neurally*, by nerve cells in the hypothalamus which send their impulses down the infundibulum to the pituitary. The pituitary gland produces many hormones. The one involved in stress is *adrenocorticotrophic hormone* (ACTH: see text).

STAGE 1 OF THE GAS: THE ALARM REACTION

The *alarm reaction* is triggered by the perception and evaluation of a stimulus as a stressor, and the body is mobilised for action. In the initial *shock phase*, the body responds with a drop in blood pressure and muscle tension. This very brief phase is replaced by the *countershock phase*, an alerting response to possible threat or physical injury. The bodily reactions in this phase are initiated by the *hypothalamus* (see Box 4.1, page 61) and regulated by the *sympathetic branch of the ANS* (see Box 4.2, page 62) and the *endocrine system* (see Box 4.3 above).

When a stressor is perceived, the hypothalamus exerts two *parallel* effects. The first involves the pituitary and adrenal glands (the *hypothalamic–pituitary–adrenal axis*). The second involves the sympathetic branch of the ANS (the *sympatho–adrenomedullary axis*).

The hypothalamic–pituitary–adrenal axis

The hypothalamus initiates the release of *corticotrophic-releasing hormone* (CRH), one of the 'releasing hormones' identified in Box 4.3, via the infundibulum. This stimulates the anterior pituitary gland to secrete *adrenocorticotrophic hormone* (ACTH: see Box 4.3). ACTH acts on the body's *adrenal glands*. These are located just above the kidneys, and consist of an outer layer (the adrenal *cortex*) and an inner core (the adrenal *medulla*). The adrenal cortex is essential for the maintenance of life, and its removal results in death. ACTH acts on the adrenal cortex, causing it to enlarge and release *corticosteroids* (or *adrenocorticoid hormones*).

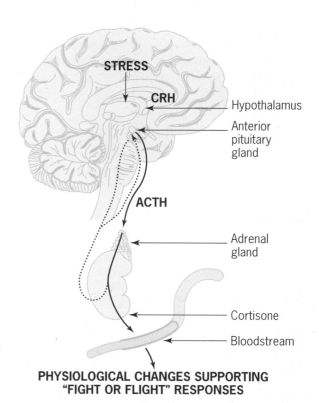

Figure 4.3 *Hormonal system known as the hypothalamic–pituitary–adrenal axis is active* (solid arrows in diagram) *in response to stress. As well as functioning outside the nervous system, the hormones released in response to pituitary hormones feed back to the pituitary and hypothalamus* (dotted arrows in diagram). *There they deliver inhibitory signals that keep hormone manufacture from becoming excessive*

The adrenal cortex secretes as many as 20 different hormones. One group of corticosteroids it releases are *glucocorticoid hormones*. These include *corticosterone*, *cortisone*, and *hydrocortisone*, which control and conserve the amount of *glucose* in the blood (*glucogenesis*). In general, corticosteroids promote muscle development and stimulate the liver to release stored sugar. This latter effect influences the body's ability to produce energy quickly (and hence steroids have been taken by athletes and bodybuilders to enhance performance). Corticosteroids also help fight *inflammation* (see page 66) and allergic reactions (e.g. difficulty in breathing). Because of the role played by the hypothalamus, pituitary and adrenal glands, this system is called the *hypothalamic–pituitary–adrenal axis*. The axis is extremely sensitive to environmental change, yet its effects die away rapidly if a stimulus is harmless (Green, 1994).

PAUSE FOR THOUGHT

Think of a situation in which you felt 'under stress'. List the physical changes and sensations you were aware of at the time and shortly afterwards. What *functions* might these changes and sensations serve?

The sympatho–adrenomedullary axis

The hypothalamus also activates the *sympathetic branch* of the ANS. This causes the adrenal *medulla* (hence 'sympatho–adrenomedullary axis') to enlarge and release *adrenaline* and *noradrenaline*, the 'stress hormones'. These mimic the action of the sympathetic branch (they are *sympathomimetics*), and initiate and maintain a heightened pattern of physiological activity as shown in Table 4.1. Adrenaline is manufactured exclusively by the adrenal medulla, whilst noradrenaline is also produced at other sites in the body. Noradrenaline raises blood pressure by causing blood vessels to become constricted. It is also carried by the bloodstream to the anterior pituitary, where it triggers the release of yet more ACTH. This prolongs the response to stress, and has the effect of preparing the body to deal efficiently with threat (Hayward, 1998).

The heightened pattern of physiological activity described in Table 4.1, which corresponds to Cannon's (1927) *fight-or-flight response* (see Box 4.2, page 62), cannot be maintained for long. If the stressor is removed, physiological activity returns to baseline levels. However, because the noradrenaline released by the adrenal medulla *prolongs* adrenaline's action, sympathetic arousal continues for a period even if the stressor itself is short-lived. If the stressor continues, then at some point the *parasympathetic branch* of the ANS (see Figure 4.2, page 62) is activated to try and slow down the internal organs (such as the heart) that were activated by the sympathetic branch.

Table 4.1 *Some of the sympathetic branch physiological activities heightened by the 'stress hormones'*

- *Heart rate accelerates* and *blood pressure increases*. This results in blood being sent to parts of the body that will need it for strenuous activity.
- *Glucose* is released from the *liver* to provide fuel for quick energy.
- *Respiration rate* accelerates to supply more oxygen to the muscles.
- *Muscles* are tensed in preparation for an adaptive response (such as running away).
- *Blood coaguability* increases so that blood will clot more quickly.
- *Perspiration* occurs to cool the body and allow more energy to be burned.
- *Digestion* is inhibited, which makes more blood available to the muscles and brain.
- Some *tissue* is broken down to provide energy-giving sugars.
- *Blood* moves from the internal organs to the skeletal musculature.

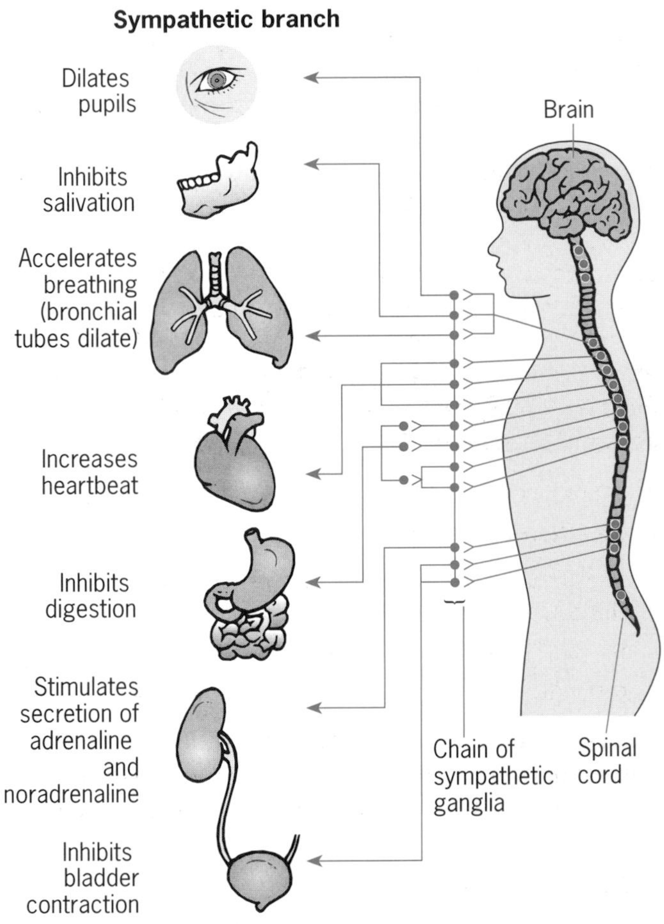

Figure 4.4 *Some of the organs affected by the sympathetic branch of the ANS (see also text above)*

STAGE 2 OF THE GAS: THE RESISTANCE STAGE

If a stressor cannot be dealt with, or it continues, the body begins to recover from the initial alarm reaction and starts coping with the situation. Although endocrine and sympathetic activities drop slightly, they are still higher than normal as the body continues to draw on its resources. This is the *resistance stage* of the GAS. If the stressor can be adequately dealt with, or is terminated, physiological damage is unlikely. However, the action of corticosteroids aggravates the natural inflammatory reaction, and the *immune* system (the system that helps us combat disease: see pages 66–68) is less responsive to infection or physical damage. Additionally, the replacement of cells which have a high turnover is inhibited. This is *immunosuppression*. So, whilst an organism *appears* to be able to defend itself against the stressor, its body's resources are being *depleted* as they are used faster than they are replaced.

STAGE 3 OF THE GAS: THE EXHAUSTION STAGE

Once ACTH and corticosteroids are circulating in the bloodstream, they tend to inhibit the further release of ACTH from the pituitary gland (through a *negative feedback system*). If the stressor is removed during the resistance stage, blood sugar levels will gradually return to normal and, as noted above, physiological damage is unlikely. However, if the stressor cannot be dealt with, or is prolonged or repeated, higher brain centres will override the negative feedback system and *maintain* the pituitary–adrenal excitation. The adrenal glands enlarge, and lose their stores of adrenal hormones. Because the body's resources are being continually drained, several effects occur, including the following:

- tissues begin to show signs of wear-and-tear;
- muscles become fatigued;
- blood sugar levels drop (and in extreme cases produce *hypoglycaemia*);
- the endocrine glands, kidneys and other organs are damaged.

In this *exhaustion stage*, what Selye calls *diseases of adaptation* (and what others call *stress-related illnesses*) occur. Some of these are discussed further on pages 66–69.

PAUSE FOR THOUGHT

Is there more to stress than the GAS? How might *psychological factors* modify our reactions to stressors, and what sorts of *psychological effects* could stressors have?

A BRIEF EVALUATION OF SELYE'S RESEARCH

Selye's GAS is useful in explaining the physiology of stress. However, his claim about the *non-specific* pattern of responses produced by stressors has been challenged. Some stressors produce patterns of physiological activity different from those of other stressors (Taylor, 1990). Also, research into the GAS was based on the study of non-humans' (and principally rats') responses to stressors. Selye's concentration on the body's physiological responses to largely non-social stressors ignored the role of *psychological factors* in the stress response. Much of the physiological activity in response to a stressor is likely to be determined by the *psychological impact* of the stressor rather than its actual presence. Selye also neglected the *psychological effects* of stressors.

Box 4.4 Some psychological factors in, and effects of, stress

- Stressors exert several effects on *cognitive processes*, some of which are negative. For example, a person experiencing a stressor might be easily *distracted* from a task, and perform more poorly (although as Selye acknowledges, *eustress* (see page 60) can be beneficial, at least up to a point). The *primary appraisal* of a stressor involves deciding whether it has positive, neutral or negative implications. If it is decided that it has negative implications, it is assessed according to how challenging, threatening or harmful it is. After this, *secondary appraisal* occurs. This involves considering whether our abilities will allow us to overcome the challenge or threat assessed earlier. Whether or not stress is experienced depends on these two appraisals.

- Stress is also associated with *negative emotional states*, including anger, hostility, embarrassment, depression, helplessness, and anxiety. People who cannot cope effectively with *anxiety* are more susceptible to a variety of mental and physical disorders.

- Stress affects *behaviour* in several ways. Some behaviours involve an attempt to confront the stressor, whilst others involve withdrawing from it (and the terms 'fight' and 'flight' respectively can be used to describe these). Yet other behaviours involve efforts to adapt to the stressor by, for example, taking avoiding action whenever it occurs. All of these are attempts to *manage* or *reduce* the effects of stressors. Stress management is discussed in detail on pages 77–82.

RESEARCH INTO THE RELATIONSHIP BETWEEN STRESS AND ILLNESS

A general way of trying to understand why stress is bad for us is to look at it from an *evolutionary* perspective. The sympathetic branch of the ANS responds as a unit, so when it is stimulated, generalised undifferentiated arousal occurs (Green, 1994). This was probably extremely important in our evolutionary past, when our ancestors were frequently confronted by life-threatening dangers, and is why the fight-or-flight response evolved. However, whilst an accelerated heart rate might have been necessary to send blood to the muscles when confronted by a sabre-tooth tiger, it might be quite irrelevant to most *everyday stressors*. Although most stressors don't present us with physical danger, our nervous and endocrine systems have evolved in such a way that we typically react to them *as if they did*. Although this reaction might have been an *adaptive* response for our ancestors, it may have become *maladaptive* today.

A large body of evidence suggests that stress plays a *causal* role in several types of illness, although any illness can, of course, have a purely physical cause. Amongst others, a link *evidently* exists between stress and headaches, asthma, cancer, cardiovascular disorders, hypertension, and the malfunctioning of the immune system. This section considers research into the relationship between stress and the *immune system* and *cardiovascular disorders*.

PAUSE FOR THOUGHT

Most of us typically catch a cold during the winter months. However, it is not unusual to see students sneezing and coughing before, during and after their examinations, when other people are apparently fit and healthy. How could this observation be explained?

STRESS AND THE IMMUNE SYSTEM

As noted earlier (see page 65), the *immune system* helps to combat disease. It is a collection of billions of specialised cells distributed throughout the bloodstream, which move in and out of tissues and organs. White blood cells (*leucocytes*) form the basis of the cell population in the immune system. There are many types of leucocyte, but they all function to seek, repel, and destroy *antigens* (bacteria, viruses, and other hazardous foreign bodies). Some cells produce and secrete *antibodies*, which bind to antigens and identify them as targets for destruction. They also form 'memories' of how to fight the antigens they encounter, which is why *vaccines* are effective. A diagrammatic representation of the immune system is shown in Figure 4.5 (see page 67).

The immune system also plays a role in *inflammation*. When an injury occurs, blood vessels first contract in order to stem bleeding. Shortly afterwards they dilate, allowing more blood to flow to the damaged area (hence the redness and warmth that characterises inflammation). The blood carries leucocytes to combat foreign bodies that might use the injured area to gain access to the body. However, if the immune system is *suppressed*, we are much more vulnerable to the effects of foreign bodies. If the immune system becomes *over-reactive*, it turns on itself and attacks healthy body tissues (Hayward, 1999).

As noted earlier (see page 63), corticosteroid production increases when the body is exposed to a stressor. Although intermittent corticosteroid production has negligible effects on the immune system, persistent production, as occurs in the GAS, impairs its functioning by interfering with antibody production. This decreases inflammation and suppresses leucocyte activity.

The study of psychological factors (especially stress) and their effects on the immune system is called *psychoneuroimmunology*. Stressful events have been linked to several infectious illnesses, including *influenza, herpes*, and the *Epstein–Barr virus* (of which extreme tiredness is a major characteristic). Of course, stress itself does not *cause* infectious illness, but it apparently increases susceptibility to infectious agents such as bacteria and viruses by temporarily weakening immune defences. Stressors that apparently compromise or 'down-regulate' the immune system include examinations, the death of a spouse and marital discord (Evans *et al.*, 1997: see also pages 70–72). In non-humans, separation from the mother, electric shocks, and exposure to loud noise have all been shown to cause immunological deficiencies.

It is likely that, at least in humans, some negative effects can be attributed to differences in lifestyle (e.g. smoking and drinking: Marusic *et al.*, 1999). However, it also seems likely that stress can exert a *direct* effect on the immune system. *Corticosteroid* production is one factor involved. Another is *secretory immunoglobulin A*, (sIgA), a substance found in tears, saliva, bronchial and other bodily secretions, and which is one of the body's first lines of defence against influenza. A third factor is *interleukin-b*, a protein produced soon after tissue injury, which regulates the remodelling of connective tissue in wounds and the production of collagen (the tough fibrous tissue in scars).

In one study of interleukin-b, two groups of participants underwent small skin biopsies on their arms. Compared with a non-stressed control group, it took

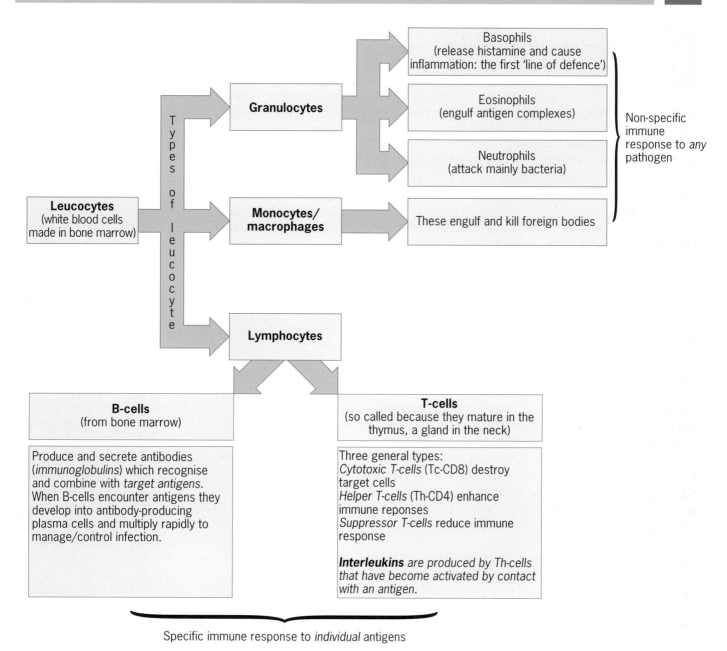

Figure 4.5 *The immune system (Adapted from Hayward, 1998)*

significantly longer for the wound to heal in people caring for relatives with dementia (Sweeney, 1995). In another study, Kiecolt-Glaser *et al.* (1995) compared the rate of wound healing in a group of 'high-stress' women, who were caring for relatives with Alzheimer's disease, with a 'stress-free' matched group. Complete wound healing typically took nine days longer in the former than the latter. The fact that stress impairs the body's ability to heal and its response to infectious diseases, has potentially important clinical consequences for people undergoing and then recovering from major surgery.

There may also be a link between stress, the immune system, and *endorphins*, morphine-like substances which are produced by the endocrine system as the body's own natural painkillers. Whilst the exact role of endorphines in the reaction to stress is unclear, they might help to mediate the body's coping response to stressful stimuli. This is supported by the finding that when people are given *naloxone* (a drug that blocks the effects of endorphins), they show signs of increased anxiety, depression, irritability, and difficulty in concentrating.

However, evidence from non-human studies indicates that endorphins also *inhibit* the immune system, and promote the growth of tumours. Interestingly, the chronic use of painkillers by humans (which might be comparable to the increase in endorphin levels in response to a stressor) is associated with increased incidence of infection and several immunological abnormalities. These include a decrease in cells which defend the body primarily against fungi and viral infections, and absorb dead or foreign material.

Box 4.5 Acute and chronic stressors and the immune system

Acute stressors include speaking in public and working to deadlines, whilst *chronic stressors* include separation, divorce and caring for others. Interestingly, whilst chronic stressors are associated with a *decrease* in defensive agents like sIgA, acute stressors are associated with an *increase* in these agents. According to Evans *et al.* (1997), the *sympatho–adrenomedullary axis* (see page 64) regulates the defence system in response to acute stressors, and this may be a normal part of the body's adaptation to life's psychological challenges. With chronic stressors, the *hypothalamic–pituitary–adrenal axis* (see page 63) takes over, and causes immunosuppressive effects via corticosteroid production.

PAUSE FOR THOUGHT

Do you get impatient when you are stuck in a traffic jam or waiting in a queue at a supermarket? Do you hurry other people to get on with what they're trying to say? Do you insist on winning games rather than just having fun? Do you get irritated when other people are late for a meeting with you? *Do you think these reactions and behaviours might be harmful to a person who performs them?*

STRESS AND CARDIOVASCULAR DISORDERS

Cardiovascular disorders, such as heart disease and disorders of the circulatory system, are known to be associated with certain 'risk factors'. These include diet, alcohol consumption, smoking, obesity, and lack of physical activity. However, since these risk factors account for only half of all diagnosed cases, others must be involved. One of them appears to be stress.

In the late 1950s, Friedman and Rosenman examined the relationship between diet and coronary heart disease (CHD). They found that American men were far more susceptible to heart disease than American women, even though there was apparently no difference between the sexes in dietary terms. Friedman and

Rosenman speculated that *job-related stress* might be a factor, since most of the men worked but most of the women did not. When the researchers sent out questionnaires to people who had had a heart attack, and asked them what they thought had caused their own heart attacks and those of people they knew, their responses appeared to mirror Friedman and Rosenman's speculation.

In a later study investigating job-related stress, Friedman and Rosenman monitored the *blood-clotting speed* and *serum cholesterol levels* (two warning signs in coronary heart disease) of 40 tax accountants over several months. For a time, the levels were within normal range. However, as the deadline for filing tax returns approached, they rose dangerously and then returned to normal after the deadline.

Key STUDY

Box 4.6 Type A and non-Type A

Friedman & Rosenman (1974) undertook a nine-year study involving over 3000 initially healthy 39–59-year-old men. On the basis of their responses about eating habits and ways of dealing with stressful situations, the men were divided into two roughly equal groups called *Type A* and *non-Type A*. Type A individuals tended to be ambitious, competitive, easily angered, time-conscious, hard-driving, and demanding of perfection in both themselves and others. Non-Type A individuals tended to be relaxed, easygoing, not driven to achieve perfection, forgiving, and not easily angered.

Friedman and Rosenman found that even when risk factors such as smoking and drinking were taken into consideration, 70 per cent of the 257 who died during the nine years after the study began were Type A individuals. Other research, conducted in other countries, has *sometimes* also found that Type A individuals have a greater *relative risk* of developing CHD. However, the role of the *Type A personality* (or *Type A behaviour pattern*) in 'coronary proneness' has been challenged. For example:

• Type A people may engage *more frequently* in behaviours that are known risk factors (e.g. smoking), and may be more *psychologically reactive* to stress. Both of these could contribute to their coronary proneness.

• Type A behaviour might even be a *response* to, rather than a cause of, physiological reactivity. Even when they are unconscious and undergoing surgery, Type A people show higher blood pressure levels than non-Type A people experiencing the same surgery. This suggests a *predisposition* to respond with heightened physiological activity to a stressor's presence. If so, Type A behaviour could be seen as a way of *coping* with heightened physiological activity.

- It has been proposed that there is actually no difference between Type A and non-Type A men in the incidence of heart attacks and death rates. Indeed, Type A men might actually be at a *lower risk* of recurrent heart attacks than non-Type A men (Cramb, 1997).

The contradictory findings in this area of research might be reconciled if certain Type A characteristics, such as *cynicism*, *hostility*, and an *aggressively reactive temperament*, are actually more influential than others (as some researchers have proposed). Also, Type A individuals may be *'hardier'* than non-Type As (see pages 79–80 for a discussion of the role played by *hardiness* in stress reduction).

Clearly, the relationship between stress and CHD is not straightforward. Stress *itself* cannot cause CHD or any other illness (see page 66), and exactly how it is linked is not known. One proposal is that chronic stress, involving repeated episodes of increased heart rate and blood pressure, produces *plaque formation* in the cardiovascular system. Additionally, stress may increase *blood cholesterol* levels through the action of adrenaline and noradrenaline on the release of free fatty acids. This produces a 'clumping' of cholesterol particles leading to clots in the blood and artery walls, and narrowing of the arteries. In turn, raised heart rate is related to a more rapid build-up of cholesterol on artery walls. High blood pressure results in small lesions in the artery walls, and cholesterol tends to get trapped in these lesions (Holmes, 1994).

Box 4.7 Stress and hypertension

Consistent with the likely role played by the sympathetic branch of the ANS, stress might be linked to cardiovascular disorders because of its apparent role in *hypertension* (the medical term for chronically high blood pressure). This currently accounts for seven per cent of all deaths world-wide. Blood flow through the veins increases when ANS activity is heightened. This can cause both a hardening and a general deterioration in blood vessel tissues, leading to heart disease, stroke and kidney failure. Although several factors contribute to hypertension, the role of stress has been demonstrated in several studies.

For example, Harburg *et al.* (1973) measured the blood pressure of Americans from 'high' and 'low' stress areas of Detroit. 'High' stress areas were defined as those in which population density, crime rates, poverty and divorce were greatest. The highest blood pressures were found in those living in the highest stress areas.

Section Summary

- Stress can be defined as a pattern of negative physiological states and psychological processes occurring in situations where people perceive threats to their well-being which they may be unable to meet.

- Selye found that non-humans respond in a physiologically non-specific way to any stressor. He called the response the **general adaptation syndrome** (GAS).

- The GAS is an interaction between the **central nervous system** (especially the **hypothalamus**), **autonomic nervous system** (especially the **sympathetic branch**) and **endocrine system** (especially the **pituitary gland**).

- The first stage of the GAS, the **alarm reaction**, is characterised by physiological activity that prepares the body for 'fight or flight'. Two parallel effects exerted by the hypothalamus involve the pituitary and adrenal glands (the **hypothalamic–pituitary–adrenal axis**) and the autonomic nervous system's sympathetic branch (the **sympatho–adrenomedullary axis**).

- In the **resistance stage**, the body is less aroused, but continues to draw on its resources above the normal levels. The **exhaustion stage** occurs when the stressor can no longer be managed. This results in bodily damage and **diseases of adaptation**.

- The GAS is a useful approach to the physiology of stress. However, its application to humans is weakened because it ignores the role played by **cognitive processes** in the stress response.

- Cognitive processes include **primary appraisal**, in which negative implications of a potential stressor are assessed, and **secondary appraisal**, which involves an assessment of one's ability to overcome the potential stressor's challenge.

- **Cognitive responses** to a stressor include distractibility and impaired task performance. **Emotional responses** include anger, hostility, embarrassment, and depression. Stressors produce various **behavioural responses**, including confrontation, withdrawal, adaptation and avoidance, all of which are attempts to manage/reduce the effects of stressors.

- Stress might contribute to several types of illness, including **cardiovascular disorders** and malfunctioning of the **immune system**.

- **Psychoneuroimmunology** is the study of the effects of psychological factors (especially stress) on immune system functioning. The production of **corticosteroids**, **secretory immunoglobulin A** and

interleukin-b have all been shown to be 'down-regulated' by **chronic stressors**.

- **Acute stressors** are associated with 'up-regulation' of corticosteroid production, and this may be a normal part of the body's adaptation to psychological challenges.

- The relationship between stress and cardiovascular disorders could be a consequence of personality type (**Type A**), and some evidence supports this. However, other evidence is less supportive, and if a relationship does exist it is a complex one.

- Stress could be linked to cardiovascular disorders because of its apparent role in **hypertension**. Increased blood flow through the veins can cause both a hardening and a general deterioration in the tissue of blood vessels.

Self-Assessment Questions

1 a Describe the role played by the autonomic nervous system in the general adaptation syndrome (GAS). *(6 marks)*

   b Describe **two** research studies which suggest that stress plays a role in cardiovascular disorders.
   (6 marks + 6 marks)

   c 'Stress itself does not cause infectious illnesses, but it is likely that it increases the susceptibility to infectious agents by temporarily weakening immune defences.'
   Assess the relationship between stress and the malfunctioning of the immune system. *(12 marks)*

2 a Outline the three stages in Selye's general adaptation syndrome (GAS). *(6 marks)*

   b Describe **two** research studies into the relationship between stress and the immune system.
   (6 marks + 6 marks)

   c 'Since risk factors such as smoking account for only half of all diagnosed cases of cardiovascular disorders, other factors must be involved. One of them appears to be stress.'
   To what extent does stress play a role in cardiovascular disorders? *(12 marks)*

Stressors: Sources of Stress

Many *stressors* have been identified. These include *frustration* (being blocked from a desirable goal), *conflict* (the experience of two or more competing or contradictory motives or goals) and *pain*. In this section, however, attention will be paid to *life changes* and *workplace stressors*.

LIFE CHANGES

It is not surprising that the stimuli identified above have been associated with stress. However, it is not just *negative* stimuli that cause stress, as anyone who has tried to ensure that everything is organised for a family holiday would agree. Whilst preparing for pleasant events mobilises our energies, it also places great demands on our resources.

PAUSE FOR THOUGHT

Identify life changes/life events, both pleasant and unpleasant, which people might consider to be stressful. Are they equally stressful, or is it possible to rank order them from most to least stressful?

Holmes & Rahe (1967) examined the hospital records of 5000 patients and identified 43 *life events*, of varying seriousness, that appeared to cluster in the months preceding the onset of their illnesses. Holmes and Rahe worked on the assumption that stress is created by undesirable *or* desirable events which require *change*. Accordingly, they used these 43 events to construct their *social readjustment rating scale* (SRRS), a measure of 'normal life stresses'. Assigning an arbitrary value of 50 'life change units' to 'marriage', they asked people to assign a value to each of the other events according to the amount and intensity of readjustment they perceived them to require *relative* to getting married. Most events were judged to be *less* stressful than getting married. However, some, including the death of a spouse (100 units), divorce (73 units) and marital separation (65 units), were judged to be *more* stressful. The original SRRS is shown in Table 4.2.

Holmes and Rahe found a relationship between high SRRS scores for events occurring in the preceding year and the likelihood of experiencing some sort of physical illness within the following year. For example, a person scoring 200–300 life change units appeared to have a 50 per cent chance of developing an illness, whilst for a score of more than 300, the probability rose to around 80 per cent. According to Cohen *et al.* (1998), high SRRS scores are associated with various physical and psychological problems. The more serious include heart disease, cancer, and relapses amongst those diagnosed with mental disorders.

PAUSE FOR THOUGHT

Is it reasonable to conclude that life changes *cause* illness? What are the limitations of the SRRS as a measuring device?

A BRIEF EVALUATION OF HOLMES AND RAHE'S RESEARCH

Although their research has been influential, several important points should be made.

- Even though some studies suggest a relationship between life changes and the likelihood of someone experiencing illness, the *overall* relationship is small and does not predict with any certainty future problems with illness and disease. Partly, this is due to the SRRS's simplistic approach to measurement, in which mean values are simply added up to produce a total score. Also, people *differ* in their ability to withstand the effects of potential stressors, because some people *appraise* events differently to others (see page 60). For

Table 4.2 *To complete the scale, identify those events which you have experienced over the last 12 months, and then add up the life change units associated with them. Note, though, that whilst the events identified by Holmes and Rahe may, to varying degrees, be stressful, it is highly unlikely (though not impossible) that many items on the original SRRS will apply to the typical student following a course in psychology! Note also that by today's standards, a $10,000 (£6,500) mortgage is not as big a debt as it was in the 1960s.*

Rank	Life event	Mean value
1	Death of spouse	100
2	Divorce	65
3	Marital separation	65
4	Jail term	63
5	Death of close family member	63
6	Personal illness or injury	53
7	Marriage	50
8	Fired at work	47
9	Marital reconciliation	45
10	Retirement	45
11	Change in health of family member	44
12	Pregnancy	40
13	Sex difficulties	39
14	Gain of new family member	39
15	Business readjustment	39
16	Change in financial state	38
17	Death of close friend	37
18	Change to different line of work	36
19	Change in number of arguments with spouse	35
20	Mortgage over $10,000	31
21	Foreclosure of mortgage or loan	30
22	Change in responsibilities at work	29
23	Son or daughter leaving home	29
24	Trouble with in-laws	29
25	Outstanding personal achievement	28
26	Wife begins or stops work	26
27	Begin or end school	26
28	Change in living conditions	25
29	Revision of personal habits	24
30	Trouble with boss	23
31	Change in work hours or conditions	20
32	Change in residence	20
33	Change in schools	20
34	Change in recreation	19
35	Change in church activities	19
36	Change in social activities	18
37	Mortgage or loan less than $10,000	17
38	Change in sleeping habits	16
39	Change in number of family get-togethers	15
40	Change in eating habits	15
41	Vacation	13
42	Christmas	12
43	Minor violations of the law	11

example, divorce might be stressful for one person, but might significantly lower the stress experienced by another. Simply adding up the values assigned to each life change does not take into account differences in how potential stressors are appraised.

- Research using the SRRS is typically *retrospective*, and asks people to *recall* both their illnesses and the life events that occurred during, say, the preceding twelve months. One way this might produce unreliable data is if a person who was under stress, for whatever reason, focused on minor physiological sensations and reported them as 'symptoms of illnesses' (Davison & Neale, 1994).

- Research with the SRRS is also *correlational* rather than experimental (see Chapter 7, page 139). The fact that two variables share a relationship does not necessarily mean that changes in one *cause* changes in the other. Several alternative explanations of the relationship are possible. For example, it could be that people who are predisposed towards physical or psychological problems experience more life changes than those not predisposed. So, a particular medical disorder might itself *cause* sexual problems, changes in sleeping habits, and so on. These life changes could therefore be the *result* of physical or psychological ill-health as much as the *cause* of them.

- Various life changes could also cause changes in behaviour which are not conducive to good health. A person experiencing marital separation, for example, might begin to drink heavily and/or act in other ways that increase the risk of illness. The relationship between life changes and illness might be more subtle than the direct link claimed by Holmes and Rahe.

- Holmes and Rahe's original assumption, that stress is caused by *any* event which requires change, has also been challenged. *Positive* life changes may be *less* disturbing than negative life changes. This is apparently true even if the number of life change units assigned to an event on the SRRS is high. For example, a 'major change in the health of a family member' (44 life change units) is less stressful if the change is for the better than the worse. Related to this is the finding that the *undesirable aspects* of events are at least as important as the fact that they change people's lives. The 'top ten' events on the SRRS (to which most life change units are assigned) have a largely negative 'feel' about them. This implies that the SRRS might be confusing 'change' with 'negativity'.

Box 4.8 'Hassles' as stressors

According to Kanner *et al.* (1981), it is the less dramatic, but often everyday events in life, that are most stressful. Such events include being stuck in traffic, arguing with a partner, and even having to meet some social obligation you would rather not. Kanner *et al.* have called such irritants, ranging from minor annoyances to fairly major pressures, problems or difficulties, *hassles*.

The *hassles scale* is a 117-item questionnaire that is used to examine the relationship between hassles and health. High scores have been found to be related to both physiological and psychological ill-health, and the scale appears to be a better predictor of both physical and psychological health than scores on the SRRS. By contrast, high scores on Kanner *et al.*'s *uplifts scale* (which consists of 135 items, including 'relating well with spouse/lover' and 'meeting your responsibilities') are *inversely* related to physiological and psychological ill-health.

WORKPLACE STRESSORS

PAUSE FOR THOUGHT

Are all occupations likely to be equally stressful? Who in an organisation is most likely to experience stress, the 'executives' or those 'on the shop floor'? What sorts of things might cause people to experience stress in the workplace?

The relationship between stress and the workplace, along with the relationship between workplace stressors and health, was first systematically investigated in the 1970s. Studies indicate that some occupations are more stressful than others. Four of the most stressful are nursing, social work, teaching, and working in the police force. In *nursing*, some sources of stress are intrinsic to the job. These include:

- having to deal constantly with the pain, anxiety and death of patients;

- having to support patients and their families, often with little appropriate training;

- needing to maintain high concentration levels for long time periods;

- being in the 'front line' when major disasters occur, as in the Paddington rail disaster (1999).

Whilst the popular perception is that managers and senior executives are most susceptible to stress ('*executive stress*'), the picture is actually very complicated (Lazarus, 1999). Some evidence suggests that people on the 'bottom rung' in an organisation are most susceptible, even when factors such as smoking habits are controlled for. For example, Marmot *et al.* (1997) found that men and women in clerical and office support positions were much more likely to develop cardiovascular disorders than those in administrative positions. Of all the potential contributory factors explored by Marmot *et al.*, a *low degree of control* emerged as the biggest (confirming other findings obtained from both human and non-human studies: see pages 80–81).

Figure 4.6 *Dealing on the floor of the stock exchange is one of many stressful occupations*

The interaction between occupational and other factors such as the environment is complex (Marmot & Wilkinson, 1999). What seems to be clear, though, is that *all* employees suffer from some degree of stress as a result of their work and the environment in which the work is done, although women are confronted with *more* and *different* employment-related stressors than men (Long & Khan, 1993). Many employment-related stressors have been identified. Some of these and their effects are identified in Table 4.3.

Table 4.3 *Some effects of employment-related stressors*

- **Work overload/underload:** *Quantitative overload* is having too much to do, or having to be excessively quick or productive. *Qualitative overload* occurs when work is too difficult or demands excessive attention. Both are associated with anxiety and frustration. *Quantitative underload* (not having enough to do) and *qualitative underload* (when skills and abilities are under-utilised) are both associated with boredom, frustration, low job satisfaction and lack of commitment.

- **Role ambiguity/commitment:** *Role ambiguity* occurs when an employee is unclear about his/her work-role in an organisation. It is associated with frustration and anxiety. *Role conflict* occurs when a person is required to do something that conflicts with his/her beliefs, or when s/he has to perform two incompatible roles. Role conflict has been shown to be associated with physical illness (e.g. cardiovascular disorders, peptic ulcers).

- **Job insecurity/redundancy:** Both of these are associated with anxiety, which is heightened by feelings of unfairness, because the organisation still requires commitment but does not offer it to the employee. Lack of a career structure has also been shown to be associated with poor physical health.

- **Degree of latitude/control:** *High decision latitude/control*, in which employees make decisions about work practices or problems, can be stressful depending on the outcome of the decisions made. However, *low decision latitude/control* is associated with low self-esteem, anxiety, depression, apathy, exhaustion, and symptoms of coronary heart disease.

- **Interpersonal relationships/support:** *Poor interpersonal relationships/supports* are associated with high anxiety, job tension and low job satisfaction. *Bullying* and *violence* at work are associated with stress, absenteeism and poor mental health. *Good interpersonal relationships/supports* from superiors, subordinates and peers or colleagues, by contrast, promote health for the individual and the organisation.

(Based on Hayward, 1996)

Some of the stressors identified above have been linked with potentially harmful behaviours in those affected by them. Chen & Spector (1992), for example, gave 400 employees questionnaires about job stressors, frustration, satisfaction, and potentially harmful behaviours (such as aggressive acts, interpersonal violence, theft and substance abuse). One important finding was that the relationship between stressors and behaviour was greatest for the more directly aggressive actions like sabotage, hostility and intention to quit. Theft and absence showed only a moderate relationship with stressors, a finding which suggests that stress might not be the principle reason for their occurrence. Interestingly, substance abuse (e.g. alcohol) was *not* related to stress, although it has been shown to be in other research (Begley, 1998). Whether stressors *trigger* aggression, or aggressive employees *interpret* jobs as having high stress levels, has yet to be determined.

Key STUDY

Box 4.9 Are working mothers more stressed than non-working mothers?

A further area of interest is the *home/work interface*. Kahn & Cuthbertson (1998) compared the stress experienced by working mothers with mothers who were full-time homemakers. Although there were few differences between the two on various measures of physical and mental health, full-time homemakers experienced *more* depression than working mothers, and reported greater stress when spouses did not contribute to childcare or general household chores. By contrast, stress *decreased* in working mothers because spouses appeared to be more willing to undertake domestic tasks (see Chapter 3).

INDIVIDUAL DIFFERENCES WHICH MODIFY THE EFFECTS OF STRESSORS

In a study of English women who had undergone mastectomies as a result of being diagnosed with breast cancer, Greer *et al.* (1979) found that those who reacted either by denying what had happened, or by showing a 'fighting spirit', were significantly more likely to be free of cancer five years later than women who stoically accepted it or felt helpless.

Much evidence indicates that people do differ in their responses to potentially stressful situations, and that some are more vulnerable than others. This is hardly surprising. In their definition of stress (see page 60), Lazarus & Folkman (1984) use the phrase '*where people perceive threats to their well-being*'. Their definition implies, correctly, that stressors cannot be defined objectively (independently of the person experiencing the stress). As noted previously (see page 65), perhaps the biggest weakness of Selye's research is that it ignored *psychological processes*, and failed to acknowledge that much of the physiological response to stress is not directly determined by the actual presence of the stressor, but by its psychological *impact*. This section considers the role of *personality*, *culture*, and *gender* as individual differences which *modify* the effects of stressors.

Personality

Some of the research into the *Type A personality* (or *behaviour pattern*) was described in the section on stress and cardiovascular disorders. Although early studies indicated that Type A individuals have a higher risk of developing cardiovascular disorders than non-Type A individuals, more recent research has disputed this. As

noted on page 69, the contradictory findings might be reconciled if certain Type A characteristics, such as *anger* and *hostility*, are more important than others.

Booth-Kewley & Friedman (1987) have shown that *hostility* is a better single predictor of coronary heart disease than the Type A pattern as a whole. However, whether hostility *causes* coronary heart disease or is merely *related* to it, has yet to be resolved. Possibly, both personality (in the form of Type A and hostility) *and* genetic factors that lead to hostility and arousal, are involved in the development of cardiovascular disorders. Even so, the fact that not all Type A personalities succumb to cardiovascular disorders and at least some non-Type A personalities do, suggests that other physiological and/or psychological factors play a role.

Temoshok (1987) has proposed the existence of a *Type C personality*, who has difficulty expressing emotion and tends to suppress or inhibit emotions, particularly negative ones like *anger*. Although Type C personality characteristics have been linked to *cancer*, there is no convincing evidence that they *cause* cancer. However, such characteristics might influence cancer's progression, and thereby influence the survival time of cancer patients. The Type C personality has also been linked with decreased sperm production. The hormones produced in stressful situations could inhibit the manufacture of hormones necessary for healthy sperm production (Norton, 1999).

Box 4.10 Types D and ER

In addition to Types A and C, there may be other personality types more susceptible to the negative effects of stress. The *Type D personality* is an anxious, gloomy and socially inept worrier. Research indicates that ten years after 87 men had suffered heart attacks, those who scored high on measures of social ineptness and anxiety were four times more likely to have had further attacks. The *Type ER personality* ('emotional responder') is highly volatile, at one time being extremely happy and at another in the depths of despair. It has been shown that the mood swings of Type ER heart patients reduced blood flow to the heart, which increased the risk of another attack by four times. Yet another, but so far un-named, personality type is pessimistic, has low self-esteem, and lacks control over events in his/her life. Evidently, heart attack victims with these characteristics are three times more likely to suffer a second attack. Clearly, there is much to learn about the role of personality in the predisposition to stress and illness.

(Adapted from Burne, 1999)

Culture

An important variable which might interact with personality is *culture*. For example, competitiveness and striving for success are common goals in capitalist societies, but less common in more traditional, communal ones. Culture might even exert an effect on its own. One further criticism of Holmes and Rahe's SRRS (see pages 70–72) is that it does not take account of cultural and ethnic differences in the kinds of potential stressors to which people are exposed. For example, the physical and mental health of African-Americans is generally poorer than that of white Americans. Whilst this is partly accountable for in terms of the direct negative effects of poverty (e.g. poor diet, education and medical care), there are also many psychological stressors involved, many of which are more or less directly related to *racism* (see Box 4.11).

Acculturative stress (Anderson, 1991) refers to the emotional challenges posed by discrepancies between the values, beliefs, norms and behaviours of African-Americans and those of the majority white community, in which African-Americans often live as outcasts and strangers. Anderson distinguishes between three types of stressor:

*   Level 1 (*chronic*) stressors include racism, over-crowding, poor living conditions and noise;
*   Level 2 (*major life events*) stressors include those identified in the SRRS (see Table 4.2, page 71);
*   Level 3 (*daily events, hassles*) includes the sorts of stressors identified by Kanner *et al.* (1981: see Box 4.8, page 72).

Acculturative stress can be present at all three levels. However, it occurs most often at Level 3. On a day-to-day basis, African-Americans face pressures to become assimilated into the mainstream white society. At the same time, they face obstacles to assimilation and the compromise of their sense of African-American identity as a result of successful assimilation.

Box 4.11 The puzzle of hypertension in African-Americans

Thirty-five per cent of black Americans suffer from hypertension, and it accounts for 20 per cent of deaths among blacks in America. This is twice the figure for whites. It is popularly supposed that black Americans are 'intrinsically susceptible', because of some vaguely defined aspect of their genetic make-up. However, whilst psychological and social stresses are extremely difficult to measure, especially across cultures, there is little dispute that blacks in North

America and Europe face a unique kind of stress – *racial discrimination*. Although the long-term effects of racism on blood pressure are unknown, it is possible that the relationships between races in the continental United States place greater 'insults' on the cardiovascular system than it does elsewhere in the world.

(Based on Cooper *et al.*, 1999)

Gender

At every age from birth to 85 and beyond, more men die than women. However, despite this lower *mortality rate*, women have higher *morbidity rates*, and are more likely to suffer generalised poor health and specific diseases. For example, women have higher rates of diabetes, amnesia, gastrointestinal problems and rheumatoid arthritis. They also visit their doctor more often, and use more prescribed drugs. The lower mortality rate might be explained in terms of a biological mechanism possessed by women which protects them from life-threatening diseases. For example, *estrogen* may protect against coronary heart disease, since hormone replacement therapy lowers mortality from it (perhaps by maintaining raised levels of *high-density lipoprotein* (*HDL*), the 'good cholesterol').

Key STUDY
Box 4.12 Adrenaline and the sexes

Frankenhauser (1983) found that compared with male students, female students *failed* to show a significant increase in adrenaline output when faced with a stressful situation (doing an intelligence test). Females' relative unresponsiveness might contribute to their higher life expectancy, because they may experience less stress-related damage during their lifetimes. Frankenhauser *et al.* (1991) found that female engineering students and bus drivers showed *male* patterns of adrenaline response to stressors, suggesting that *socialisation* into *gender roles* might be the important variable, rather than any biological sex difference.

Another explanation for the difference in male and female mortality rates could lie in the finding that women are less likely than men to be Type A personalities (see Box 4.6, page 68). They are also less *hostile* than men. The Type A behaviour pattern might reflect the traditional male gender role (which emphasises achievement, mastery, competitiveness, not asking for help or emotional support, a tendency to become angry and express this anger when frustrated, and an excessive need for control). These attributes could be linked to men's greater vulnerability to cardiovascular disorders and other stress-related health risks (Davison & Neale, 1994).

Finally, whilst the mortality rate in men from cardiovascular disorders has declined over the last 30 years or so, it has stayed fairly constant for women. So, the mortality rate gap between the sexes is decreasing. This might be explained in terms of *lifestyle changes*, in that lifestyle differences between the sexes are decreasing, with women smoking and drinking more than they used to (Davison & Neale, 1994).

Section Summary

- Many **stressors** have been identified. Two of these are **life changes** and certain aspects of the **workplace**.

- Holmes and Rahe's **social readjustment rating scale (SRRS)** is a measure of 'normal life stresses', and some research indicates that high SRRS scores are associated with various physical and psychological problems.

- The SRRS is, however, a simplistic measuring device, and does not take into account differences in the way people **appraise** stressors. Additionally, research using the SRRS is **retrospective** and **correlational**.

- **Hassles** are less dramatic, but often everyday, life events. They may be more influential as stressors than life changes. Kanner *et al.*'s '**hassles scale**' appears to be a better predictor of physical and psychological ill-health than scores on the SRRS.

- Some occupations are more stressful than others, and the interaction between occupational and other factors is complex. However, all employees suffer some degree of stress as a result of their work and the environment in which it is done.

- Many employment-related stressors have been identified. These include **work overload/underload, role ambiguity/commitment, job insecurity/redundancy, degree of latitude/control** and **interpersonal relationships/support**.

- Some employment-related stressors are associated with potentially harmful behaviour in those affected by them, especially more directly aggressive actions like **sabotage**, **hostility** and **intention to quit**. However, whether stressors trigger aggression has yet to be discovered.

- One individual difference which might modify the effects of stress is **personality**. Different personality types (**Types A, C, D** and **ER**) may be especially vulnerable to stressors.

- It is likely that there are **cultural** and **ethnic differences** in the kinds of potential stressors to which people are exposed. Many of these are more or less directly related to **racism**.

- **Gender** is another important individual difference. Women seem to be relatively unresponsive to stress-producing situations, which might explain their longer average life expectancy. Women are also less likely than men to be Type A personalities, although the gap in death rates from CHD between men and women is closing.

Self-Assessment Questions

3 a Describe **one** research study into life changes as sources of stress. *(6 marks)*

   b Describe how culture and gender can modify the effects of stressors. *(6 marks + 6 marks)*

   c 'All employees suffer from some degree of stress as a result of their work.'

      Assess the relationship between stress and the workplace. *(12 marks)*

4 a Describe how culture can modify the effects of stress. *(6 marks)*

   b Describe **two** research studies into the effects of life changes as sources of stress. *(6 marks + 6 marks)*

   c 'Some personality types are more vulnerable than others to the effects of stressors.'

      To what extent is stress modified by personality type? *(12 marks)*

Critical I S S U E

Stress Management

On the basis that stress almost certainly plays a role in at least some illnesses, it is important to find ways in which it can be managed, and its impact on health minimised. One way to manage stress is to eliminate the factors causing it. However, since there are so many factors that can act as stressors, this is not realistic. Many ways of managing and reducing stress have been devised. Lefcourt *et al.* (1997), for example, have proposed that *humour* can help because it stimulates *endorphin* production (see page 67). This section examines some other approaches to stress management.

PHYSICAL APPROACHES TO MANAGING THE NEGATIVE EFFECTS OF STRESS

Psychotherapeutic drugs

As shown earlier, the body's response to a stressor involves the activation of the sympathetic branch of the ANS (see Box 4.2, page 62). Several methods exist for reducing the physiological effects of stress. One is the use of *drugs* which act directly on the ANS. In cases of chronic stress, *anxiolytic* (anxiety-reducing) drugs are commonly used. The *benzodiazepine* group of anxiolytics includes *chlordiazepoxide* (*Librium*) and *diazepam* (*Valium*). The mode of activity of these drugs and other anxiolytics are described in detail in Gross *et al.* (2000).

PAUSE FOR THOUGHT

What sorts of dangers might be associated with the long-term use of drugs to manage stress?

Although anxiolytic drugs are effective in reducing the physiological effects of stress in the majority of those who take them, they are associated with various *side-effects* such as drowsiness and lethargy. They may also cause *physical dependence* (the body becomes dependent on their presence). If the drug is stopped, various problems occur, such as insomnia, tremors and convulsions. These are the symptoms of *withdrawal* (or *abstinence syndrome*). Anxiolytics are also associated with *tolerance*, that is, an increasing amount of the drug is needed to achieve the same initial effect. Together, physical dependence and tolerance define the medical syndrome *drug addiction*. For these reasons alone, other methods of reducing physiological responses to stress would seem preferable.

Biofeedback

The body is not designed to allow us to be consciously aware of subtle feedback about internal physiological states occurring when we experience stress. *Biofeedback* aims to provide some of this information so that, at least to a degree, we can learn to bring internal physiological states under *voluntary control* and hence modify them. A biofeedback machine provides precise information (or *feedback*) about certain autonomic functions, such as heart rate, muscle tension and blood pressure. The feedback may be presented in auditory and/or visual form. For example, heart-rate changes may be indicated by a tone whose pitch varies, and/or a line on a television monitor that rises or falls when heart rate increases or decreases. The person is then taught to use a psychological technique (such as *meditation*: see Box 4.15, page 78) or some physical response (such as *muscle relaxation*: see page 78) to try to reduce the biofeedback machine's readings.

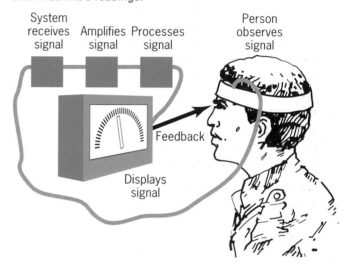

Figure 4.7 *One type of biofeedback apparatus*

Key S T U D Y

Box 4.13 Biofeedback and stress-related disorders

The fact that some people can apparently regulate certain internal body processes has led to biofeedback being used with many types of stress-related disorders. These include migraine and tension headaches and hypertension. For example, Bradley (1995) cites a study in which college students suffering from tension headaches were given seven 50-minute sessions using electromyogram (EMG) biofeedback (feedback about muscle tension). They were also urged to practice bringing the muscle tension under control when free of headaches and at the first sign of a headache. Compared with a similar group of students, given no treatment until the study was over, and another group who engaged in '*pseudomeditation*', the EMG biofeedback produced significant reductions in muscle tension and headaches.

Although biofeedback can be effective, several disadvantages are associated with it:

- Unlike some methods, biofeedback requires a physiological measuring device. Because biofeedback and techniques not requiring specialised equipment (e.g. *relaxation*: see below) are *equally* effective in stress reduction, those techniques would appear to be more preferable.

- Regular practice appears to be needed for the development and maintenance of any beneficial effects (although this is also true of some other methods).

- Whilst biofeedback may eventually enable a person to recognise the symptoms of, say, high blood pressure, without the need for the machine, it is not known *exactly* how biofeedback works.

- Some critics argue that biofeedback itself exerts no effects, and that the important factor is a person's *commitment* to reducing stress and the active involvement of a stress therapist!

Physical activity and exercise

In a study of London bus drivers and conductors, Morris (1953) found that conductors, who moved around the bus collecting fares, were far less likely to suffer from cardiovascular disorders than the constantly seated drivers. Other research has confirmed Morris' conclusion that *physical activity and exercise* are beneficial in stress management (Anshel, 1996).

All activity is apparently useful in reducing the incidence of stress-related illnesses. Physiologically, exercise promotes fitness. Although fitness is a complex concept, one benefit of being fit is that the body uses more oxygen during vigorous exercise, and pumps more blood with each beat. Consequently, circulation is improved and the heart muscles strengthened. Psychologically, exercise might also be therapeutic, since sustained exercise can reduce depression and boost feelings of self-esteem.

Box 4.14 Exercise and workplace stressors

Daley & Parfitt (1996) measured mood states, physical well-being, job satisfaction and absenteeism among the employees of a British food retail company. Some employees were members of a corporate health and fitness club, some were on the waiting list, and some were non-members. Club members scored highest on the measures, suggesting that workplace health-promotion programmes, which give the opportunity to exercise during the day, can have beneficial effects on employees' physical *and* psychological health.

PSYCHOLOGICAL APPROACHES TO MANAGING THE NEGATIVE EFFECTS OF STRESS

Relaxation

Physiological responses to stress can also be managed through *relaxation*. Jacobson (1938) observed that people experiencing stress tended to add to their discomfort by tensing their muscles. To overcome this, Jacobson devised *progressive relaxation*. In this, the muscles in one area of the body are first tightened and then relaxed. Then, another group of muscles is tightened and relaxed and so on until, progressively, the entire body is relaxed (and note that this technique is an important component in *systematic desensitisation*, a therapeutic method used to treat phobias: see Gross *et al.*, 2000).

Once a person becomes aware of muscle tension, and can differentiate between feelings of tension and relaxation, the technique can be used to control stress-induced effects. Progressive relaxation lowers the arousal associated with the alarm reaction (see page 63), and reduces the likelihood of recurrent heart attacks. However, the method probably only has long-term benefits if it is incorporated into a person's lifestyle as a regular procedure, since it would require a *cognitive change*, namely seeing calmness and relaxation as essential features of life (Green, 1994).

Box 4.15 Meditation

Another relaxation technique is *meditation*. In this, a person assumes a comfortable position and, with eyes closed, attempts to clear all disturbing thoughts from the mind. A single syllable, or *mantra*, is then silently repeated. At least some people who use meditation believe it helps them to relax. Indeed, Wallace & Fisher (1987) found that meditation reduces oxygen consumption and induces electrical activity in the brain indicative of a calm mental state. Both progressive relaxation and meditation reduce blood pressure, and the fact that both techniques do not require specialised equipment gives them, as noted earlier, an advantage over biofeedback.

Stress inoculation training

Cognitive restructuring is a general term referring to various methods of changing the way people *think* about their life situations and selves, in order to change their emotional responses and behaviour. This approach to stress reduction is based on the *cognitive model of abnormality* (see Chapter 5, pages 96–97) which focuses on the role of disturbed and irrational thoughts, expectations and attitudes, and their effects on behaviour. One approach to reducing stress by changing cognitions is

Meichenbaum's (1976, 1997) *stress inoculation training* (or *self-instructional training*: SIT).

Meichenbaum's approach assumes that people sometimes find situations stressful because they think about them in *catastrophising ways*. SIT consists of three stages. The first, *cognitive preparation* (or *conceptualisation*) involves the therapist and person exploring the ways in which stressful situations are thought about and dealt with, and whether the strategies used have been successful. Typically, people react to stress by offering negative self-statements like 'I can't handle this'. This '*self-defeating internal dialogue*', as Meichenbaum calls it, aggravates an already stressful situation.

The second stage, *skill acquisition and rehearsal*, attempts to replace negative self-statements with incompatible positive coping statements. These, which Meichenbaum calls '*preparation statements*', are then learned and practised.

Box 4.16 Some coping and reinforcing self–statements used in SIT

Preparing for a stressful situation

- What is it you have to do?
- You can develop a plan to deal with it.
- Just think about what you can do about it; that's better than getting anxious.
- No negative self-statements; just think rationally.
- Don't worry; worry won't help anything.
- Maybe what you think is anxiety is eagerness to confront it.

Confronting and handling a stressful situation

- Just 'psych' yourself up – you can meet this challenge.
- One step at a time; you can handle the situation.
- Don't think about fear; just think about what you have to do. Stay relevant.
- This anxiety is what the therapist said you would feel. It's a reminder to you to use your coping exercises.
- This tenseness can be an ally, a cue to cope.
- Relax; you're in control. Take a slow deep breath.
- Ah, good.

Coping with the fear of being overwhelmed

- When fear comes, just pause.
- Keep the focus on the present; what is it that you have to do?
- Label your fear from 0 to 10 and watch it change.
- You should expect your fear to rise.
- Don't try to eliminate fear totally; just keep it manageable.
- You can convince yourself to do it. You can reason fear away.
- It will be over shortly.

- It's not the worst thing that can happen.
- Just think about something else.
- Do something that will prevent you from thinking about fear.
- Describe what is around you. That way you won't think about worrying.

Reinforcing self-statements

- It worked; you did it.
- Wait until you tell your therapist about this.
- It wasn't as bad as you expected.
- You made more out of the fear than it was worth.
- Your damn ideas – that's the problem. When you control them, you control your fear.
- It's getting better each time you use the procedures.
- You can be pleased with the progress you're making.
- You did it!

(From Meichenbaum, 1976)

The final stage of SIT, *application and follow-through*, involves the therapist guiding the person through progressively more threatening situations that have been rehearsed in actual stress-producing situations. Initially, the person is placed in a situation that is moderately easy to cope with. Once this has been mastered, a more difficult situation is presented. According to Meichenbaum (1997), the 'power-of-positive-thinking' approach advocated by SIT can be successful in bringing about effective behaviour change, particularly in relation to the anxiety associated with exams and pain.

Developing hardiness

As noted previously, people differ widely in their ability to resist a stressor's effects. One characteristic that apparently helps resist stress, and which could have been discussed as an individual difference in the effects of stress (see pages 74–76) is *hardiness*. According to Kobasa (1979, 1986), 'hardy' and 'non-hardy' individuals differ in three main ways. Hardy people:

- are highly *committed*, or more deeply involved, in whatever they do, and see activities associated with their endeavours as being meaningful;

- view change as a *challenge* for growth and development, rather than a threat or burden;

- see themselves as having a strong sense of *control* over events in their lives, and feel they can overcome their experiences (in Rotter's, 1966, terms, they have a *high internal locus of control*: see Box 4.18, page 81).

Critical ISSUE

By *choosing* to be in stress-producing situations, interpreting any stress as making life more interesting, and being in control, the amount of stress experienced can be regulated. People high in hardiness tend to be healthier than those low in hardiness, even though the amount of stressful experiences they have been exposed to does not differ (Pines, 1984).

PAUSE FOR THOUGHT

Presumably, stress would be reduced if hardiness could be increased? How could a person be made more hardy?

One approach to increasing hardiness is *teaching* people to identify the physical signs of stress (e.g. tenseness), since a stressor cannot be dealt with if it cannot be identified. Kobasa calls this *focusing*. Even if we can identify stressors, the way they are dealt with might not be beneficial. Another approach is to try and make a more realistic assessment of life's stresses. This involves examining a stressful experience in terms of how it could have been more and less effectively dealt with. Kobasa calls this *reconstructing stressful situations*.

Kobasa's third approach, *compensation through self-improvement*, derives from her view that perceived abilities to bring about change have important effects on our capacity to withstand stress. Kobasa proposes that when a stressor's effects cannot be avoided, or otherwise dealt with, we should take on some other challenge which *can* be dealt with. This allows us to experience the *positive* aspects of coping with a stressor. What Bandura (1984) calls *self-efficacy expectations* regulate problem-solving, and allow us to 'bounce back' more readily from failure. Life's stressors are consequently experienced as being less stressful.

The role of control in the perception of stress

As noted above, a sense of control is one of the ways in which 'hardy' people differ from 'non-hardy' people. Many studies on non-humans have shown that *uncontrollable* situations are highly stressful. For example, Weiss (1972: see Figure 4.8) found that if two rats simultaneously received electric shocks, but one could turn a wheel to terminate the shocks, the one that could not terminate the shocks displayed a lowered immunity to disease and was more susceptible to peptic ulcers.

Most of us prefer to have control over events in our lives, even when those events are unpleasant, and perceived control is important in determining how much stress we experience. To appreciate this, you only have to think how stressful it is having someone else use a needle to remove a splinter in your finger compared with using the needle yourself. Indeed, when people are asked to classify the life events on the SRRS (see Table 4.2, page 71) as either 'controllable' or 'uncontrollable', only the latter are correlated with subsequent onset of illness.

Rat 1
(Escapable shock)

Rat 2
(Inescapable shock)

Rat 3
(No shock – control)

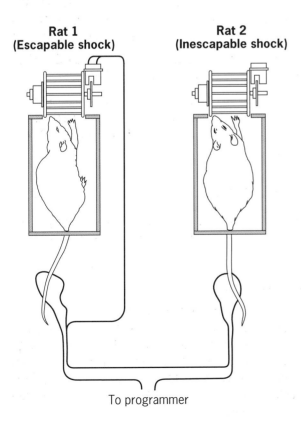

To programmer

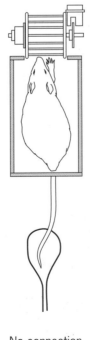

No connection

Figure 4.8 *The rat on the left (Rat 1) can terminate the programmed shock by turning the wheel. Also, turning the wheel between shocks will postpone the shock. The rat in the middle (Rat 2) is electrically wired in series to Rat 1 – when Rat 1 receives a shock, Rat 2 simultaneously receives a shock of the same intensity and duration. The actions of Rat 2 do not affect the shock sequence. The electrodes on the tail of Rat 3 (the Control) are not connected, and this rat does not receive shocks at any time. At the end of the experimental session, gastric lesions are measured in each rat. (Adapted from Weiss, 1972)*

Box 4.17 Learned helplessness

When events over which we have no control are aversive, *learned helplessness* occurs (Seligman, 1975). This is a generalised expectation that events are independent of our control, and has been demonstrated in both non-humans and humans. For example, if dogs are placed in a situation in which they cannot avoid receiving electric shocks, they fail to learn to escape when placed in a situation in which electric shocks *can* be avoided. Similarly, when humans are exposed to uncontrollable loud noise, their performance is poor and continues to be poor even when the situation is changed and the loud noise *can* be controlled (Hiroto & Seligman, 1975). According to Seligman, human *depression* can be explained in terms of learned helplessness (see Gross *et al.*, 2000).

When people believe that an unpleasant event *can* be predicted, modified or terminated, it is *less* likely to be perceived as stressful. For example, laboratory studies of pain stimulation of teeth indicate that increases in anxiety raise sensitivity to pain. As a result, some dentists use 'stop signals', in which patients are instructed to raise a hand the moment they feel discomfort, which signals the dentist to stop whatever s/he is doing. Similar strategies are used in other settings where patients are receiving physical treatment. These have the effect of minimising the mismatch between expectations and experiences, and encourage cognitive activity of a 'coping' rather than 'catastrophising' kind.

Moreover, the mere *knowledge* that there is control is apparently sufficient to reduce stress. Glass & Singer (1972) exposed one group of participants to loud noise, and told them they could stop the noise by pressing a button, although they were urged not to use the button if at all possible. A second group was exposed to the same noise but had no control button. Even though the participants in the first group never pressed the button, they showed less evidence of stress that those in the second group who lacked the option of control.

Box 4.18 Locus of control

Related to learned helplessness is Rotter's (1966) concept of *locus of control*. This refers to our perceived sense of control over our behaviour. It is measured along a dimension running from high *internal* to high *external control*, and assessed using Rotter's *locus of control scale*. As noted on page 79, 'hardy' people tend to have a high internal locus of control. This means they tend to take responsibility for their own actions and view themselves as having control over their 'destiny'. High externals, by

contrast, tend to see control as residing elsewhere ('destiny' is out of their hands), and attribute both success and failure to outside forces. Johnson & Sarason (1978) found that life events' stress was more closely related to psychiatric symptoms (in particular, depression and anxiety) among those identified as high externals.

In general, then, it is better to have control than not to have it. However, as Wade & Tavris (1993) have observed:

'Believing that an event is controllable does not always lead to a reduction in stress, and believing that an event is uncontrollable does not always lead to an increase in stress. The question must always be asked: Control over what?'.

Wade and Tavris distinguish between two types of control:

- In *primary control*, people try to influence existing reality by changing other people, events or circumstances. This is the approach typically used by Westerners – if you don't like something, change it, fix it, or fight it. The emphasis on primary control encourages self-expression, independence, and change, at a possible price of self-absorption.

- In *secondary control*, people try to accommodate to reality by changing their own perceptions, goals, or desires. The Eastern approach emphasises secondary control – if you have a problem, learn to live with it or act in spite of it. The emphasis on secondary control leads to acceptance and serenity, at a possible price of self-denial and stagnation.

No one form of control is better or healthier than the other. Rather, both have their place. As Wade and Tavris note:

'Most problems require us to choose between trying to change what we can and accepting what we cannot. Perhaps a secret of healthy control lies in knowing the difference'.

PAUSE FOR THOUGHT

According to Homer Simpson, 'never do today, what you can put off until tomorrow'. Is Homer's 'philosophy' a good way of dealing with stressors?

Coping strategies

Another way people differ in their abilities to resist stress is related to the *coping strategies* they use to try to manage it. Coping involves cognitive and behavioural efforts to manage specific external and/or internal demands that are appraised as taxing or exceeding our resources. Cohen & Lazarus (1979) have classified all the coping strategies a person might use into five general categories.

Table 4.4 *Cohen & Lazarus's (1979) classification of coping strategies*

Category	Strategy
1 Direct action response	Trying to change or manipulate a relationship with the stressful situation (e.g. escaping from or removing it).
2 Information seeking	Trying to understand the situation better and predict future situations related to the stressor.
3 Inhibition of action	Doing nothing may be the best course of action if the situation is seen as short-term.
4 Intrapsychic (palliative)	Reappraising the situation by, for example, coping using psychological defence mechanisms (see Chapter 5, page 94 and text below) or changing the 'internal environment' (through, for example, drugs, relaxation or meditation).
5 Turning to others	Using others for help and emotional support.

Figure 4.9 *Socialising with others in an informal and relaxed atmosphere is one way of coping with stress*

These five categories of coping overlap with Lazarus & Folkman's (1984) distinction between *problem-focused* (or *optimistic*) and *emotion-focused* (or *pessimistic*) coping strategies. In the former, some specific plan for dealing with a stressor is made and implemented, and other activities are postponed until the stressor has been reduced or terminated. This subsumes categories (1), (2) and some examples of (5) in Table 4.4. The latter involves implementing cognitive and behavioural strategies that are effective in the short term, and reduce the negative emotions associated with the stressor, but do little to reduce or eliminate its long-term effects (category (4) in Table 4.4 is an example of this).

Box 4.19 Using coping strategies

Consider, for example, revising for an examination as a potential stressor. A problem-focused coping strategy would be to organise a revision plan and then adhere to it until the examination. What Moos (1988) calls a *behavioural* emotion-focused coping strategy could be to go out drinking every night, which would avoid confronting the stressor. When the examination results are published, the stress caused by failure could be reduced by using a *cognitive* emotion-focused coping strategy, such as claiming that there was no opportunity to revise. Most of us use *combinations* of problem- and emotion-focused strategies, but some people rely almost exclusively on the latter. By teaching them more effective strategies for dealing with stressors, the amount of stress that problems create can be significantly reduced.

Coping mechanisms and *ego defence mechanisms* correspond to problem- and emotional-focused coping strategies. Savickas (1995) sees a coping mechanism as a *conscious* way of trying to adapt to stress and anxiety in a positive and constructive manner. This is achieved by using thoughts and behaviours directed towards problem-solving, seeking help from others, searching for information, recognising true feelings, and establishing goals and objectives. By contrast, ego defence mechanisms are associated with the anxiety produced by conflict, as described in Freud's psychodynamic perspective (see Chapter 5, pages 93–95).

By their nature, defence mechanisms involve some degree of distortion of reality and self-deception. Whilst they are desirable in the short term, they are unhealthy and undesirable as long-term solutions to stress. Although they reduce tension, anger, depression, and other negative emotions, they do nothing to remove or change the stressor or the fit between the person and the environment.

Section Summary

■ Physiological responses to stress can be managed through **psychotherapeutic drugs**, such as **anxiolytics**. These act directly on the ANS. However, drugs have unpleasant side effects, cause physiological dependence and produce tolerance and withdrawal symptoms.

■ **Biofeedback** is also used to manage physiological responses. It has been shown to be successful in the treatment of migraine headaches and hypertension. However, regular practice is needed for beneficial effects, and because it is not known precisely how it works, its use is limited.

■ **Relaxation** (including **meditation**) and **physical activity** and **exercise** are other ways of managing physiological responses to stress. Such practices help combat the physiological changes caused by stressors. Workplace health promotion programmes can have beneficial effects on employees' physical and psychological health.

■ Meichenbaum's **stress inoculation training** (SIT) assumes that people sometimes find situations stressful because of their misperceptions about them. SIT trains people to cope more effectively with potentially stressful situations through **cognitive preparation**, **skill acquisition and rehearsal** and **application and follow-through**.

■ What Kobasa calls **hardy** individuals use cognitive strategies which enable them to deal with stressors more effectively. These include being able to identify the physical signs of stress, realistically assessing stressors and taking on other challenges to experience the positive aspects of coping with stressors.

■ **Control** plays an important role in the perception of stress. Lack of control has adverse physical and psychological consequences. One of these is **learned helplessness**. When an event can be predicted, modified or terminated, it is less likely to be perceived as stressful. **Locus of control** is also an important factor in this respect.

■ In general, it is better to have control than not to have it. **Primary control** is an attempt to influence reality by changing other people, events or circumstances. **Secondary control** is an attempt to accommodate reality by changing perceptions, goals or desires. Both have their place in stress management.

■ Cohen and Lazarus's classification of **coping strategies** overlaps with Lazarus and Folkman's distinction between **problem-focused** (or **optimistic**) and **emotion-focused** (or **pessimistic**) coping strategies.

■ Problem-focused strategies involve devising plans for dealing with stressors, and then adhering to them until the stressors have been reduced or terminated.

■ Emotion-focused strategies involve behaviours that are effective in the short term, but do little to reduce stressors' long-term effects. Most people use a combination of problem- and emotion-focused strategies, but some rely exclusively on the latter.

Self-Assessment Questions

5 a Outline **two** physiological approaches to managing the negative effects of stress. *(3 marks + 3 marks)*

 b Describe **two** ways in which 'control' plays a role in the perception of stress. *(6 marks + 6 marks)*

 c 'The negative effects of stress are much more effectively dealt with by psychological than physical methods.'

 To what extent does research support this statement?
 (12 marks)

6 a Outline **two** research studies which show how physical methods can be used to manage the negative effects of stress. *(3 marks + 3 marks)*

 b Describe **two** psychological approaches to managing the negative effects of stress. *(6 marks + 6 marks)*

 c 'All methods of stress management, physical and psychological, have both strengths and weaknesses.'

 Assess the strengths and weaknesses of physical *and/or* psychological methods of stress management.
 (12 marks)

CONCLUSIONS

This chapter began by looking at definitions of stress and the effects that stress has on the body. Selye's general adaptation syndrome is a useful approach to understanding the physiological processes that occur in response to a stressor, although his concentration on the body's response to largely non-social stressors ignores the role of psychological factors in the production of the stress response.

Research suggests that stress and illness are related. Evidence about the effects of stress on the immune system and its involvement in cardiovascular disorders indicates that stress may be causally related to some illnesses. Two important stressors are life changes and those occurring in the workplace. Much research has been conducted to identify the ways in which these stressors affect people. However, people differ in their responses to potentially stressful situations, and three important individual differences are personality, culture and gender.

There are many methods by which stress can be managed. Some involve managing physiological responses to stressors, whilst others attempt to manage stress by changing cognitions or behaviour. All of these methods are effective to some degree.

WEB ADDRESSES

http://www.fisk.edu/vl/Stress
http://www.stressfree.com/
http://onhealth.com/
http://www.uiuc.edu/departments/mckinley/health-info/stress/stress.html
http://www.unl.edu/stress/
http://www.clas.ufl.edu/users/gthursby/stress/
http://amwa-doc.org/publications/WCHealthbook/stressamwa-ch09.html
http://futurehealth.org/stresscn.html
http://stats.bls.gov/opub/ted/1999/Oct/wk4/art03.htm
http://www/workhealth.org/prevent/prred.html

5 *Abnormality*

INTRODUCTION AND OVERVIEW

Although many psychologists study *normal* psychological processes, some are interested in *abnormal* psychological processes. This, of course, assumes that it is both possible and meaningful to distinguish between normal and abnormal. This chapter is divided into three parts. The first examines some of the ways in which abnormality has been *defined*, and some of the limitations associated with these definitions. The second looks at four different models (or *paradigms*) in abnormal psychology. Each of these places a different interpretation on abnormality's causes and how it should best be *treated*. One of the models is biological (the *medical model*) and three are psychological (the *psychodynamic, behavioural* and *cognitive models*). The final part of this chapter looks at *anorexia nervosa* and *bulimia nervosa*, two eating disorders. The clinical characteristics of these disorders are described, and explanations of them discussed in terms of the biological and psychological models.

Defining Psychological Abnormality

'ABNORMALITY': TWO ILLUSTRATIVE EXAMPLES?

William Buckland (1784–1856) was an interesting man. He was Oxford University's inaugural professor of geology, and the first person in England to recognise that glaciers had once covered much of the northern part of the United Kingdom. Buckland supervised the laying of the first pipe drains in London, and was responsible for introducing gas lighting to Oxford. He also ate bluebottles, moles and, on being shown it by a friend, the embalmed heart of the executed King Louis XIV of France.

In 1994, a reader of *The Daily Telegraph* was moved to write to the newspaper following his observations of a fellow passenger on the London to Sidcup train:

'Opposite sat an ordinary-looking, well-dressed man in his mid-thirties who was reading a book called *Railway Systems of North Africa*. The man closed his book and wedged it between himself and another passenger. Bending down, he untied the laces of his right shoe, removed it and placed it on the carriage floor. He then removed his right sock and placed it on his lap. Oblivious to the stares of fellow passengers, he then undid his left shoe-lace, removed the shoe, placed it on the floor beside its companion, transferred his left sock to his right foot, and put the sock from his right foot onto his left foot. For half a minute he inspected his handiwork and, presumably satisfied, donned his shoes, tied up their laces, retrieved his book and continued reading'. (Davies, 1994)

Figure 5.1 *William Buckland: a connoiseur of fine cuisine?*

PAUSE FOR THOUGHT

Eating bluebottles and moles, washed down with some bats' urine (a behaviour for which William Buckland was also known), might strike you as being a little 'odd'. Swapping over socks in a crowded railway carriage might also appear 'a little strange'. Perhaps these behaviours seem 'odd' or 'strange' because *most* of us do not do them. But would it be enough to label someone as being 'abnormal' *just* because they behave in ways *most* of us don't, or don't behave in ways *most* of us do?

DEFINING ABNORMALITY IN TERMS OF 'STATISTICAL INFREQUENCY'

By definition, abnormality means *'deviating from the norm or average'*. Perhaps the most obvious way to define abnormality is in terms of *statistically infrequent* characteristics or behaviours. This definition has some appeal. For example, if the average height of a given population of adults is 5'8", we would *probably* describe someone who was 7'6" or 3'3" as being 'abnormally' tall or short respectively. When people *behave* in ways the vast majority does not, or do not behave in ways the vast majority does, we often label them abnormal.

Unfortunately, there are limitations to using a purely statistical approach to defining abnormality. One is that it fails to take account of the *desirability* of a behaviour or characteristic. Eating moles and drinking bats' urine is statistically infrequent *and* (probably) undesirable. But what about preparing to sit A level maths at the age of five, as Zuleika Yusoff did in 1999. Zuleika may even better her sister, Sufiah, who started university at 13, and her brother Iskander, who began his university course aged 12. Since the majority of people don't start an A level course when they are five, Zuleika is in the minority, and would therefore be defined as 'abnormal' according to the statistical infrequency definition (as, indeed, would Mozart, who performed his own concerto aged three!).

Another limitation to the statistical infrequency definition is that there are people involved in a range of undesirable behaviours in all cultures:

'Americans [engage in various] socially undesirable behaviour patterns, from mild depression to child abuse, [and] if it were possible to add up all the numbers, it would become clear that as many as one out of every two people would fall into at least one of these categories'. (Hassett & White, 1989)

Figure 5.2 *Zuleika Yusoff, a child prodigy, but abnormal by the statistical infrequency definition of abnormality*

These behaviour patterns, which characterise half the American population, would be *normal* in a statistical sense, but they are also regarded as *mental disorders*. Moreover, we cannot know just how *far* from the average a person must deviate before being considered abnormal. If a population's average height is 5'8", a decision must be made about *when* a person becomes abnormally tall or short. Such decisions are difficult both to make and justify.

Clearly, then, it is not sufficient to define abnormality *solely* in terms of statistical infrequency, although this is sometimes what we do. A useful definition of abnormality needs to take more into account than just the statistical infrequency of behaviours or characteristics.

DEFINING ABNORMALITY AS A 'DEVIATION FROM IDEAL MENTAL HEALTH'

A second approach is to identify the characteristics and abilities (which may or may not be statistically infrequent) that people *should* possess in order to be considered *normal* (Parker *et al.*, 1995). Abnormality is then defined as deviating from these characteristics, either by not possessing them or by possessing characteristics that should not be possessed. Several 'ideals' have been proposed. Jahoda (1958), for example, identifies *individual choice, resistance to stress, an accurate perception of reality*, and *self-actualisation* as some characteristics of ideal mental health.

This approach also has some appeal, since at least some of Jahoda's ideals would probably be shared by everybody. However, they are so demanding that almost everybody would be considered abnormal to some degree, depending on how many of them they failed to satisfy. According to Maslow (1968), only a few people achieve *self-actualisation*, defined as a level of psychological development in which the realisation of full personal potential takes place. Consequently, most of us would be considered abnormal on that criterion (and if most of us are abnormal and therefore in the majority, *being abnormal is normal* by the statistical infrequency definition, because it is a majority behaviour or characteristic!).

PAUSE FOR THOUGHT

Is it possible to construct a list of ideals that *everyone* would agree with?

Box 5.1 Value judgements and mental health

Lists of ideals defining mental health are *value judgements*, reflecting the beliefs of those who construct them. Someone who hears voices when nobody is there may well be unhealthy as far as some people are concerned. However, the person who hears the voices, *and welcomes them*, would define him- or herself as being perfectly normal and healthy. A culture that emphasised co-operation between its members, rather than competition between them, would reject Jahoda's view that *individual choice* is part of *ideal* mental health. This problem does not arise when judgements are made about *physical health*, since such judgements are neither moral nor philosophical. What physical health is can be stated in anatomical and physical terms. If there are no abnormalities present, a person is judged to be in 'ideal' health (Szasz, 1960).

Another reason for questioning the deviation from ideal mental health definition is that it is *bound by culture*. Whilst different cultures have *some* shared ideals about what constitutes mental health, some ideals are not shared. For example, soccer is popular on the island of Java. The Javanese, though, play with a ball that has been soaked in petrol and then set alight. Provided that the game is played near water and the players' legs are shaved, they consider playing soccer like this to be 'healthy'.

However, those who define abnormality in terms of 'ideal mental health' would argue that there ought to be some sort of *universal standard* to which we should all aspire, irrespective of culture:

'Does it really make sense to say that murder and cannibalism are [healthy] just because some society has approved them? And if it is, then why not apply the same standards to communities within society? Murder is a popular activity among Baltimore youth. Shall we say that, in that city, murder is healthy?' (Chance, 1984)

Figure 5.3 *Soccer the Javan way: mentally healthy or not?*

Even if Chance's points are accepted, the deviation from ideal mental health definition also changes over time *within* a particular culture (it is *era-dependent*). Seeing visions was a sign of healthy religious fervour in thirteenth-century Europe, but now seeing such visions might be a sign of *schizophrenia* (Wade & Tavris, 1993).

PAUSE FOR THOUGHT

Can you think of any circumstances in which eating bluebottles might be 'healthy'?

A final problem with the deviation from ideal mental health definition is that it is limited by the *context* in which a behaviour occurs. For example, it is 'healthy' to walk around wearing a steel hat if one works on a building site, but it is probably less 'healthy' to do this if one is a waiter in a restaurant. Faced with the choice between a highly nutritious salad and a plate of mole and bluebottles, the former would be a healthier choice. In the absence of an alternative, however, mole and bluebottles might be better than nothing at all! So, defining abnormality as a deviation from 'ideal mental health' can sometimes be helpful, but like the previous definition it too has limitations.

DEFINING ABNORMALITY AS A 'FAILURE TO FUNCTION ADEQUATELY'

According to this definition (which overlaps with the one just discussed), every human being should achieve some sense of personal well-being and make some contribution to a larger social group. Any individual who fails to function adequately in this respect is seen as being 'abnormal'. Sue *et al.* (1994) use the terms *practical* or *clinical criteria* to describe the ways in which individuals fail to function adequately, since they are often the basis on which people come to the attention of psychologists or other interested professionals.

Personal distress or discomfort

One way in which people can come to a professional's attention is if they are experiencing *personal distress* or *discomfort*:

'People do not come to clinics because they have some abstract definition of abnormality. For the most part, they come because their feelings or behaviours cause them distress'. (Miller & Morley, 1986)

Such feelings or behaviours might not be obvious to other people, but may take the form of intense *anxiety*, *depression*, and a *loss of appetite*. Unfortunately, whilst such states might cause personal distress, we could not use personal distress *by itself* as a definition of abnormality, since certain states causing such distress might be *appropriate responses* in particular circumstances. Examples here include experiencing anxiety in response to the presence of a real threat, and depression as a response to the death of a loved one. We would not consider such responses to be abnormal, *unless* they persisted long after their source was removed or after most people would have adjusted to them.

Moreover, some forms of *mental disorder* are not necessarily accompanied by personal distress. For example, some people engage in repeated acts of crime and violence, but have no feelings of guilt or remorse (*dissocial personality disorder*). With *substance-related disorders*, the consequences of, say, excessive use of alcohol, may be strenuously denied by the user.

Others' distress

Although certain psychological states might not cause personal distress, they may be *distressing to others*. For example, a person who tried to assassinate the Prime Minister might not experience any personal distress at all. However, the fact that such a person is a threat to *others* also constitutes a failure to function adequately.

Maladaptiveness

Even someone who does not experience personal distress, or is not distressing to others, would be failing to function adequately if the behaviour was *maladaptive*, either for the individual concerned or society. Maladaptiveness prevents the person from efficiently satisfying social and occupational roles. Some mental disorders, such as the substance-related disorders mentioned previously, are defined in terms of how the (ab)use of the substance produces social and occupational difficulties, such as marital problems and poor work performance.

Bizarreness

We could also include a behaviour's *bizarreness* as an example of a failure to function adequately. Unless it actually is true that the Martians, in collusion with the CIA, *are* trying to extract information from someone, it would be hard to deny that a person making such claims was behaving bizarrely, and hence failing to function adequately.

Unexpected behaviour

Finally, *unexpected behaviour* could be included as a failure to function adequately (Davison & Neale, 1994). This involves reacting to a situation or event in ways that could not be *predicted* or *reasonably expected* from what is known about human behaviour. If a person behaves in a way which is 'out of all proportion to the situation', then we might say that s/he was failing to function adequately. An example would be a person who reacted to some trivial event by attempting to commit suicide.

Box 5.2 Predictability and adequate functioning

If we have generalised expectations about how people will typically react in certain situations, then behaviour is *predictable* to the extent that we know about the situation. However, since different situations have more (or less) powerful effects on behaviour, we cannot say that all situations are equal in terms of our abilities to predict how a person will behave. In some situations, individual differences will determine what behaviours occur. This, of course, makes it more difficult to predict what will happen.

As a result, we could argue that a person was functioning adequately if behaviour was *partially predictable*, and failing to function adequately if behaviour was *always extremely unpredictable* or *always extremely predictable*. For example, a person who was always extremely unpredictable would be difficult to interact with, since interaction involves making assumptions and having expectations about what responses will occur. A person who always acted so predictably that s/he seemed to be unaffected by any situation would also strike us as being 'odd', and may give the impression that we were interacting with a *machine* rather than another human being.

PAUSE FOR THOUGHT

Would you consider William Buckland and the passenger on the train to be abnormal, if abnormality is a 'failure to function adequately'?

Although Buckland's behaviour might not have caused him distress, it might have been distressing to others. However, given his prominent position at Oxford University, and other things we know about him from page 85's brief description, we would probably not call his behaviour maladaptive. His eating of Louis XIV's heart was unexpected, at least to the friend who showed him it (and, incidentally, had paid a grave robber a large sum of money for it). Whether Buckland was partially or extremely unpredictable is hard to assess from descriptions of him in historical documents. As far as bizarreness is concerned, we would have to question whether his eating and drinking habits constituted adequate functioning.

The passenger on the train was not, presumably, distressed by his own behaviour, nor does it seem from the letter writer's account that other passengers were. More contentious, perhaps, is whether the behaviour was maladaptive. As with William Buckland, it is difficult to assess predictability, but we would probably accept that the behaviour was bizarre. If you disagree, you are gaining first hand experience of just how difficult it is to define abnormality!

For some psychologists, and other professionals, the failure to function adequately definition is the most useful single approach and closest to 'common sense'. However, as with the other definitions, there are problems in defining abnormality in this way. Using the distress of others as a failure to function adequately is a double-edged sword. Sometimes, it can be a 'blessing', in that one person's distress at another's behaviour can, occasionally, literally be a 'life-saver' (as when someone lacks *insight* into his/her own self-destructive behaviour). Sometimes, however, it can be a 'curse', as when, say, a father experiences distress over his son's homosexuality, whilst the son feels perfectly comfortable with it.

The meaning of the phrase '*out of all proportion to the situation*', used when unexpected behaviour was described as a failure to function adequately, can be questioned. For Davison & Neale (1994: see page 88), unexpected behaviours are apparently those involving an *over-reaction*. However, a behaviour which is out of all proportion can also equally refer to an *under-reaction*.

PAUSE FOR THOUGHT

Can the meaning of 'bizarreness' (see page 88) also be questioned? Are there circumstances in which apparently bizarre behaviours are actually *beneficial* to those who perform them?

Some behaviours, *in general*, would be considered *bizarre*. However, under certain conditions and contexts, the perpetrators could justify them in terms of their own survival, or the political or religious meanings attached to them. As Houston *et al.* (1991) have remarked:

'Whether or not we agree with the justifications, the events in context give them a meaning that is generally not attributed to individual abnormality. Even less atrocious behaviours, such as jumping off a cliff on a motorcycle or dressing up in the clothing of the opposite sex, are not inherently abnormal; depending on their contexts, and in certain situations, such behaviours may even be entertaining and profitable for those performing them'.

Figure 5.4 *As 'Lily Savage' demonstrates, cross-dressing can sometimes be both entertaining for others and profitable for the cross-dresser*

DEFINING ABNORMALITY AS A 'DEVIATION FROM SOCIAL NORMS'

All societies have standards, or *norms*, for appropriate behaviours and beliefs (that is, expectations about how people should behave as well as what they should think). It is helpful to think of these in terms of a *continuum of normative behaviour*, from behaviours which are *unacceptable*, *tolerable*, *acceptable/permissible*, *desirable*, and finally those that are *required/obligatory*. A fourth way of defining abnormality is in terms of *breaking* society's standards or norms.

In Britain, there is a norm for queuing, at least in some social situations. For example, it is accepted and 'normal' to stand in line when waiting for a bus, a bank clerk, or a MacDonald's hamburger. Indeed, in Britain, people will readily wait in line, even when it is not entirely necessary! (Collett, 1994). However, in other social situations such a norm does not, at least explicitly, operate. In pubs, for example, the British form 'invisible queues', expecting the person behind the bar to remember who is next. A person who breaks the norm, and 'pushes in', can expect to be 'punished' by others in the queue. For example, a person who pushes in at a bus stop will be reminded that a norm has been broken, and even in a pub, people who have been frequently overlooked by the bar person will eventually point this out.

Figure 5.5 *Queueing: a social norm in Britain, but not in some other societies*

PAUSE FOR THOUGHT

Can you think of any behaviours which deviate from the norms of our society but are also *statistically frequent*? If so, would this mean that most people are abnormal?

It is true that behaviour which deviates from social norms is sometimes also statistically infrequent. Drinking bats' urine, and swapping over one's socks on a crowded train, would be examples. However, some behaviours which are considered to be *socially unacceptable* in our culture are actually statistically *frequent*. Research indicates high 'confession rates' amongst people asked if they have engaged in a prosecutable offence without actually being convicted for it. If abnormality is defined as a 'deviation from social norms', most people would be 'abnormal' (and if abnormality is defined in terms of statistical *infrequency*, criminal behaviour is *normal* because it is statistically frequent!).

Box 5.3: Time to confess?

Below is a list of 15 criminal acts which you *might* have committed, but were not prosecuted for. Are *you* abnormal according to the deviation from social norms definition?

- Riding a bicycle without lights after dark.
- Travelling on a train or bus without a ticket, or deliberately paying the wrong fare.
- Letting off fireworks in the street.
- Fighting with another person in the street.
- Breaking or smashing things in a public place (e.g. whilst on a bus).
- Carrying a weapon (e.g. a knife) in case it is needed in a fight.
- Breaking the window of an empty house.
- Dropping litter in the street.
- Buying something cheap, or accepting something as a present, knowing that it has been stolen.
- Deliberately taking something from someone else and keeping it.
- Stealing school/college property worth more than 50p.
- Stealing goods worth more than 50p from an employer.
- Trespassing somewhere, such as a railway line or private gardens.
- Lying about your age to watch an 18 film at a cinema.
- Consuming illegal substances (e.g. cannabis).

Like other definitions, the deviation from social norms definition is also *bound by culture*. British car drivers are typically hesistant about 'crashing' traffic lights, and usually wait until the light has turned green before proceeding. As Collett (1994) notes:

> '... it is not unusual to see drivers in England waiting patiently for the lights to turn green, even at the dead of night, when there isn't another car around for miles'.

For Italians, however, such behaviour is abnormal. Provided that there are no cars around, and no chance of being apprehended, the red lights will be ignored. Traffic lights are only there to be obeyed when other cars or the police are around. Thus, Italians view traffic regulations as 'flexible guidelines', something they can afford to ignore, provided the police do not cause trouble and nobody gets hurt.

Key STUDY

Box 5.4 Social norms in the Trobriand islanders

In Western cultures, the sons of a deceased father are not expected to clean his bones and distribute them amongst relatives to wear as ornaments. Malinowski (1929), however, found that amongst Trobriand islanders such behaviour was expected and hence 'normal'. Indeed, a widow who did not wear her former husband's jawbone on a necklace was failing to behave in accordance with her culture's expectations, and was considered abnormal. Perhaps a culture exists where William Buckland's eating and drinking habits would fail to raise an eyebrow, or where the changing over of one's socks on a railway journey is the norm.

The deviation from social norms definition is further weakened by the fact that it, too, is era-dependent. As values change, so particular behaviours move from being considered abnormal to normal, back to abnormal again, and so on. Some behaviours today tend to be viewed as differences in lifestyle rather than as signs of abnormality, the smoking of marijuana being, perhaps, one such example (Atkinson *et al.*, 1993).

As with other definitions, it can be helpful to use the idea of violating societal norms or expectations as a way of defining abnormality. By itself, however, it cannot serve as a complete and acceptable definition.

SO WHAT IS 'ABNORMALITY'?

All the definitions of abnormality considered have strengths and weaknesses. All are helpful as ways of conceptualising abnormality, but none on its own is

sufficient. Indeed, not all the characteristics of the definitions discussed are necessarily evident in those behaviours which are classified as mental disorders. Indeed, any of the behaviours classified as being mental disorders may reflect only one, or a combination, of the characteristics.

Different definitions carry different implications, and there is certainly no consensus on a 'best definition' (Sue *et al.*, 1994). Sue *et al.* have suggested that a *multiple perspectives* (or *multiple definitions*) view is one way of approaching the very difficult task of defining abnormality. A truly adequate understanding of what abnormality is can probably only be achieved through a comprehensive evaluation of all points of view.

Section Summary

- One way of defining abnormality is in terms of characteristics/behaviours that are **statistically infrequent** (the **deviation from statistical norms definition**). However, this does not take into account the **desirability** of a characteristic or behaviour.

- The definition also fails to recognise that in all cultures large numbers of people may engage in behaviours that constitute mental disorders. A further problem is the failure to identify how far a person must deviate before being 'abnormal'. Such decisions are difficult to make and justify.

- The **deviation from ideal mental health definition** proposes that abnormal people do not possess characteristics that mental healthy people do, or possess characteristics that mentally healthy people do not.

- This definition relies on **value judgements** about what constitutes ideal mental health. It is also **bound by culture**, **era-dependent**, and limited by the **context** in which behaviour occurs.

- Abnormality has also been defined as a **failure to function adequately** (by not achieving some sense of personal well-being and making some contribution to a larger social group). Experiencing **personal distress/discomfort**, causing **distress to others**, and behaving **maladaptively**, **bizarrely** or **unexpectedly** are often the reasons why people come to the attention of psychologists and other professionals.

- Many consider the failure to function adequately definition as being the most useful single approach, and the one closest to common sense. However, none of the above on its own constitutes an adequate definition of abnormality, since bizarre behaviour, for example, might actually allow a person to function adequately in a particular context.

■ Another way of defining abnormality is in terms of a **deviation from social norms**. Abnormality is seen as behaving in ways society disapproves of, or not behaving in ways it approves of. Like other definitions, this one is **bound by culture** and **era-dependent**. Also, since most people have behaved in ways society disapproves of, most would be defined as 'abnormal'.

■ No one definition on its own is adequate. Behaviours that are **classified** as mental disorders do not necessarily reflect all the various definitions. A truly adequate definition can probably only be achieved through a **multiple perspectives** (**multiple definitions**) approach.

Self-Assessment Questions

1 a Describe the 'statistical infrequency' and 'deviations from social norms' definitions of abnormality.
      (3 marks + 3 marks)

   b Describe the major limitations associated with each of the definitions identified in part (a).
      (6 marks + 6 marks)

   c 'Every human being should achieve some sense of personal well-being and make some contribution to a larger social group. Any individual who fails to function in this way is abnormal.'
      To what extent can abnormality be defined as a 'failure to function adequately'? *(12 marks)*

2 a Distinguish between the 'deviation from ideal mental health' and 'failure to function adequately' definitions of abnormality. *(3 marks + 3 marks)*

   b Describe the limitations of these two ways of defining abnormality. *(6 marks + 6 marks)*

   c 'Abnormality is best defined in terms of a deviation from social norms.'
      Assess the strengths and limitations of defining abnormality in this way. *(12 marks)*

Biological and Psychological Models of Abnormality

ABNORMALITY: AN HISTORICAL PERSPECTIVE

Throughout much of human history, abnormality was regarded as a sign of 'possession' by demons or evil spirits (the *'demonological'* model of abnormality). Skeletons from the Stone Age, for example, have been discovered with egg-shaped holes in the skull. Although we cannot be certain, these holes were possibly drilled into the skull (*trephined*) to 'release' the spirits presumed to be responsible for a person's abnormal behaviour. Whether trephining was effective is debatable. However, because the skulls of some skeletons show evidence of the holes growing over, the 'operation' obviously did not inevitably lead to immediate death.

Box 5.5 The 'demonological' model of abnormality

This model was especially popular in the Middle Ages. Thousands of people (mostly women) were convicted of being 'witches', and executed for their 'crimes'. A birthmark, scar or mole on a woman's skin was interpreted as indicating that she had signed a pact with the Devil. To establish whether they were possessed, those accused underwent various tests. Based on the fact that *pure* metals sink to the bottom of a melting pot, whereas *impurities* float to the surface, it was 'reasoned' that *pure people* would sink to the bottom when placed in water, whilst *impure people*, who were in league with the Devil, would be able to keep their heads above water. 'Pure' people would, of course, die by drowning. 'Impure' people would suffer some other fate (such as being burned at the stake).

Today, the demonological model has been replaced by a number of other models of abnormality. The major models are biological (the *medical model*) and psychological (including the *psychodynamic*, *behavioural* and *cognitive* models).

THE BIOLOGICAL (MEDICAL) MODEL OF ABNORMALITY

Although some physicians in the Middle Ages called for a more rational approach to abnormality, it was not until the eighteenth century (the *Age of Enlightenment*) that the demonological model began to lose its appeal, and a different model (or perspective) emerged. Pinel, in Europe, and Dix, in America, were the pioneers of change. Rather than seeing abnormal behaviour as supernatural possession, they argued that it should be seen as a kind of *illness*, which could be treated.

Although different, this perspective was not new. The ancient Greek physician Hippocrates proposed that in what is now called *epilepsy*:

'If you cut open the head, you will find the brain humid, full of sweat and smelling badly. And in this way you may see that it is not a god which injured the body, but disease'. (cited in Zilboorg & Henry, 1941)

In the eighteenth century, the view that mental disorders are illnesses based on an organ's (the brain's) pathology was emphasised by von Haller. He believed that the brain played a central role in 'psychic functions', and that understanding could be gained by studying the brains of the insane through post-mortem dissection. Nearly one hundred years later, Griesinger insisted that *all* forms of mental disorder could be explained in terms of brain pathology.

The biological (*medical*) model's early successes were largely based on showing that certain mental disorders could be traced to gross destruction of brain tissue. More recently, the model has looked at the role played by *brain biochemistry* and *genetics* in the development of mental disorders, whilst retaining its interest in the role of brain damage in such disorders. *Biochemical theories* explain the development of mental disorders in terms of an imbalance in the concentration of *neurotransmitters*, the chemical messengers that nerve cells use to communicate with one another. *Genetic theories* derive from the observation that at least some mental disorders have a tendency to run in families. By means of DNA, the material that contains genetic codes, some disorders may be transmitted from generation to generation. Some of the methodological approaches used to study the role of genetic factors are described on pages 100–101.

PAUSE FOR THOUGHT

If the biological (medical) model sees abnormality as having physical causes, what approach to *treatment* do you think its supporters take?

Because the biological (medical) model sees mental disorders as having physical causes, the therapeutic approaches it favours are *physical*. Collectively, they are known as *somatic therapy* ('somatic' means 'of the body').

Box 5.6 Therapies based on the medical model

Three therapies favoured by the medical model are *chemotherapy* (the use of *psychotherapeutic* drugs), *electroconvulsive therapy* (ECT: electricity) and *psychosurgery* (surgical procedures). These therapies have been successful in treating various mental disorders, although their use has been extensively criticised. For example, the drugs used in chemotherapy may have unpleasant, and sometimes permanent, side-effects. Moreover, they do not provide a 'cure' for disorders, but merely *alleviate* their symptoms for as long as they remain active in the nervous system (although it should be acknowledged that this is also true for the treatment of some physical illnesses, such as diabetes).

More disturbingly, what Kovel (1978) calls '*biological directives*' have been used as *agents of social control*. Critics of chemotherapy see the zombie-like state that some psychotherapeutic drugs produce as acting like 'pharmacological strait-jackets', exerting the same effects as the actual strait-jackets they were intended to replace. Critics of ECT argue that whilst it is effective in the treatment of some mental disorders, it is not known *why* its beneficial effects occur. Supporters, however, contend that this is also true for some treatments of certain physical illnesses, and the fact that a treatment 'works' is sufficient to justify its use. Therapies based on the biological (medical) model are discussed in more detail in Gross *et al.* (2000).

PSYCHOLOGICAL MODELS OF ABNORMALITY

The psychodynamic model

The view that mental disorders have physical origins was challenged in the late nineteenth century by Sigmund Freud. Whilst Freud (1923) believed that mental disorders were caused by internal factors, he saw these as being *psychological* rather than physical in origin. He first made his claim as a way of explaining *hysteria*, a disorder in which physical symptoms (such as deafness) are experienced, but with no underlying physical cause. Freud, a qualified physician, astonished his medical colleagues by proposing that hysteria's origins lay in *unresolved* and *unconscious sexual conflicts* originating in *childhood*.

Freud believed that personality has *three* components, and that all behaviour is a product of their *interaction*:

- The *id* is present at birth. This is the impulsive, subjective and pleasure-seeking part of personality. It operates on the *pleasure principle* (which aims at the immediate gratification of instinctual needs without regard for how this is achieved).

- The *ego* develops from the id to help us cope with the external world, and is necessary for survival. It operates on the *reality principle* (which directs the gratification of the id's needs through socially acceptable means).

- The *superego* is the last component to develop, and is concerned with moral judgements and feelings. It consists of *conscience* (the source of guilt when we engage in immoral or unethical behaviours) and *ego-ideal* (against which our behaviours are measured).

When these structures are 'in balance', psychological *normality* is maintained. However, Freud saw conflict between them as always being present to some degree, and when the conflict cannot be managed, disorders arise. Freud believed that early childhood experiences shape both normal *and* abnormal behaviour. As noted earlier, he proposed that hysteria stemmed from unresolved and unconscious sexual conflicts originating in childhood, and that *all* mental disorders could be explained in this way.

According to Freud, human development passes through a series of *psychosexual stages*:

- In the *oral stage* (0–1 year), the principal sexually sensitive zone is the mouth, and the infant's greatest source of gratification is sucking.

- In the *anal stage* (1–3), the membranes of the anal region provide the major source of pleasurable stimulation.

- From 3 to 5 or 6, self-manipulation of the genitals provides the major source of pleasurable sensation. This is the *phallic stage*.

- In the *latency stage* (5 or 6–12), the child's sexual motivations recede in importance as a preoccupation with developing skills and other activities occurs.

- Finally, after puberty, the deepest feelings of satisfaction come from heterosexual relationships. This is the *genital stage*.

The nature of the conflicts and how they are expressed reflect the stage of development the child was in when the conflict occurred. To avoid the pain caused by the conflict, Freud proposed the existence of *defence mechanisms* as a way of preventing anxiety-arousing impulses and thoughts from reaching consciousness (see also Chapter 4, page 82). All of these unconsciously operating mechanisms serve to protect us by *distorting reality*, and some of them are identified below:

- **Repression**: Forcing a dangerous/threatening memory/idea/feeling out of consciousness and making it unconscious.

- **Displacement**: Redirecting an emotional response from a dangerous object to a safe one. For example, anger towards one's boss might be redirected towards the family dog.

- **Denial**: Refusing to acknowledge certain aspects of reality; refusing to perceive something because it is painful, distressing or threatening.

- **Rationalisation**: Giving socially acceptable reasons for thoughts or actions based on unacceptable motives; justifying your own/others' actions to yourself, and believing it.

- **Identification**: Incorporating an external object (usually another person) into one's own personality, making them part of one's self. Coming to think/act/feel as if one were that person.

- **Regression**: Engaging in a behaviour characteristic of an earlier stage of development, such as going to bed when upset.

For Freud, mental disorders stem from the demands of the id and/or superego on the ego. If the ego is too weak to cope with such conflicts, it defends itself by *repressing* them into the unconscious. However, the conflicts do not disappear, but find expression through behaviour (and this is the disorder a person experiences). In Freud's view, it is not enough to change a person's *present* behaviour. To bring about a permanent cure, the problems *giving rise* to the behaviours must also be changed.

Box 5.7   Therapies based on the psychodynamic model

To treat mental disorders, Freud developed *psychoanalysis*. The first aim of this is to *make the unconscious conscious*. Through a 'therapeutic regression', the person experiencing psychoanalysis is directed to re-experience *repressed* unconscious feelings and wishes frustrated in childhood. This takes place in the 'safe' context of the *psychoanalyst's* consulting room, and the person is encouraged to experience the feelings and wishes in a more appropriate way, with a 'new ending'. Providing disturbed people with *insight* (self-knowledge and self-understanding) enables them to adjust successfully to their deep-rooted conflicts, and deal with them in a 'more mature way'.

Although psychoanalysis is the main therapy based on the psychodynamic model, there are many variations on it. These include *psychoanalytically oriented psychotherapies* and *psychodynamic approaches to group therapy*, such as *psychodrama* and *transactional analysis*. Some of the therapies based on the psychodynamic model are discussed in more detail in Gross *et al.* (2000).

The psychodynamic model has been both influential and controversial, and its assumptions, and the therapies based on it, have been subject to much criticism. Despite the model's claim to have explanatory power, experimental support for it is weak. Freud's lack of scientific rigour in developing the model, most notably his dependence on *inference* rather than objective *evidence*, has also attracted criticism.

PAUSE FOR THOUGHT

Would it be valid to propose a theory of *child development* based exclusively on the study of adults, and would it be valid to propose a theory of *normal* development based on the treatment of emotionally disturbed individuals?

The sample of people on which Freud based his theory was actually quite a narrow one, consisting largely of upper-middle-class Viennese women aged between 20 and 44, all of whom had serious emotional problems. Although restricted and atypical samples can sometimes be helpful and illuminating, critics argue that Freud's was too narrow to formulate a model of personality development in *children* and of *normal* psychological development.

The psychodynamic model has also been criticised for its *reductionist* interpretation of life. In its purest form, the model sees people as being driven by 'animal instincts' which are beyond their control. Because 'the die is cast in early life', we are seen as being helpless to change ourselves (which also makes the model *deterministic*).

The behavioural model

Both the biological (medical) and psychodynamic models explain mental disorders in terms of *internal* factors, their difference being that the former sees disorders as having underlying *physical* causes, whilst the latter sees their causes as being psychological. By contrast, the behavioural model sees disorders as *maladaptive behaviours*, which are *learned* and *maintained* in the same way as adaptive behaviours. According to this model, the best way of explaining mental disorders is to look at the *environmental conditions* in which a particular behaviour is displayed.

Pavlov and classical conditioning

At the beginning of the twentieth century, Ivan P. Pavlov discovered a learning process which is now called *classical conditioning* (and sometimes *Pavlovian* or *respondent conditioning*). In this, a stimulus which does not normally elicit a particular response will eventually come to do so if it is *reliably* paired with a stimulus that does elicit that response. For example, a hungry dog does not ordinarily salivate when it hears a bell, but it does when it sees some food. Pavlov found that if the sound of the bell *reliably* preceded the sight of the food, the dog would eventually *associate* the former with the latter, and would salivate as soon as the bell sounded, in anticipation of seeing food. The principles and procedures of classical conditioning are described in detail in Gross *et al.* (2000).

Classical conditioning's role in *human learning* was taken up by Watson (1913), who is credited with recognising its importance as a potential explanation of how mental disorders develop.

Key **S T U D Y**

Box 5.8 **Classically conditioning a fear response**

In an experiment which would today be regarded as unethical (see Chapter 6, pages 128–132), Watson & Rayner (1920) classically conditioning a fear response in a young child called Albert. According to Jones (1925):

'Albert, eleven months of age, was an infant with a phlegmatic disposition, afraid of nothing "under the sun" except a loud noise made by striking a steel bar. This made him cry. By striking the bar at the same time that Albert touched a white rat, the fear was transferred to the white rat. After seven combined stimulations, rat and sound, Albert not only became greatly disturbed at the sight of the rat, but this fear had spread to include a white rabbit, cotton wool, a fur coat and the experimenter's [white] hair. It did not transfer to wooden blocks and other objects very dissimilar to the rat'.

Figure 5.6 *A very rare photograph of John Watson and Rosalie Rayner during the conditioning of Little Albert*

Watson and Rayner showed that a *phobia* could be *acquired* through classical conditioning. For some psychologists, classical conditioning explains the *acquisition* of *all* abnormal fears:

> 'Any neutral stimulus, simple or complex, that happens to make an impact on an individual at about the same time a fear reaction is evoked, acquires the ability to evoke fear subsequently ... there will be generalisation of the fear reactions to stimuli resembling the conditioned stimulus'. (Wolpe & Rachman, 1960)

Thorndike, Skinner and operant conditioning

At the same time that Pavlov was researching classical conditioning, Edward Thorndike observed that animals tended to *repeat* behaviours when they were associated with *pleasurable consequences*, but would *not repeat* behaviours associated with *unpleasurable consequences*. Thorndike's work was taken up by B.F. Skinner, who coined the term *operant conditioning* (also known as *instrumental conditioning*). An *operant behaviour* is a voluntary and controllable one. For example, when we find ourselves in a situation in which our physiological activity changes in an uncomfortable way, we cannot 'will' it to return to normal. We can, however, *operate* on our environment to change it. Operant conditioning is discussed in detail in Gross *et al.* (2000).

According to the behavioural model, when we develop a fear of something, we avoid it, and this reduces the fear. In Skinner's terms, the avoidance behaviour is *reinforcing* because it reduces the fear. Because avoidance is associated with the pleasurable consequence of the fear being reduced, avoidance behaviour is *maintained* through operant conditioning.

PAUSE FOR THOUGHT

If the principles of classical and operant conditioning can be used to explain the origins and maintenance of mental disorders, what approach to *treatment* would supporters of the behavioural model take?

Box 5.9   Therapies based on the behavioural model

The behavioural model focuses on the behavioural problem itself, rather than historical reasons for its development (which the psychodynamic model sees as being of major importance). Consequently, behavioural therapists attempt to change behaviour by systematically applying learning principles.

Some behavioural therapies are based on classical conditioning. Collectively, these are called *behaviour therapy*, and include techniques such as *implosion therapy, flooding, systematic desensitisation, aversion therapy*, and *covert sensitisation*. Other behavioural therapies are based on operant conditioning, and are known collectively as *behaviour modification techniques*. These include *behaviour shaping* and *token economies*.

Behavioural therapies have been extremely influential. Irrespective of whether they use classical or operant conditioning, all have at least two things in common:

*   A treatment's success or failure is based on specific and *observable* changes in behaviour.
*   All behaviourally oriented therapists are committed to the idea that the value of any therapy must be assessed by conducting controlled experimental studies of its effectiveness.

The cognitive model

Both classical and operant conditioning require that people actually *perform* behaviours for them to be learned. However, whilst accepting the principles of conditioning, *social learning theorists* point out that certain behaviours can be acquired simply by *watching* them being performed. Bandura (1969) called this *observational learning*, and his approach to understanding and treating mental disorders represents a link between the behavioural and cognitive models of abnormality (see Gross *et al.*, 2000).

Like the psychodynamic model, the cognitive model is concerned with internal processes. However, instead of emphasising the role of unconscious conflicts, the cognitive model focuses on internal events such as *thoughts, expectations* and *attitudes* that accompany, and in some cases cause, mental disorders. The cognitive model developed partly from dissatisfaction with the behavioural model's concentration on overt behaviour, to the neglect of thoughts and interpretations.

Instead of concentrating on environmental conditions, the cognitive model proposes that *mediating processes*, such as thoughts, interpretations and perceptions of ourselves, others and the environment, are important in causing mental disorders. The cognitive model became influential in the 1950s, but recognition of the importance of cognitive factors in mental disorders is not new. For example, Shakespeare's *Hamlet* expresses this when he says: 'there is nothing either good or bad, but thinking makes it so'.

PAUSE FOR THOUGHT

Are there any ways in which humans could be likened to *computers*? Do humans always think about things in a *rational* way?

One cognitive approach to understanding behaviour sees people as *information processors* (see Chapter 1, page 2, and Chapter 2, page 11). The information processing approach likens the mind to a computer. As with computers, information (based on our perceptions) is put into the system, stored, manipulated and later retrieved from it. According to this view, disorders occur when the input–output sequence is disturbed in some way. For example, the faulty storage or manipulation of information may lead to a 'distorted output' or a 'lack of output'.

Another cognitive approach sees some mental disorders as stemming from irrational and maladaptive *assumptions* and *thoughts*. Beck (1967) calls these *cognitive errors*, whilst Meichenbaum (1976) uses the term *counterproductive self-statements*. One application of the cognitive model has been to *depression*. For example, Beck (1974) argues that disorders like depression are often 'rooted' in the maladaptive ways people think about themselves in the world. Depressed people characteristically think in a *negative way*, and are likely to view minor (or even neutral) events as self-devaluing or hopeless. Beck believes that such illogical thoughts deepen the depression and lower a person's motivation to take constructive action. Some examples of irrational thinking contributing to depression are:

- **Magnification and minimisation**: Some people *magnify* difficulties and failures, whilst minimising their accomplishments and successes. For example, a student who gets a low mark in one exam might magnify that and minimise achievements in others.

- **Selective abstraction**: People sometimes arrive at conclusions based on only one rather than several factors that could have made a contribution. For example, the goalkeeper of a beaten football team may blame himself, despite the fact that other team members also played badly.

- **Arbitrary inference**: A person arrives at a conclusion about him/herself, despite the absence of any supporting evidence for it. For example, a student who misses a lecture might see him/herself as incompetent, despite the fact that the bus to college was late.

- **Overgeneralisation**: A person arrives at a sweeping conclusion based on a single and sometimes trivial event. For example, a student might conclude that s/he is unworthy of a place at university, because his/her application form contained a minor mistake.

Box 5.10 Therapies based on the cognitive model

Since the cognitive model sees mental disorders as arising from 'faulty thinking' and since, to a large degree, our behaviour is controlled by the way we think, the most effective way to change maladaptive behaviours is to change the cognitions that underlie them.

Wessler (1986) defines cognitively-based therapies as a set of treatment interventions in which human cognitions are assigned a central role. Beck's therapy, for example, aims to alter the way depressed people think about their situations, and to challenge beliefs about their worthiness, inadequacy and inability to change their circumstances. This approach is characteristic of all therapeutic approaches based on the cognitive model. According to Beck & Weishaar (1989), such therapies involve highly specific learning experiences designed to teach people to:

- monitor their negative, automatic thoughts (cognitions);

- recognise the connection between cognition, emotion and behaviour;

- examine the evidence for and against distorted automatic thoughts;

- substitute more reality-oriented interpretations for these biased cognitions;

- learn to identify and alter the beliefs that predispose them to distort their experiences.

The cognitive model attempts to identify, and then change, the maladaptive thoughts and beliefs that occur in many different situations and with many different disorders. The cognitive model and its therapies are therefore less mechanical and more 'in tune' with people's conscious experiences than other models. Not surprisingly, supporters of the 'mechanistic' behavioural model have been the most critical of the cognitive model. Skinner (1990), for example, saw it as a return to *'unscientific mentalism'*, and warned that, because cognitive phenomena are not observable, they cannot possibly form the foundations of a scientific psychology. Arguing from a *humanistic* perspective, Corey (1991) proposes that human behaviour is more than thoughts and beliefs and that, in a sense, the cognitive model is as 'mechanistic' as the behavioural model in reducing human beings to 'the sum of their cognitive parts'.

Despite these reservations, psychology's current emphasis on the role of cognition suggests that the cognitive model will continue to be influential as a way of both explaining and treating mental disorders.

Section Summary

■ Psychologists disagree about abnormality's **causes** and the best way to **treat** it. Four major models of abnormality are the **biological (medical)**, **psychodynamic**, **behavioural**, and **cognitive**.

■ The **biological (medical) model** views abnormality as having an underlying **physical cause**, a kind of **illness** which can be treated **medically**. Some mental disorders are caused by **brain damage**, although the model also sees **genes** and **brain biochemistry** as being directly involved.

■ The approaches to treatment favoured by the medical model are collectively known as **somatic therapy**. Three of these are **chemotherapy**, **electroconvulsive therapy**, and **psychosurgery**. All have been subjected to much criticism.

■ The **psychodynamic model** sees mental disorders as being caused by internal psychological factors, namely, **unresolved**, **unconscious**, **childhood conflicts**.

■ One approach to therapy is **psychoanalysis**. This involves re-experiencing repressed childhood feelings and wishes. Psychoanalysis aims to provide **insight**, which provides a more mature way of coping with deep-rooted conflicts.

■ The psychodynamic model has been criticised for its lack of scientific rigour and experimental evidence. Freud's theory of psychological development was based on a biased sample, and his emphasis on 'animal instincts' as a source of all behaviour is **reductionist** and **deterministic**.

■ According to the **behavioural model**, disorders are **learned maladaptive behaviours**. The learning processes involved are **classical** and **operant conditioning**. Evidence suggests that some disorders (e.g. **phobias**) can be explained in conditioning terms.

■ Therapies based on the behavioural model focus on maladaptive behaviours, and try to change them without establishing their causes and history. Success is measured in terms of changes in specific and observable **behaviours**. Any therapy's value must be assessed by conducting controlled experimental studies of its effectiveness.

■ **Social learning theorists** view some behaviours as being acquired through **observational learning**. This approach emphasises the role of thoughts, interpretations and other cognitions as **mediating processes** between the individual and the environment.

■ Social learning theory is a link between the behavioural and **cognitive models** of abnormality. The **information processing** approach compares the mind to a computer. Disorders occur when the 'input–output' sequence is disturbed in some way. Other cognitive approaches see mental disorders as stemming from **irrational assumptions** or **counterproductive self-statements**.

■ The cognitive model sees the changing of the 'faulty thinking' underlying maladaptive behaviour as the most logical and effective approach to treatment. All cognitively-based therapies involve cognitive **restructuring**.

Self-Assessment Questions

3   a   Outline the biological (medical) and behavioural models in terms of their views on the causes of abnormality. *(3 marks + 3 marks)*

    b   Describe how the biological (medical) and cognitive models approach the treatment of mental disorders. *(6 marks + 6 marks)*

    c   'The psychodynamic model of abnormality has been both influential and controversial.'
      Critically consider the application of the psychodynamic model to the understanding of abnormal behaviour. *(12 marks)*

4   a   Distinguish between the psychodynamic and cognitive models of abnormality in terms of their views on how abnormality should be treated.
(3 marks + 3 marks)

    b   Describe how the psychodynamic and cognitive models of abnormality explain the causes of mental disorders. *(6 marks + 6 marks)*

    c   'There are strengths and weaknesses associated with all models of abnormality.'
      Assess the strengths and limitations associated with any **two** models of abnormality. *(12 marks)*

Eating Disorders:
Anorexia Nervosa and Bulimia Nervosa

Eating disorders are characterised by physically and/or psychologically harmful eating patterns. In the ICD-10 classificatory system of mental disorders (see Gross *et al.*, 2000), they are classified as *'behavioural syndromes associated with physiological disturbances and physical factors'*. Although there are several types of eating disorder, two broad categories are *anorexia nervosa* and *bulimia nervosa*. This section describes the clinical characteristics of these disorders, and discusses explanations of them offered by biological and psychological models of abnormality.

ANOREXIA NERVOSA (AN)

Although the characteristics of what is now called anorexia nervosa (AN) have been known about for several hundred years, it is only recently that the disorder has attracted much interest. One source of this is the popular press, which has given publicity to the condition, and in particular its effects on entertainers such as Jane Fonda and, tragically, Karen Carpenter and Lena Zavaroni. This interest is the result of a greater public knowledge of the disorder and the recent increase in its incidence (although Fombonne, 1995, argues that the increase can be attributed to changes in diagnostic criteria concerning weight loss: see below).

AN occurs primarily in females, and female anorectics outnumber males by a factor of 15:1. The disorder usually has its onset in adolescence, the period between 14 and 16 being most common. However, the onset sometimes occurs before adolescence or later in adult life. For example, Lask & Bryant-Waugh (1992) have reported cases in children as young as eight, whilst Boast *et al.* (1992) investigated 25 'late-onset' female anorectics whose average age was 32. Estimates of AN's incidence vary. American data suggest that one in 250 females may experience the disorder (Lewinsohn *et al.*, 1993). In Britain, the figure has been estimated at one to four in 100, with around 70,000 people recognised as anorectic (Murray, 1999).

Key (S T U D Y)
Box 5.11 A case of anorexia nervosa

Frieda had always been a shy, sensitive girl who gave little cause for concern at home or in school. She was bright and did well academically, although she had few friends. In early adolescence, she was somewhat overweight, and teased by her family that she would never get a boyfriend until she

lost some weight. She reacted to this by withdrawing and becoming very touchy. Her parents had to be careful about what they said. If offended, Frieda would throw a tantrum and march off to her room.

Frieda began dieting. Initially, her family was pleased, but gradually her parents sensed all was not well. Under pressure, she would take her meals to her room and later, having said that she had eaten everything, her mother would find food hidden away untouched. When her mother caught her deliberately inducing vomiting after a meal, she insisted they go to the family doctor. He found that Frieda had stopped menstruating a few months earlier. Not fooled by the loose, floppy clothes that Frieda was wearing, he insisted on carrying out a full physical examination. Her emaciated body told him as much as he needed to know, and he arranged for Frieda's immediate hospitalisation.

(Adapted from Rosenhan & Seligman, 1984)

As Box 5.11 illustrates, AN is characterised by a prolonged refusal to eat adequate amounts of food, which results in deliberate weight loss. As 'Frieda''s case shows, body weight loss is typically accompanied by the cessation of menstruation (*amenorrhea*). For a diagnosis of AN to be considered, the individual must weigh less than 85 per cent of normal or expected weight for height, age and sex. As a result of their significant weight loss, anorectics look emaciated. They also show a decline in general health, which is accompanied by many physical problems. These include low blood pressure and body temperature, constipation, dehydration and poor quality sleep (Nobili *et al.*, 1999). In five to 15 per cent of cases AN is fatal, and may sometimes be resistant to all forms of therapy. Depression, low self-esteem, pessimism, and feelings of insecurity and guilt also frequently feature in AN. Suicide is the most common related cause of death (Crisp, 1983).

Literally, anorexia nervosa means 'nervous loss of appetite'. However, anorectics are often both hungry and preoccupied with thoughts of food. For example, they may constantly read recipe books and prepare elaborate meals for their friends. Anorectics themselves, however, will avoid most calorie-rich foods, such as meat, milk products, sweets and other deserts, and will often limit their consumption to little more than a lettuce leaf and carrot. Although anorectics do not experience deficiencies in taste, they show reduced pleasure in eating and an aversion to the oral sensation of fat.

Box 5.12 Restricting and binge eating/purging types

AN is also characterised by an intense fear of being over-weight, which does not diminish even when a large amount of weight has been lost. As a consequence of this fear, anorectics take extreme measures to lose weight. In the DSM-IV classificatory system (see Gross *et al.*, 2000), two sub-types of AN are identified, both of which involve a refusal to maintain a body-weight above the minimum normal weight. The *restricting type* loses weight through constant fasting and engaging in excessive physical activity. The *binge eating/purging type* alternates between periods of fasting and 'binge eating' (see below), in which normally avoided food is consumed in large quantities. The guilt and shame experienced as a result of the 'binge' leads the anorectic to use laxatives or self-induced vomiting to expel ingested food from the system.

One other characteristic of AN is a *distorted body image*, in which the anorectic does not recognise his/her body's thinness. Even though their appearance may show protruding bones, many anorectics still see themselves as 'being fat', and deny that they are 'wasting away'. As Bruch (1978) has observed:

> 'anorectics vigorously defend their gruesome emaciation as not being too thin ... they identify with the skeleton-like appearance, actively maintain it and deny its abnormality'.

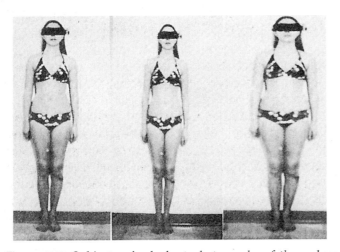

Figure 5.7 *Subjects who look at photographs of themselves through an anamorphic lens can adjust the lens until they see what they believe is their actual image. A subject may alter her actual image (left) from 20 per cent thinner (middle) to 20 per cent larger (right). Most anorectics overestimate their body size (From Comer, 1998)*

The fact that many people who would be diagnosed as anorectic do not perceive themselves as having a problem, suggests that data relating to both the incidence and prevalence of the disorder should be treated with caution (Cooper, 1995).

EXPLANATIONS OF AN

Biological (medical) model

Modern biological models see dysfunction in the *hypothalamus* (see Chapter 4, page 61) as being involved in AN. Certainly, psychological research indicates that the hypothalamus plays an important role in the regulation of eating. When the neurotransmitter *noradrenaline* acts on part of the hypothalamus, non-human animals begin eating and show a marked preference for carbohydrates. The neurotransmitter *serotonin*, by contrast, apparently induces satiation and suppresses appetite, especially for carbohydrates. Any condition which increased serotonin's effects would presumably decrease eating. However, there is not yet sufficient evidence to indicate whether hypothalamic dysfunction and changes in neurotransmitter levels are *causes* of AN, *effects* of it, or merely *correlates* (Hinney *et al.*, 1999).

PAUSE FOR THOUGHT

Some psychological disorders might be inherited, just as some physical disorders are. How could the role of genetic factors in AN be explored?

There is a tendency for AN to run in families, with first- and second-degree relatives of anorectics being significantly more likely to develop the disorder compared with the same type of relative in a control group of non-anorectics (Strober & Katz, 1987). This has led to the proposal that AN may have a *genetic* basis. One method of studying the inheritance of characteristics involves comparing the *resemblance* of monozygotic (MZ or *identical*) twins and dizygotic (DZ or *non-identical*) twins. With continuous characteristics (e.g. intelligence test scores), resemblance is defined in terms of the strength of the correlation (see Chapter 7, pages 160–162) between the twins on whatever has been measured. However, AN is probably *discontinuous* (a person either is anorectic or is not), and resemblance is defined in terms of a *concordance rate*. If two twins are anorectic, they are *concordant* for AN. If one is anorectic and other is not, they are *discordant*.

Askevold & Heiberg (1979) reported a 50 per cent concordance rate for MZs brought up in the *same* environment, which they see as strong evidence that genes play a role. However, in the absence of concordance rates for MZs and DZs raised in *different* environments, this claim is difficult to evaluate. Holland *et al.* (1984) reported a concordance rate of 55 per cent for MZs brought up in the same environment, and seven per cent for DZs. According to Gorwood *et al.* (1998), the 'vulnerability component' of AN that can be attributed to genetic factors is around 70 per cent, although it has yet to be established which, or how many, 'candidate genes' are involved.

Figure 5.8 *The much publicised English anorectic twins, Samantha and Michaela Kendall. Despite receiving treatment in the USA, Samantha eventually died. Michaela died three years later*

Box 5.13 AN and brain damage

Other biological hypotheses suggest that some cases of AN are a consequence of brain damage at or before birth (Cnattingius *et al.*, 1999). According to Lask (cited in Kennedy, 1997), a blood-flow deficiency in the part of the brain which governs visual perception, appetite and the sense of fullness, explains why anorectics see themselves as fat when they are thin. However, people with this deficiency would need other triggers to develop the disorder. These might include stress, a perfectionist personality and a society that promoted thinness (see below and Box 5.15, page 102).

Psychological models

There are several explanations of AN based on the *psychodynamic* model. One proposes that the disorder represents an unconscious effort by a girl to remain pre-pubescent. As a result of overdependence on the parents, some girls might fear becoming sexually mature and independent. As noted previously, AN is associated with amenorrhea, and psychodynamic theorists sees this as enabling the anorectic to circumvent growing up and achieving adult responsibilities. To achieve puberty, we must attain a particular level of body fat, and evidence suggests that anorectics will eat, provided they do not gain weight.

Another psychodynamic account proposes that the disorder may allow a girl to avoid the issue of her sexuality. The weight loss that occurs prevents the rounding of the breasts and hips, and the body takes on a 'boy-like' appearance. Psychodynamic theorists propose that this might be a way of avoiding the issue of sexuality in general, and the prospect of pregnancy in particular.

A third psychodynamic account sees AN as an attempt by adolescents to *separate* themselves from their parents, and establish their own *identities*. Bruch (1991) argues that the parents of anorectics tend to be domineering, and the disorder represents an attempt to gain a sense of *autonomy* and *control*. Many female anorectics are 'good girls', who do well in school and are co-operative and well-behaved. Bruch argues that this leads them to feel they have no choices and are being controlled by the desires and demands of others. For Bruch, 'such children experience themselves as not ... owning their own bodies'. One way of exerting individuality is to assume control over what is most concretely one's self – the body. Thinness and starvation, then, are signs of self-control and independence.

Box 5.14 Dysfunctional families and AN

According to Minuchin *et al.* (1978), AN is the result of *dysfunctional family systems*. For example, in families where there is marital discord, an adolescent who develops AN might bring the dissenting partners closer together again, as a result of their shared concerns. Another way in which AN might develop is through what Minuchin *et al.* call an *enmeshed family pattern*. In this, family members are overinvolved with each other's affairs and overconcerned with details of one another's lives. Adolescence may pose a problem because it threatens to expose a family's apparent 'closeness' as a facade. The development of AN in the adolescent may enable the family to maintain an illusion of being harmonious, because its members have a focus which unites them. However, the evidence in this regard is unclear (Gowers & North, 1999).

As well as lacking supportive evidence, two observations challenge psychodynamic accounts of AN:

- Some seem to apply only to females. It is impossible to see how avoiding the prospect of pregnancy could apply to male anorectics.

- All of the accounts have difficulty in explaining AN's occurrence *after* adolescence.

The *behavioural* model sees AN as a *phobia* concerning the possibility of gaining weight. Indeed, AN might be more appropriately called *weight phobia* (Crisp, 1967). The phobia is assumed to be the result of the impact of *social norms*, *values* and *roles*. For example, Garner *et al.* (1980) found that the winners of Miss America and the centrefolds in *Playboy* magazine have been consistently below the average female weight, and became significantly more so in the period from 1959 to 1978. This trend has continued into the 1990s (Wiseman *et al.*, 1992).

PAUSE FOR THOUGHT

In what ways might the *media* contribute to the development of AN?

According to Hill (cited in Uhlig, 1996), women's fashion magazines play a part in shaping young girls' perceptions of desirable figures, but are not as influential as classmates, mothers and toys. According to Hill:

'[Sindy] is now unashamedly blonde, pointedly thin, [and] dressed immaculately … Not only does 90s' Sindy depict the ideal appearance and lifestyle of 90s' women, she does so for girls only halfway to puberty'.

Thus, the *cultural idealisation* of the slender female (as represented by toys and 'supermodels', and as portrayed by toy companies and the media) may be one cause of the fear of being fat (Petkova, 1997). If women are encouraged to see slimness as desirable, through, say, its promotion in the media, then seeing their bodies as larger than they are (*distorted body image*: see page 100) may encourage dieting to try to achieve that goal.

In one study of media influence, Hamilton & Waller (1993) showed eating-disordered and non-eating-disordered women photographs of idealised female bodies as portrayed in women's fashion magazines. The non-eating-disordered women were not affected by the nature of the photographs they saw. However, the eating disordered women were, and overestimated their own body-sizes more after they had seen such photographs than after they had seen photographs of neutral objects. According to Fairburn *et al*'s. (1999) *cognitive–behavioural theory* of the maintenance of AN, the tendency in Western societies to judge self-worth in terms of shape and weight is superimposed on the disorder's central feature of a need to control eating.

In some occupations, such as ballet-dancing and modelling, there is considerable pressure on women to be thin, and the incidence of AN in these occupations is *higher* than in the general population (Alberge, 1999). However, not *all* ballet-dancers, models and so on, who diet to be slim develop eating disorders (Cooper, 1995). Nevertheless, for Wooley & Wooley (1983):

'an increasingly stringent cultural standard of thinness for women has been accompanied by a steadily increasing incidence of serious eating disorders in women'.

Support for the claim that societal norms can be influential in this respect comes from evidence about eating disorders in other cultures. In some non-Western cultures (including China, Singapore and Malaysia), the incidence of AN is much *lower* than in Western societies (Lee *et al.*, 1992). Additionally, cases of AN reported in black populations of Western and non-Western cultures are significantly lower than those in white populations (Sui-Wah, 1989), but apparently increasing amongst populations where concerns about thinness have increased (Rogers *et al.*, 1997).

Key (S T U D Y)

Box 5.15 AN via TV

A sudden increase in eating disorders among teenage girls in Fiji may be linked to the arrival of television on the island in 1995. Since TV's introduction, there has been a sharp rise in indicators of disordered eating. Seventy-four per cent of Fijian teenage girls reported feeling 'too big or fat' in a 1998 survey conducted 38 months after the country's one television station began broadcasting.

Traditionally, Fijians have preferred a 'robust, well-muscled body' for both sexes. However, with the advent of the television station, which features American shows such as *ER* and *Melrose Place*, adolescent girls may have become seduced by Western ideals of beauty.

(Adapted from Fearn, 1999)

If Western cultural values are important in AN, then it might reasonably be assumed that members of non-Western populations who 'Westernise' themselves would be at highest risk of developing AN. However, Mumford *et al.* (1991) found that Asian girls living in Bradford from the most *traditional* families (as determined by Asian language and dress) were *more* likely to be diagnosed as anorectic. Mumford *et al.* argue that girls from traditional families experience greater *intergenerational family conflict* than those from families who have already adopted a Western outlook and values, and that this plays a major role in the development of eating disorders among Asian girls in Britain.

Box 5.16 AN and the blind

One puzzling observation which is difficult for theories to account for is the development of AN in people unable to see. As noted previously (see page 100), body image disturbance is one of the 'hallmarks' of AN. However, Yager *et al.* (1986) describe the case of a 28-year-old woman, blind from age two, who had become anorectic at age 21. Touyz *et al.* (1988) report a case of AN in a woman blind from birth. Although neither research team offered a satisfactory explanation for their findings, both agreed that blindness either from birth or a very early age does not preclude AN's development, and that people do not have to be actually able to see themselves to desire a slimmer physique (see also Box 5.13, page 101).

BULIMIA NERVOSA (BN)

Literally, bulimia comes from the Greek *bous* meaning 'ox' and *limos* meaning 'hunger'. The disorder was first extensively investigated by Russell (1979), who saw it as 'an ominous variant' of AN. BN is characterised by periodic episodes of 'compulsive' or 'binge' eating, involving the rapid and seemingly uncontrolled consumption of food, especially that rich in carbohydrates.

The binge is terminated either by abdominal pain or, in the case of the *purging type*, by expulsion of food using diuretics, laxatives or self-induced vomiting. Some bulimics begin their binges by eating coloured 'marker' foods and, after they have finished, will continue purging until the marker has re-emerged (Colman, 1987). A typical binge might include the consumption of a large amount of ice-cream, packets of crisps, a pizza and several cans of fizzy drink. As well as their high calorific content, most foods consumed by bulimics have textures that aid rapid consumption. Thus, food tends to be 'wolfed down' rather than chewed properly. With the *non-purging type*, strict dieting or vigorous exercise (rather than regular purging) occurs.

'Binge eating' itself is actually quite common and many people admit to indulging occasionally. In BN, however, the frequency of such behaviour is much higher, averaging at least two or three times a week, and sometimes as often as 40 times a week.

Box 5.17 A case of BN

Miss A. was a 22-year-old single clerk who was referred by her doctor for treatment of 'psychiatric problems'. She had a three-year history of uncontrolled over-eating. Although she was not originally obese, she disliked her 'square face' and developed a sensitive personality. After failing an examination and being unable to study in further education, she started to relieve her boredom and comfort herself by over-eating. Her binges occurred four times per week and lasted one to three hours each.

Triggers included feelings of emptiness and critical remarks from others. On average, she secretly consumed 800 g of bread and biscuits. Such episodes were followed by abdominal bloating, guilt and dysphoria (inappropriate emotional feelings). There was nausea, but no vomiting. She took excessive laxatives (usually prune juice) to purge and 'calm' herself, restricted food intake, and exercised excessively in the next one to two days. Her body-weight fluctuated by up to 4 kg per week, but her menstrual cycle was normal.

Examination revealed a girl who was fully conscious of what she was doing, and who felt helpless over the 'attacks of over-eating'. She desired a body weight of 45 kg and disparaged her waistline and square face, which made her 'look like a pig'. She found food dominated her life, and likened her problem to heroin addiction. There was a persistent request for laxatives.

(Adapted from Lee *et al.*, 1992)

Most bulimics are women, and BN affects nearly 50 times more women than men (Emmett, 1996). The disorder typically begins in adolescence or early adulthood, and generally appears later than in AN, although as with AN there have been reports of pre-pubertal BN (Stein *et al.*, 1998). BN is also more frequent than AN, and may affect as many as five per cent of the population. However, a substantially larger percentage can be identified as 'sub-clinical' bulimics (Franko & Omori, 1999).

Like anorectics, bulimics have what the ICD-10 classificatory system calls 'an intrusive fear of fatness', and they are unduly concerned with body-weight and shape (hence they take the drastic steps described above to control their weight). Whilst the discrepancy between actual and desired body-weight is generally no greater than among non-bulimics, the discrepancy between *estimations* of body-size and desired size is substantial (Cooper, 1995). Although bulimics are mostly able to maintain a normal body-weight, they tend to fluctuate between weight gain and weight loss. The binge–purge behaviour is usually accompanied by guilty feelings. The purging of food produces feelings of relief, and a commitment to a severely restrictive diet which ultimately fails.

Clearly, bulimics recognise their eating behaviour is abnormal and feel frustrated by it. However, they are unable to control the behaviour voluntarily. Because of the guilty feelings, bingeing and purging are usually carried out in secret and, consequently, many bulimics go unrecognised even to close friends and family (Hay *et al.*, 1998). Moreover, because there is not a constant weight loss, and because the bulimic's eating habits may appear normal in public, the estimate given for the number of cases must be treated cautiously.

Purging does, however, produce some effects that might be noticeable to others. These include:

- a 'puffy' facial appearance (a consequence of swollen parotid glands caused by vomiting);

- a deterioration in tooth enamel (caused by the stomach acid produced when vomiting occurs);

- the development of calluses over the back of the hand (caused by rubbing the hand against the upper teeth when the fingers are pushed into the throat to induce vomiting).

Other associated physiological effects include digestive tract damage, salivary gland enlargement, dehydration and nutritional imbalances. Psychological effects include anxiety, sleep disturbances and depression (Stice, 1999: see below).

PAUSE FOR THOUGHT

How are AN and BN *similar*, and how do they *differ*? Draw up a list of their similarities and differences.

EXPLANATIONS OF BN

Although AN and BN differ in several ways, because they *share* many characteristics, some researchers believe they can be explained in the *same way*. Garner (1986) has argued that it is seriously misleading to consider the disorders as psychologically dissimilar. Echoing Garner, Bee (1992) describes them as 'variations on a basic theme' rather than distinctly different disorders. As well as sharing many psychological traits (such as perfectionism: Fairburn *et al.*, 1999), anorectics and bulimics also share the goal of maintaining a sub-optimal body-weight. Moreover, a particular individual may often move *between* the two disorders in the quest for thinness.

Biological (medical) model

As mentioned previously (see page 100), dysfunction in the hypothalamus has been implicated in AN. Hypothalamic dysfunction may also be involved in BN. A decrease in the neurotransmitter *serotonin*, whose apparent effect is to induce satiation and suppress appetite (see page 100), would presumably permit unrestrained eating to occur. It may therefore be no coincidence that bulimics often display low levels of serotonin (Wilcox, 1990).

Box 5.18 Hormones, endorphins, genes and BN

Hormones (see Chapter 4, page 62), such as *cholecys-tokinin octapeptide* (CCK-8) and *endorphins* (see page 67)

---

may also play mediating roles (Lauer *et al.*, 1999). For example, *plasma endorphins* are raised in people with BN. However, whether the raised levels are a cause or a result of BN remains to be established. Additionally, the evidence for a genetic basis to BN is much weaker than that for AN. Kendler *et al.* (1991), for example, have reported a concordance rate (see page 100) of only 23 per cent for MZs and nine per cent for DZs, and the role played by genetic factors remains unclear (Wade *et al.*, 1999).

Psychological models

Many of the explanations that have been proposed for AN can also be applied to BN. However, one psychological approach to understanding BN is Ruderman's (1986) *disinhibition hypothesis*. This distinguishes between 'unrestrained' and 'restrained' eaters, the latter being people who constantly monitor their weight and constantly diet. Sometimes, 'restrained' eaters believe they have overeaten, a belief that may be accompanied by the thought that, since the diet has been broken, there is no reason why more should not be eaten. This *disinhibition* leads to the consumption of more food, which is followed by purging in an attempt to reduce the weight gained by the binge eating. As well as breaking a diet, other *disinhibiting factors* include alcohol. For Ruderman, the food intake pattern of highly weight-conscious people is characterised by an all-or-nothing rigidity, which makes them susceptible to binge eating.

Box 5.19 Parental domination and BN

Bruch's (1991) perspective on AN (see page 101) has also been applied to BN. As well as *ego deficiencies* (a poor sense of autonomy and self-control), Bruch argues that parental domination also produces *perceptual and cognitive disturbances*, and the affected child is unable to distinguish between its own internal needs (whether hungry or satiated) and to identify its own emotions or fatigue levels (Comer, 1998). This view is supported by Halmi's (1995) finding that bulimics have trouble distinguishing hunger from other bodily needs or emotions. So, when they are anxious or upset, they mistakenly believe they are also hungry, and respond by eating (Comer, 1998).

The view that both BN and AN have a *single* cause is unlikely to be true, given that both biological and psychological models can claim some degree of experimental support. Perhaps both disorders can best be explained in terms of a *multidimensional-risk perspective* (Comer, 1998), in which a combination of the explanations presented here account for their development and maintenance.

Section Summary

■ **Anorexia nervosa** (AN) occurs more frequently in females than males, and usually appears in adolescence. It is characterised by a prolonged refusal to eat adequate amounts of food, resulting in deliberate weight loss.

■ To be diagnosed as **anorectic**, an individual must weigh less than 85 per cent of normal/expected weight for height, age and sex. There are many physical consequences of AN. In five to 15 per cent of cases, AN is fatal.

■ Because of their fear of being overweight, anorectics take extreme measures to lose weight. The **restricting type** engages in constant fasting/excessive physical activity, whilst the **binge eating/purging type** alternates between periods of fasting and 'binge eating', food being expelled by laxatives or self-induced vomiting.

■ Damage to the **hypothalamus** might cause AN. In non-humans, hypothalamic stimulation by **noradrenaline** produces eating, and a preference for carbohydrates. **Serotonin** produces the opposite effect. **Brain damage** before or after birth has also been implicated in AN. However, whether changes in neurotransmitter levels and other biological factors are causes, effects or correlates of AN is unclear.

■ **Genetic** factors might be involved in AN. **Concordance rates** are higher in MZ than DZ twins, but it has yet to be established which, or how many, 'candidate genes' are involved.

■ There are several **psychodynamic** explanations of AN, including accounts based on **parental domination** and an **enmeshed family pattern**. Although some observations are consistent with such explanations, there is little supportive experimental evidence. Some explanations only apply to females, and all focus on AN exclusively as an adolescent disorder.

■ The **behavioural** model sees AN as a **phobia** of gaining weight, resulting from the impact of social norms, values and roles. The current cultural idealisation of the 'slender female' may be one cause of a fear of being fat.

■ A lower incidence of AN in other cultures supports the behavioural view, as do studies indicating that media portrayal of female bodies influences attitudes and body-size estimations.

■ One difficulty for all explanations of AN is its occurrence in people blind from birth. This finding makes a **distorted body image**, as one of the disorder's main characteristics, difficult to explain.

■ Most **bulimics** are women, and **bulimia nervosa** (BN) usually begins in adolescence or early adulthood. The **purging type** is characterised by frequent episodes of compulsive/binge eating, ended either by abdominal pain or the use of diuretics, laxatives and/or self-induced vomiting. The **non-purging type** counteracts the food intake either by strict dieting or vigorous exercise.

■ Like anorectics, bulimics are unduly concerned with their body weight/shape. Although able to maintain a normal body weight, they tend to fluctuate between gain and loss. Bulimics recognise their eating behaviour is abnormal, but cannot control it.

■ AN and BN may be distinct disorders or 'variations on a theme'. Anorectics and bulimics share many psychological traits, along with the goal of maintaining a sub-optimal body weight. The same person may also alternate between the two disorders.

■ **Hypothalamic dysfunction**, **neurotransmitters**, **hormones** and **endorphins** may all play mediating roles in BN. For example, elevated **plasma endorphin** levels have been found in bulimics, although whether these are a cause, consequence or correlate of the disorder is unknown. The role played by **genetic factors** in BN is also unclear.

■ The **disinhibition hypothesis** proposes that when 'restrained eaters' believe they have overeaten, their eating becomes 'disinhibited'. This is followed by purging to reduce the weight gained. Highly weight-conscious people display all-or-nothing rigidity, making them susceptible to binge eating.

■ **Parental domination** may also play a role in BN by disturbing perception and cognition. Bulimics have trouble distinguishing hunger from other needs or emotions. When they are anxious or upset, they mistakenly believe they are also hungry, and respond by eating.

■ AN and BN probably have more than one cause. A better approach to understanding them might be in terms of a **multidimensional-risk perspective**, in which a combination of explanations account for their origin and maintenance.

Self-Assessment Questions

5 a Outline some clinical characteristics of anorexia nervosa and bulimia nervosa. *(3 marks + 3 marks)*

b Describe **two** research studies into the causes of anorexia nervosa. *(6 marks + 6 marks)*

c 'Anorexia nervosa is better explained in terms of psychological rather than biological factors.'

To what extent do psychological factors explain the causes of anorexia nervosa? *(12 marks)*

6 a Describe **two** ways in which anorexia nervosa differs from bulimia nervosa. *(3 marks + 3 marks)*

b Describe **one** research study which suggests that anorexia nervosa has a biological cause, and **one** research study which suggests that its cause is psychological. *(6 marks + 6 marks)*

c 'It is unlikely that anorexia nervosa or bulimia nervosa can be explained by any single model of abnormality.'

Using research, evaluate **two** models of abnormality in terms of how they explain anorexia nervosa *or* bulimia nervosa. *(12 marks)*

CONCLUSIONS

This chapter began by looking at some of the ways in which abnormality has been defined. Several definitions were identified. However, although all are useful, the limitations of each were exposed. No one definition on its own is sufficient, and a truly adequate definition of abnormality can probably only be achieved through a multiple perspectives (multiple definitions) approach.

As well as being unable to agree on what abnormality is, psychologists also disagree on what causes it (whatever it is), and how it should best be treated. Several biological and psychological models were presented,

each of which places a different interpretation on abnormality's causes, the focus (or goals) of therapy, and the methods used to achieve those goals.

Two types of eating disorder are anorexia nervosa and bulimia nervosa. The final part of this chapter described their clinical characteristics, and looked at attempts by biological and psychological models of abnormality to explain them. Although each model is supported by some evidence, the two eating disorders are probably best explained in terms of a multidimensional-risk perspective, in which a combination of the various models' explanations account for their development and maintenance.

WEB ADDRESSES

http://apsa.org
http://www.bfskinner.org/
http://plaza.interport.net/nypsan/Freudarc.html
http://www.usm.maine.edu/psy/gayton/333/3_03.html
http://www.noah.cuny.edu/wellconn/eatingdisorders.html
http://www.phe.queensu.ca/anab/
http://www.mentalhealth.com/dis/p20-et01.html
http://mentalhelp.net/factsfam/anorexia.htm
http://www.priory-hospital.co.uk/htm/bulimi.htm
http://www.edreferral.com/bulimia_nervosa.htm

UNIT 3

Social Psychology and Research Methods

6 *Social Influence*

INTRODUCTION AND OVERVIEW

It is impossible to live amongst other people and not be influenced by them in some way. Sometimes, other people's attempts to change our behaviour or thoughts is very obvious, as when, for example, a traffic warden tells us not to park our car in a particular place. If we do as we are told and move the car, we are demonstrating *obedience*, which implies that one person (in this example, the traffic warden, who is an *authority figure*) has more social power than others (*motorists*).

However, on other occasions social influence is less direct, and may not involve any explicit requests or demands at all. For example, when your choice of clothes or taste in music is influenced by what your friends wear or listen to, you are showing *conformity*. Your peers (equals) exert pressure on you to behave (and think) in particular ways, a case of the majority influencing the individual.

The first part of this chapter discusses research studies into conformity (*majority influence*), including the work of Sherif and Asch. Under certain conditions, however, majorities can be *influenced* by minorities (*minority influence*), and here the work of Moscovici has been important. Explanations of both majority and minority influence will be considered.

The second part of this chapter examines research into *obedience to authority*, much of which has been conducted by Milgram. It considers issues of experimental and ecological validity associated with such research, explanations of psychological processes involved in obedience, and the reasons we are sometimes blindly obedient to others, and how we might behave more *independently*.

The final part of this chapter considers the *ethical issues* that have arisen from research into social influence, such as the use of deception, protecting participants from harm, and informed consent, and the ways in which psychologists deal with these issues.

Conformity and Minority Influence

CONFORMITY

What is conformity?

Conformity has been defined in a number of ways. For Crutchfield (1955), it is 'yielding to group pressure'. Mann (1969) agrees with Crutchfield, but argues that it may take different forms and be based on motives other than group pressure.

Zimbardo & Leippe (1991) define conformity as:

'a change in belief or behaviour in response to real or imagined group pressure when there is no direct request to comply with the group nor any reason to justify the behaviour change'.

PAUSE FOR THOUGHT

What do these definitions have in common?

Group pressure is the common denominator in definitions of conformity, although none of them specifies particular groups with particular beliefs or practices. Pressure is exerted by those groups that are important to the individual at a given time. Such groups may consist of 'significant others', such as family or peers (*membership groups*), or groups whose values a person admires or aspires to, but to which s/he does not actually belong (*reference groups*).

Conformity, then, does not imply adhering to any particular set of attitudes or values. Instead, it involves yielding to the real or imagined pressures of *any* group, whether it has majority or minority status (van Avermaet, 1996).

EXPERIMENTAL STUDIES OF CONFORMITY

Sherif (1935) used a visual illusion called the *autokinetic effect*, in which a stationary spot of light in an otherwise darkened room *appears* to move. He asked participants to estimate how far the light moved. In one experiment, participants first made their estimates privately and then as members of a group. Sherif found that their individual estimates *converged* (they became more *alike* when made in a group). Thus, a *group norm* developed which represented the average of the individual estimates.

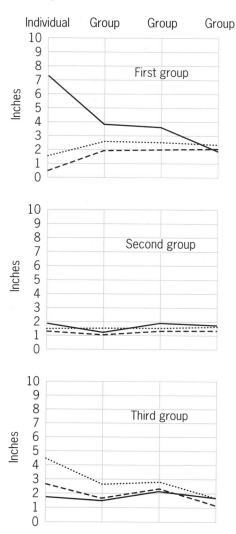

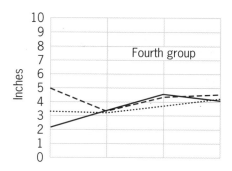

Figure 6.1 *Median judgements of the apparent movement of a stationary point of light given by participants in Sherif's (1935) experiment. In the data shown, participants first made their estimates alone ('individual'), and then in groups of three on three occasions ('group'). The figure shows the estimates given by four groups. Sherif also found that when the procedure was reversed, that is, participants made three estimates in groups followed by an estimate alone, the 'individual' estimates did not deviate from one another (From Sherif, 1936)*

Evaluating Sherif's experiment

According to Brown (1996), although Sherif's study is one of the classics of social psychology, it seems to raise questions rather than provide answers:

- In what sense can Sherif's participants be described as a *group*?

- Can we speak of *group norms* without any direct interaction taking place or participants seeing themselves as engaged in some kind of joint activity?

In post-experimental interviews, participants all denied being influenced by others' judgements. They also claimed that they struggled to arrive at the 'correct' answers on their own. In other words, they did *not* consider themselves part of a group (although there is always doubt about taking participants' reports about the motivation for their behaviour at face value).

Whilst Sherif believed that his study demonstrated conformity, Asch (1951) disagreed. According to Asch, the fact that Sherif's task was *ambiguous* (there was no right or wrong answer) made it difficult to draw conclusions about conformity in group situations. In Asch's view, the best way to measure conformity was in terms of a person's tendency to agree with other people who unanimously give the *wrong answer* on a task where the solution is obvious and unambiguous. Asch devised a simple perceptual task that involved participants deciding which of three comparison lines of different lengths matched a standard line.

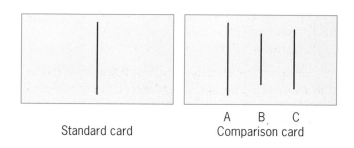

Figure 6.2 *An example of the line-judgment task devised by Asch*

In a pilot study, Asch tested 36 participants individually on 20 slightly different versions of the task shown in Figure 6.2. They made a total of only three mistakes in the 720 trials (an error rate of 0.42 per cent).

PAUSE FOR THOUGHT

What was the purpose of the pilot study? What conclusions do you think Asch drew from its results?

The purpose of the pilot study (which involved participants who would not take part in the actual experiment) was to establish that the tasks really were simple and their answers obvious and unambiguous. Asch concluded that they were. Because his procedure for studying conformity can be adapted to investigate the effects of different variables on conformity, it is known as the *Asch paradigm*.

Box 6.1 The Asch paradigm

Some of the participants who had taken part in Asch's pilot study (see text) were asked to act as 'stooges' (accomplices of the experimenter). The stooges were told that they would be doing the tasks again, but this time in a *group*. They were also told that the group would contain one person (a *naïve participant*) who was completely ignorant that they were stooges.

On certain *critical trials*, which Asch would indicate by means of a secret signal, all the stooges were required to say out loud the same *wrong answer*. In Asch's original experiment, the stooges (usually seven to nine of them) and the naïve participant were seated either in a straight line or round a table (see Figure 6.3). The situation was rigged so that the naïve participant was always the last or last but one to say the answer out loud.

On the first two trials (called *neutral trials*), all the stooges gave the *correct answers*. However, the next trial was a critical trial (the stooges *unanimously* gave a wrong answer). This happened a further 11 times (making 12 critical trials in total), with four additional neutral trials (making six in total) between the critical trials.

The important measure in the Asch paradigm is whether the naïve participant conforms, and gives the same wrong answer as the unanimous stooges on the *critical* trials, or remains independent and gives the obviously correct answer. Asch found a *mean* conformity rate of 32 per cent, that is, participants agreed with the incorrect majority answer on about one-third of the critical trials.

Figure 6.3 *A naïve participant (number 6), having heard five stooges give the same incorrect answer, offers his own judgement as to which of the three comparison lines matches a stimulus line*

As shown in Table 6.1, there were also wide *individual differences*:

- no one conformed on all the critical trials, and 13 of the 50 participants (26 per cent) never conformed;
- one person conformed on 11 of the 12 critical trials, and about three-quarters conformed at least once.

Table 6.1 *The findings from Asch's original experiment*

No. of conforming responses made	No. of people making those responses
0	13
1	4
2	5
3	6
4	3
5	4
6	1
7	2
8	5
9	3
10	3
11	1
12	0

Given that the task was simple and unambiguous, such findings indicate a high level of conformity. As van Avermaet (1966) has remarked:

'the results reveal the tremendous impact of an "obviously" incorrect but unanimous majority on the judgements of a lone individual'.

How did the naïve participants explain their behaviour?

After the experiment, the naïve participants were interviewed. The interviews revealed several specific reasons for conformity. For example, some participants claimed that they wanted to act in accordance with what they imagined were the experimenter's wishes. Others wished to convey a favourable impression of themselves by 'not upsetting the experiment' (which they believed they would have done by disagreeing with the majority).

Some, who had no reason to believe that there was anything wrong with their eyesight, claimed they genuinely doubted their own judgements; they wondered if they were suffering from eye-strain, or if the chairs had been moved so that they could not see the task material properly. Others denied being aware of having given incorrect answers – they had, without realising it, used the stooges as 'marker posts' (Smith, 1995).

Some said that they 'didn't want to appear different', or 'didn't want to be made to look a fool' or 'inferior'. For them, there was clearly a discrepancy between the answer they gave in the group and what they *privately believed*. Whilst they knew the answer they were giving was wrong, they nonetheless went along with the views of the majority (see page 114).

Asch showed that the participants were justified in fearing potential ridicule if they gave a different answer from the other group members. When a *single stooge* in a group of 16 naïve participants gave the wrong answer on the critical trials, they reacted with sarcasm and laughter.

Factors affecting conformity

Using the Asch paradigm, researchers have manipulated particular variables in order to see if they increase or decrease the amount of conformity reported in Asch's original experiment.

Box 6.2   Some factors affecting conformity

Group size: With one stooge and the naïve participant, conformity is very low (3 per cent), presumably because it is a simple case of the participant's 'word' against the stooge's. With two stooges, conformity rises to 14 per cent. With three stooges, it reaches the 32 per cent which Asch originally reported. After

that, however, further increases in group size do *not* produce increases in conformity. In fact, with very large groups conformity may drop dramatically (Asch, 1955). One reason for this is that participants become (quite rightly) suspicious.

Unanimity: Conformity is most likely to occur when the stooges are unanimous in their answers. When one stooge is instructed to disagree with the majority judgement, conformity decreases (Asch, 1956). The stooge need not even share the naïve participant's judgement (the stooge may, for example, be wearing thick glasses, indicating a visual impairment). Thus, just *breaking the unanimity* of the majority is sufficient to reduce conformity (Allen & Levine, 1971). For Asch (1951), unanimity is more important than group size:

'a unanimous majority of three is, under given conditions, far more effective [in producing conformity] than a majority of eight containing one dissenter'.

Additionally, when a stooge begins by giving the correct answer but then conforms to the majority, conformity *increases* again.

Task difficulty, ambiguity and familiarity with task demands: With *difficult tasks*, as when the comparison lines are all similar to the standard line, conformity increases (Asch, 1956). This is because the task becomes more *ambiguous* (and, therefore, more like the tasks used by Sherif).

The more *familiar* we are with a task's demands, the less likely we are to conform. For example, women are more likely to conform to group pressure on tasks involving the identification of tools, whereas men are more likely to conform on tasks involving the identification of cooking utensils (Sistrunk & McDavid, 1971).

Gender and other individual differences: The claim that women conform more than men has been disputed. As seen above, *both* women and men are more likely to conform when the task is unfamiliar, and men conform as much as women when their conformity or independence will be kept private. However, when conformity or independence will be made known to the group, men conform *less* (Eagly & Steffen, 1984), presumably because conformity is inconsistent with the 'macho' stereotype.

Conformity has also been found to be higher amongst those who have low self-esteem, are especially concerned about social relationships, have a strong need for social approval, and are attracted towards other group members.

Evaluating Asch's contribution to the study of conformity

One of the earliest criticisms of Asch was that his paradigm was both time-consuming (in terms of setting up the situation) and uneconomical (in the sense that only one naïve participant at a time is involved). Crutchfield (1954) attempted to overcome both of these problems.

Box 6.3   Crutchfield's procedure

Participants are seated in a cubicle which has a panel with an array of lights and switches (the *Crutchfield device*). Questions can be projected on to a wall, and the participant can answer them by pressing switches. The participant is told that the lights on the panel represent the responses given by other participants. In fact, this is not true, and the lights are controlled by an experimenter who has a 'master panel' in another cubicle. Of course, the participant does not know this, and the arrangement removes the need for stooges. It also allows several participants in different cubicles to be tested at once. Crutchfield tested over 600 people in total.

Amongst many findings were those indicating that college students agreed with statements which, in other circumstances, they would probably not have agreed with. These included:

- 'The life expectancy of American males is only 25 years.'
- 'Americans sleep four to five hours per night and eat six meals a day.'
- 'Free speech being a privilege rather than a right, it is only proper for a society to suspend free speech when it feels itself threatened.'

Were Asch's findings a reflection of the times?

Other psychologists have not always replicated Asch's findings, even in America where the original research was conducted. For example, Larsen (1974) found significantly *lower* conformity rates among American students, but five years later Larsen *et al.* (1979) reported rates similar to Asch's. How can these changes be explained?

The early 1950s was the McCarthyism era in America. This is named after the US Senator Joseph McCarthy, who claimed to have unearthed an anti-American Communist plot. This resulted in a witch-hunt of alleged Communist sympathisers, which included academics and Hollywood stars. Under these social and political conditions, high conformity is to be expected (Spencer & Perrin, 1998). By the early 1970s, there was a

more liberal climate, but this may have changed again by the late 1970s.

In Britain, Perrin & Spencer (1981) found very low rates of conformity among university students, in a period of self-expression and tolerance. As Spencer & Perrin (1998) say:

'The Asch findings are clearly an indicator of the prevailing culture'.

PAUSE FOR THOUGHT

Perrin & Spencer (1981) tested young offenders on probation, with probation officers as stooges. How do you think conformity rates with these participants compared with those of Asch? Explain your answer.

We might expect the general social and political climate in Britain in the early 1980s to have had a different impact on university students than on young offenders. Additionally, the stooges were adult authority figures, which means that the group was *not* composed of peers (or equals). Not surprisingly, conformity rates were much higher than for the undergraduates and were similar to those reported by Asch.

It is also possible that *experimenters* exert an influence. As Brown (1985) has noted, experimenters may also have changed over time. Perhaps their expectations of the amount of conformity that will occur in an experiment are unwittingly conveyed to the participants, who respond accordingly (see Chapter 7, page 151).

Cross-cultural studies of conformity

As shown in Table 6.2 (see page 113), the vast majority of conformity studies using the Asch paradigm have been carried out in Britain and America. However, using a special statistical technique called *meta-analysis*, Bond & Smith (1996) were able to compare the British and American studies with the small number carried out in other parts of the world. After all relevant factors have been taken into account, the studies can be compared in terms of an *averaged effect size*, in this case, the conformity rate.

PAUSE FOR THOUGHT

Are there any patterns in the conformity rates (averaged effect size) in Table 6.2? For example, are those countries with the highest and lowest conformity geographically and/or culturally related?

According to Smith & Bond (1998), the countries represented in Table 6.2 can be described as *individualist* (such as the US, the UK and other Western European countries) or *collectivist* (such as Japan, Fiji and the African countries). In *individualist* cultures, one's identity is defined by

Table 6.2 *Asch conformity studies by national culture (based on Bond & Smith, 1996; taken from Smith & Bond, 1998)*

Nation	Number of studies	Averaged effect size
Asch's own US studies	18	1.16
Other US studies	79	0.90
Canada	1	1.37
UK	10	0.81
Belgium	4	0.91
France	2	0.56
Netherlands	1	0.74
Germany	1	0.92
Portugal	1	0.58
Japan	5	1.42
Brazil	3	1.60
Fiji	2	2.48
Hong Kong	1	1.93
Arab samples (Kuwait, Lebanon)	2	1.31
Africa (Zimbabwe, Republic of the Congo [Zaire], Ghana	3	1.84

personal choices and achievements, whilst in *collectivist* cultures it is defined in terms of the collective group one belongs to (such as the family or religious group). As might be expected, the tendency is for *more* conformity in *collectivist* cultures (see Box 6.7, page 116).

Majority or minority influence in Asch-type experiments?

Typically, the findings from experiments using the Asch paradigm have been interpreted as showing the impact of a (powerful) majority on the (vulnerable) individual (who is usually in a minority of one). Whilst the stooges are, numerically, the majority, Asch himself was interested in the social and personal conditions that induce individuals to *resist* group pressure (In 1950s' America, this group pressure took the form of McCarthyism: see page 112).

Spencer & Perrin (1998) ask if reports of Asch's experiments have *overstated* the power of the majority to force minority individuals to agree with obviously mistaken judgements. Indeed, Moscovici & Faucheux (1972) argued that it is more useful to think of the naïve participant as *the majority* (s/he embodies the 'conventional', self-evident 'truth') and the stooges as *the minority* (they

reflect an unorthodox, unconventional, eccentric and even outrageous viewpoint). In Asch's experiments, this minority influenced the majority 32 per cent of the time, and it is those participants remaining independent who are actually the conformists!

Is the majority always right?

Looked at from Moscovici and Faucheux's perspective, Asch-type experiments suggest how new ideas may come to be accepted (*innovation*), rather than providing evidence about maintenance of the *status quo*. If groups always followed a *majority decision rule* ('the majority is always or probably right, so best go along with it'), or if social influence were about the inevitable conforming to the group, where would innovation come from? (Spencer & Perrin, 1998: see Box 6.7, page 116).

According to Moscovici (1976), there is a *conformity bias* in this area of research, such that all social influence is seen as serving the need to adapt to the *status quo* for the sake of uniformity and stability. However, change is sometimes needed to adapt to changing circumstances, and this is very difficult to explain given the conformity bias. Without *active minorities*, social and scientific innovations would simply never happen (van Avermaet, 1996).

How do minorities exert an influence?

Moscovici (1976) reanalysed the data from one of Asch's (1955) experiments, in which he varied the proportion of *neutral* to *critical* trials. In the original experiment this proportion was 1:2 (see Box 6.1, page 110). For example, when the proportion was 1:6, the conformity rate was 50 per cent, but when it was 4:1 it dropped to 26.2 per cent.

Moscovici interpreted these findings in terms of *consistency*. When there were more critical than neutral trials, the stooges (who embody the *minority* viewpoint) appear *more* consistent as a group, and this produces a *higher* conformity rate. They are more often agreeing with each other about something unconventional or novel, which makes it more likely that they will change the views of the majority (as represented by the naïve participant). For example, Moscovici & Lage (1976) instructed a stooge minority of two to consistently describe a blue-green colour as green. The majority's views changed to that of the minority, and this effect persisted even when further colour judgements were asked for after the stooges left the experiment.

> **Box 6.4 Why are consistency and other factors important in minority influence?**
>
> According to Hogg & Vaughan (1998), consistency has five main effects:
>
> 1 It disrupts the majority norm, and produces uncertainty and doubt.

2 It draws attention to itself as an entity.

3 It conveys the existence of an alternative, coherent point of view.

4 It demonstrates certainty and an unshakeable commitment to a particular point of view.

5 It shows that the only solution to the current conflict is the minority viewpoint.

Minorities are also more 'persuasive' if they:

- are seen to have made significant personal/material sacrifices (*investment*);
- are perceived as acting out of principle rather than ulterior motives (*autonomy*);
- display a balance between being 'dogmatic' (*rigidity*) and 'inconsistent' (*flexibility*);
- are seen as being *similar* to the majority in terms of age, gender and social class, particularly if minority members are categorised as part of the ingroup.

WHY DO PEOPLE CONFORM?

One attempt to account for conformity was provided by Deutsch & Gerard (1955). They argued that to explain group influence it was necessary to distinguish between *informational social influence* (ISI) and *normative social influence* (NSI).

PAUSE FOR THOUGHT

Why do people conform? By looking back at Sherif's and Asch's experiments, it should be possible to identify some of the reasons people conform – at least in a laboratory situation.

Informational social influence (ISI)

According to Festinger's (1954) *social comparison theory*, people have a basic need to evaluate ideas and attitudes and, in turn, to confirm that these are correct. This can provide a reassuring sense of control over the world and a satisfying sense of competence. In novel or ambiguous situations, social reality is defined by other people's thoughts and behaviours. For example, if we are in a restaurant and unsure about which piece of cutlery to use with a particular course, we look to others for 'guidance' and then conform to their behaviours. This is ISI.

The less we can rely on our own direct perceptions and interactions with the physical world, the more susceptible we should be to influences from other people (Turner, 1991). Some of Asch's participants doubted their own perceptions and claimed that they believed

the majority opinion was correct (see page 111). This suggests that ISI occurs even in *unambiguous* situations, although these participants may have been trying to justify their submission to majority influence.

Normative social influence (NSI)

Underlying NSI is the need to be accepted by others and to make a favourable impression on them. We may conform to gain social approval and avoid rejection, and we may agree with others because of their power to reward, punish, accept, or reject us. As noted earlier, most of Asch's participants were quite clear as to the correct answer. However, if they had given what they believed to be the correct answer, they risked rejection and ridicule by the majority. So, at least some participants probably conformed because of NSI.

Key **STUDY**

Box 6.5 'Johnny Rocco' and the costs of non-conformity

Schachter (1951) provided evidence that the fear that others will reject, dislike or mistreat us for holding different opinions is justified. Groups of male university students read and discussed the case of a delinquent youth called 'Johnny Rocco'. Johnny was described as having grown up in an urban slum, experienced a difficult childhood, and often been in trouble. Participants were asked to decide whether Johnny should receive a great deal of love and affection, harsh discipline and punishment, or some combination of the two.

Johnny's case notes were written sympathetically, and participants made lenient recommendations. Included in each group, however, was a stooge who sometimes agreed with the naïve participants, and sometimes recommended that Johnny be given harsh discipline and punishment (the deviant opinion).

Participants immediately directed their comments to the deviant stooge in an attempt to get him to agree with their lenient recommendations. When these attempts failed, communication dropped off sharply and the stooge was largely ignored. After the discussion, participants were asked to assign group members to various tasks and recommend who should be included in the group. Deviant stooges were rejected, whilst those who agreed with the majority were viewed positively.

So, holding an unpopular opinion, even in a short discussion, can lead to an individual being ostracised. This suggests that, at least under some circumstances, people are justified in fearing rejection if they fail to conform.

Internalisation and compliance

Related to NSI and ISI are two major *kinds* of conformity:

- *Internalisation* occurs when a private belief or opinion becomes consistent with a public belief or opinion. In other words, we say what we believe and believe what we say. Mann (1969) calls this *true conformity*, and it can be thought of as a *conversion* to other people's points of view, especially in *ambiguous* situations.

- *Compliance* occurs when the answers given publicly are *not* those that are privately believed (we say what we do not believe and what we believe we do not say). Compliance represents a compromise in situations where people face a *conflict* between what they privately believe and what others publicly believe.

PAUSE FOR THOUGHT

a Which kind of conformity was most common in Sherif's and Asch's experiments?

b How are internalisation and compliance related to NSI and ISI?

In Sherif's experiment, participants were *internalising* others' judgements and making them their own. Faced with an ambiguous situation, participants were guided by what others believed to reduce their uncertainty. So, internalisation is related to ISI.

By contrast, most of Asch's participants knew that the majority answers on the critical trials were wrong, but often agreed with them publicly. They were *complying* with the majority to avoid ridicule or rejection. So, compliance is related to NSI.

Conformity and group belongingness

The distinction between NSI and ISI has been called the *dual process dependency model of social influence*. However, this model underestimates the role of group 'belongingness'. One important feature of conformity is that we are influenced by a group because, psychologically, we feel we belong to it. This is why a group's norms are relevant standards for our own attitudes and behaviour. The dual process dependency model emphasises the *interpersonal* aspects of conformity experiments, which could just as easily occur between individuals as group members.

Box 6.6   Referent social influence

Abrams *et al.* (1990) argue that we only experience uncertainty when we disagree with those with whom we expect to agree. This is especially likely when we regard those others as members of the same category or group as ourselves with respect to judgements made in a shared stimulus situation. Social influence occurs, then, when we see ourselves as belonging to a group and possessing the same characteristics and reactions as other group members. Turner (1991) calls this self-categorisation, in which group membership is relevant, *referent social influence*.

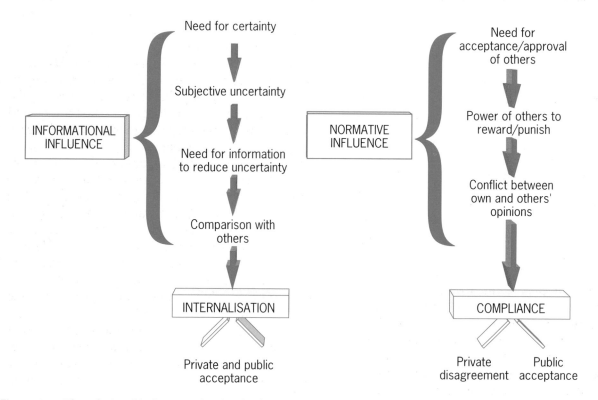

Figure 6.4 *The relationship between kinds of influence and different kinds of conformity*

The *self-categorisation* approach suggests that in Sherif's (1935) experiment, for example, participants assumed that the autokinetic effect was real, and expected to agree with each other. In support of this, it has been shown that when participants discover that the autokinetic effect is an illusion, mutual influence and convergence cease – the need to agree at all is removed (Sperling, 1946).

If, however, we believe that there *is* a correct answer, and we are uncertain what it is, then *only* those whom we categorise as belonging to 'our' group will influence our judgements. As Brown (1988) has remarked:

'there is more to conformity than simply "defining social reality": it all depends on who is doing the defining'.

According to this *self-categorisation* approach, people conform because they are group members. Abrams *et al.* (1990) found that conformity in Asch-type experiments is higher when participants see themselves as *in-group members* (stooges are introduced as fellow psychology students) than when they do not (stooges are introduced as ancient history students). This implies that what is really important is the upholding of a group norm, and *people* are the source of information about the appropriate in-group norm.

Conformity: good or bad?

PAUSE FOR THOUGHT

Is conformity always and necessarily desirable, and is failure to conform always and necessarily undesirable?

Sometimes, *dissent* is just an expression of disagreement, a refusal to 'go along with the crowd'. On other occasions, it is more creative or constructive, as when someone suggests a better solution to a problem. A refusal to 'go along with the crowd' may be an attempt to remain independent *as a matter of principle* (what Willis, 1963, calls *anticonformity*), and may betray a basic fear of a loss of personal identity.

According to Zimbardo & Leippe (1991), in most circumstances conformity serves a valuable social purpose in that it:

'lubricates the machinery of social interaction [and] enables us to structure our social behaviour and predict the reactions of others'.

For most people, though, the word 'conformity' has a *negative* connotation. As a result, it has been implicitly assumed that independence is 'good' and conformity is 'bad', a value judgement made explicit by Asch (1952). However, conformity can be highly functional, helping us to satisfy social and non-social needs, as well as being necessary (at least to a degree) for social life to proceed at all.

Since each of us has a limited (and often biased) store of information on which to make decisions, other people can often provide valuable additional information and expertise. Conforming with others under these circumstances may be a *rational judgement*. However, whilst conformity can help preserve harmony:

'there are obvious dangers to conformity. Failure to speak our minds against dangerous trends or attitudes (for example, racism) can easily be interpreted as support'. (Krebs & Blackman, 1988)

Box 6.7   Japan: a strait-jacket society

The Japanese government is encouraging people to stop being so 'typically' Japanese. An advisory panel set up by the conservative prime minister, Keizo Obuchi, advocates that Japan must abandon its obsession with conformity and equality if it is to tackle its growing social problems, such as juvenile crime, suicide, bankruptcy and unemployment. This promotion of 'individual empowerment' represents a reflection of many of Japan's core values, but the country is desperate for spontaneity, innovation and ambition. In education, for example, the panel calls for action to curb 'the excessive degree of homogeneity and uniformity'. What the panel is recommending is a shift from *collectivist* to *individualist* values (see pages 112–113).

Figure 6.5 *Almost all Japanese schoolchildren aged up to 16 wear dark-blue sailor-style uniforms and follow the same rigid curriculum and textbooks*

(Based on Watts, 2000)

Section Summary

■ The essence of conformity is yielding to real or imagined **group** (**membership** or **reference**) **pressure**. Conformity does not imply adhering to particular attitudes or values, and the group may have majority or minority status.

■ Using the **autokinetic effect**, Sherif found that individuals' estimates **converged** in a group situation. The group's estimate represented a **group norm**. However, Asch criticised Sherif's study because the task was **ambiguous**.

■ In the **Asch paradigm**, a naïve participant is led to believe that other participants ('stooges') are genuine. On **critical trials**, the stooges unanimously give incorrect answers on a task with an obviously correct answer. The crucial measurement is whether the naïve participant gives the same wrong answer as the stooges on the critical trials.

■ Asch found a mean conformity rate of 32 per cent, but there were important **individual differences**. Participants explained their behaviour in various ways. Some wondered if their eyesight was reliable, or said they conformed because they did not want to look foolish.

■ Several factors influence the amount of conformity using the Asch paradigm. These include **group size**, **unanimity**, **task difficulty**, **ambiguity** and **familiarity**. **Gender** and other individual differences can also influence how much conformity occurs.

■ A less time-consuming and more economical way of studying conformity is provided by the **Crutchfield device**. This produced similar amounts of conformity to those originally reported by Asch.

■ The amount of conformity observed in American students has fluctuated over time. In Britain, low rates of conformity have been reported in university students, but high rates in young offenders on probation. Conformity rates apparently reflect the **cultural expectations** of both participants and experimenters.

■ Most studies using the Asch paradigm have been conducted in the US or UK and other Western, **individualist** countries. However, a small number of studies carried out in non-Western, **collectivist** countries have reported **higher** conformity rates.

■ The stooges in Asch-type experiments are usually seen as the majority. However, it may be more useful to regard the naïve participant as embodying the conventional, self-evident, majority, whilst the stooges reflect an unorthodox, unconventional, **minority** opinion.

■ From this perspective, the minority influenced the majority 32 per cent of the time, and it is those participants who remained independent who were actually the conformists. This perspective is relevant to understanding how new ideas come to be accepted.

■ A **consistent minority** can change the majority's view by inducing uncertainty and doubt within the majority, drawing attention to itself as an entity, conveying the existence of an alternative point of view, and demonstrating certainty and a commitment to a particular viewpoint which represents the only solution to a current conflict.

■ Minorities are also effective if they display **investment**, **autonomy**, and a balance between **rigidity** and **flexibility**. They also have more influence if they are perceived as being similar to the majority in terms of age, gender and social category.

■ Both **informational social influence** (ISI) and **normative social influence** (NSI) operate in Asch-type experiments and other settings. Related to ISI is **internalisation/true conformity**, in which we say what we believe and believe what we say. Related to NSI is **compliance**, in which we say what we do not believe and do not believe what we say.

■ The distinction between ISI and NSI has been called the **dual process dependency model of social influence**. However, this emphasises the **interpersonal** aspect of conformity experiments and underestimates the role of **group belongingness**.

■ We may only experience uncertainty when disagreeing with those with whom we expect to agree, especially those regarded as belonging to the same category/group and sharing certain characteristics/reactions (**referent informational influence**).

■ **Dissent** may represent an attempt to remain independent as a matter of principle (**anticonformity**). Alternatively, it can be constructive and creative.

■ Conformity may be a **rational judgement** by someone lacking sufficient information and so relying on others' greater knowledge. However, failure to speak one's mind can be (mis)interpreted as support for something.

Self-Assessment Questions

1 a Explain what is meant by the terms 'conformity' and the 'Asch paradigm'. *(3 marks + 3 marks)*

   b Describe **one** research study that has investigated conformity. *(6 marks)*

   c Give **two** criticisms of this study. *(3 marks + 3 marks)*

   d 'The majority opinion will always dominate the views of those who may initially hold alternative views.'

      To what extent does research into *minority influence* support this view? *(12 marks)*

2 a Outline **two** differences between Sherif's and Asch's experimental procedures for studying conformity. *(3 marks + 3 marks)*

   b Describe **one** research study of conformity that has investigated the importance of the *unanimity* of the majority. *(6 marks)*

   c Describe **one** research study using the Asch paradigm that has been conducted outside the USA. *(6 marks)*

   d 'The only reason people agree with what others believe is that they do not want to look stupid or be the odd-one-out.'

      To what extent does psychological research support this view of why people conform? *(12 marks)*

Obedience to Authority

When people in authority tell us to do something, we tend to follow their orders. For example, Carlson (1987) cites a case in which a doctor prescribed ear-drops for a patient with an ear infection, with instructions that the nurse should 'place drops in R ear'. However, the doctor evidently did not leave a big enough gap between the 'R' (for right) and 'ear'. Neither the nurse nor the patient queried a treatment for earache which involved administering the medication *rectally*.

The more serious *social* problems that obedience can cause have been described by Milgram (1974):

'From 1933 to 1945, millions of innocent persons were systematically slaughtered on command. Gas chambers were built, death camps were guarded, daily quotas of corpses were produced with the same efficiency as the manufacture of appliances. These inhuman policies may have originated in the mind of a single person, but they could only be carried out on a massive scale if a very large number of persons obeyed orders'.

DISTINGUISHING BETWEEN CONFORMITY AND OBEDIENCE

According to Milgram (1992), both conformity and obedience involve the abdication of individual judgement in the face of some external pressure. However, there at least three important *differences* between conformity and obedience:

- In conformity, there is no *explicit* requirement to act in a certain way, whereas in obedience we are *ordered* or *instructed* to do something.

- Those who influence us when we conform are our *peers* (or *equals*), and people's behaviours become more alike because they are affected by *example*. In obedience, there is a difference in status from the outset and, rather than mutual influence, obedience involves *direction* from someone in *higher authority*.

- Conformity has to do with the psychological 'need' for acceptance by others, and involves going along with one's peers in a group situation. Obedience, by contrast, has to do with the social power and status of an authority figure in a hierarchical situation. Although we typically deny that we are conformist (because it detracts from a sense of individuality), we usually deny *responsibility* for our behaviour in the case of obedience. As a result, behaviours occur because 'I was only following orders' (an explanation given by Adolf Eichmann, director of the Nazi deportation of Jews to concentration camps).

EXPERIMENTAL STUDIES OF OBEDIENCE

Milgram's research

The original purpose of Milgram's (1963, 1974) research was to test 'the "Germans are different" hypothesis'. This has been used by historians to explain the systematic murder of millions of Jews, Poles and others by the Nazis during the 1930s and 1940s (see page 118). The hypothesis claims that Hitler could not have put his evil plans into operation without the co-operation of thousands of others, and that Germans have a basic character defect (namely, a readiness to obey authority without question, regardless of the acts demanded by the authority figure). This gave Hitler the co-operation he needed.

After piloting his research in America, Milgram planned to continue it in Germany. However, his results showed that this was unnecessary.

Milgram's participants

Milgram (1963) advertised for volunteers to take part in a study of memory and learning to be conducted at Yale University. The experiment would last about an hour, and participants would be paid $4.50. The first participants were 20–50-year-old men from all walks of life.

Public Announcement

WE WILL PAY YOU $4.00 FOR ONE HOUR OF YOUR TIME

Persons Needed for a Study of Memory

*We will pay five hundred New Haven men to help us complete a scientific study of memory and learning. The study is being done at Yale University.
*Each person who participates will be paid $4.00 (plus 50c carfare) for approximately 1 hour's time. We need you for only one hour: there are no further obligations. You may choose the time you would like to come (evenings, weekdays, or weekends).

*No special training, education, or experience is needed. We want:

Factory workers	Businessmen	Construction workers
City employees	Clerks	Salespeople
Laborers	Professional people	White-collar workers
Barbers	Telephone workers	Others

All persons must be between the ages of 20 and 50. High school and college students cannot be used.
*If you meet these qualifications, fill out the coupon below and mail it now to Professor Stanley Milgram, Department of Psychology, Yale University, New Haven. You will be notified later of the specific time and place of the study. We reserve the right to decline any application.
*You will be paid $4.00 (plus 50c carfare) as soon as you arrive at the laboratory.

- -

TO:
PROF. STANLEY MILGRAM, DEPARTMENT OF PSYCHOLOGY, YALE UNIVERSITY, NEW HAVEN, CONN. I want to take part in this study of memory and learning. I am between the ages of 20 and 50. I will be paid $4.00 (plus 50c carfare) if I participate.

NAME (Please Print). . . . .

ADDRESS . . . .

TELEPHONE NO. . . . . Best time to call you . . . .

AGE . . . . OCCUPATION . . . . SEX . . . .
CAN YOU COME:

WEEKDAYS . . . . EVENINGS . . . . . . WEEKENDS . . . .

Figure 6.6 *The advertisement used by Milgram to recruit participants for his study*

The basic procedure

When participants arrived at Yale University's psychology department, they were met by a young, crew-cut man in a grey laboratory coat who introduced himself as Jack Williams, the experimenter. Also present was a Mr Wallace, a mild and harmless-looking accountant in his late fifties. In fact, neither the experimenter nor Mr Wallace was genuine, and everything else that followed in the procedure (apart from the naïve participant's behaviour) was carefully pre-planned, staged and scripted.

The participant and Mr Wallace were told that the experiment was concerned with the effects of punishment on learning, and that one of them would be the 'teacher' and the other the 'learner'. Their roles were determined by each drawing a piece of paper from a hat. In fact, both pieces of paper had 'teacher' written on them. Mr Wallace drew first and read out 'learner', which meant that the participant would always play the 'teacher' role. All three then went to an adjoining room, where Mr Wallace was strapped into a chair with his arms attached to electrodes. These would supposedly deliver an electric shock from a generator in the adjacent room.

The teacher and experimenter then went into the adjacent room. The teacher was shown the generator, which had several switches on it, each clearly marked with voltage levels and verbal descriptions. The shocks began at 15 volts and went up in 15-volt increments to 450 volts. The teacher was then given a 45-volt shock to convince him that the generator was real. However, unknown to the teacher, this would be the only *actual* electric shock delivered during the entire experiment.

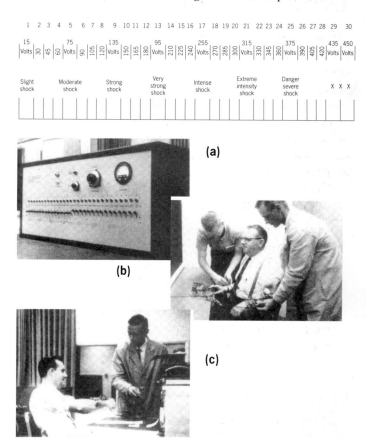

Figure 6.7 *The 'electric shock generator' used by Milgram (a) and a schematic representaion of its front panel showing the voltages and verbal labels (top). In (b), the 'learner' is strapped into his chair, and in (c), the 'teacher' receives a shock of 45 volts (from Milgram, 1974)*

The task involved the teacher reading out a list of word-pairs (such as 'blue–girl' and 'fat–neck'). The teacher then read out the first word of each pair, followed by a number of other words, one of which was the second member of the original pair. The learner had to choose the correct word by pressing one of four switches which turned on a light on a panel in the teacher's room. Each time the learner made a mistake, the teacher had to deliver a shock, and each successive mistake was punished by a shock 15 volts higher than the previous one.

In Milgram's first experiment (the *remote-victim* condition), the learner was scripted to pound loudly on the adjoining wall at 300 volts and, after 315 volts, to stop pounding and *give no further answers*. In the second experiment (the *voice-feedback* condition), the teacher heard a tape-recorded series of verbal responses that were Mr Wallace's 'spontaneous reactions' to the increasing shock levels.

Box 6.8   Mr Wallace's 'spontaneous reactions' to increasing shock levels

75, 90 and
105 volts: Makes a little grunt.
120 volts: Tells the experimenter that the shocks are becoming painful.
150 volts: Cries out: 'Experimenter, get me out of here! I won't be in the experiment any more! I refuse to go on!'.
180 volts: Shouts out: 'I can't stand the pain!'.
270 volts: Lets out an agonised scream and continues to insist on being released.
300 volts: Desperately shouts out that he will no longer provide answers.
315 volts: Lets out a violent scream and reaffirms vehemently that he will no longer provide answers.
330 volts: There is an ominous silence.

PAUSE FOR THOUGHT

If you had been one of Milgram's teacher-participants, how far up the voltage scale would you have continued to punish 'wrong answers'?

The scripted behaviours were, of course, dependent on any participant actually continuing with the experiment up to that shock level. When Milgram asked his students what they thought would happen in the experiments, a few said that *some* people would continue all the way up to 450 volts, but that most would stop at the early or middle shock range. Psychiatrists estimated that less than one per cent of teachers would administer the highest voltage, and that most would stop around 120 volts (Milgram, 1974).

The teacher had been instructed to treat a non-response from Mr Wallace as an incorrect response, so that shocks could continue to be given. When Milgram's participants showed reluctance to administer the shocks, the experimenter gave a series of scripted 'verbal prods'. These were:

- 'Please continue' (or 'please go on');
- 'The experiment requires that you continue';
- 'It is absolutely essential that you continue';
- 'You have no other choice, you *must* go on'.

The experimenter was also scripted to say that 'although the shocks may be painful, there is no permanent tissue damage', to reassure the teacher that no permanent harm was being done to the learner. The experiment was terminated *either* when the participant refused to continue *or* when the maximum 450-volt shock had been administered *four times*.

Figure 6.8 *A participant refuses to continue any further with the experiment (From Milgram, 1974)*

Milgram's results

The participants displayed great anguish, verbally attacked the experimenter, twitched nervously, or broke out into nervous laughter. Many were observed to:

> 'sweat, stutter, tremble, groan, bite their lips and dig their nails into their flesh. Full-blown, uncontrollable seizures were observed for three [participants]'. (Milgram, 1974)

Indeed, one experiment had to be stopped because the participant had a violent seizure. It is quite astonishing, then, that in the remote-victim condition every teacher went up to at least 300 volts, and *65 per cent* went all the way up to 450 volts. In the voice-feedback condition, *62.5 per cent* went all the way up to 450 volts.

To determine *why* the obedience levels were so high, Milgram conducted several variations using the voice-feedback condition as his baseline measure. In all, a further 16 variations were performed.

Box 6.9 Some variations on Milgram's basic procedure

Institutional context (variation 10): In interviews following the first experiment, many participants said they continued delivering shocks because the research was being conducted at Yale University, a highly prestigious institution. So, Milgram transferred the experiment to a run-down office in downtown Bridgeport.

Proximity and touch proximity (variations 3 and 4): In the original procedure, the teacher and learner were in adjacent rooms and could not see one another. However, in variation 3 they were in the same room (about 1.5 ft/46 cm apart), and in variation 4 the teacher was required to force the learner's hand down onto the shock plate.

Remote authority (variation 7): The experimenter left the room (having first given the essential instructions) and gave subsequent instructions by telephone.

Two peers rebel (variation 17): The teacher was paired with two other (stooge) teachers. The stooge teachers read out the list of word-pairs, and informed the learner if the response was correct. The real participant delivered the shocks. At 150 volts, the first stooge refused to continue and moved to another part of the room. At 210 volts, the second stooge did the same. The experimenter ordered the real teacher to continue.

A peer administers the shocks (variation 18): The teacher was paired with another (stooge) teacher and had only to read out the word-pairs (the shock being delivered by the stooge).

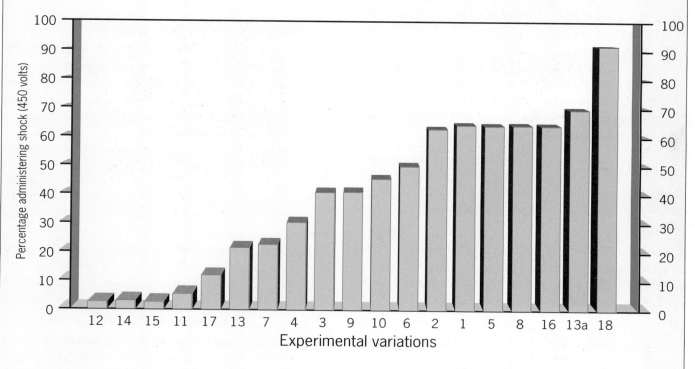

1 Remote victim	7 Remote authority	11 Subjects free to choose shock level	14 Authority as victim – an ordinary man commanding	16 Two authorities – one as victim
2 Voice feedback	8 Women as subjects	12 Learner demands to be shocked	15 Two authorities – contradictory commands	17 Two peers rebel
3 Proximity	9 The victim's limited contract	13 An ordinary man gives orders		18 A peer administers shock
4 Touch proximity	10 Institutional context			
5 New baseline				
6 Change of personnel				

Figure 6.9 *The percentage of participants administering 450-volt shocks across the 18 variations of Milgram's original experiment. Note that one experiment has two variations (13 and 13a) (From Zimbardo & Weber, 1994)*

For each of the variations described in Box 6.9, estimate the total obedience rate (those participants going all the way up to 450 volts), and try to explain why it might have been higher or lower than the 62.5 per cent in the voice-feedback condition.

- In variation 10, the obedience rate was *47.5 per cent*. This still very high figure suggests that the institutional context played some part, but was *not* a crucial factor.

- In variation 3, the obedience rate dropped to *40 per cent*, and in variation 4 it dropped further to *30 per cent*. Whilst *seeing* the effects of the shock reduces obedience, the figures are still very high.

- In variation 7, obedience dropped to *20.5 per cent*. Indeed, participants often pretended to deliver a shock or delivered one lower than they were supposed to. This suggests that they were trying to compromise between their conscience and the experimenter's instructions. In his absence, it was easier to follow their conscience.

- In variation 17, there was only *10 per cent* obedience. Most stopped obeying when the first or second stooge refused to continue. According to Milgram (1965):

    'the effects of peer rebellion are most impressive in undercutting the experimenter's authority'.

In other words, seeing other participants (our peers) disobey shows that *it is possible* to disobey, as well as *how* to disobey. Indeed, some participants said they did not realise they *could*. This is a demonstration of the effects of *conformity*.

- In variation 18, obedience rose to *92.5 per cent*. This shows that it is easier for participants to shift responsibility from themselves to the person who actually 'throws the switch'.

Explaining Milgram's results

According to Milgram (1974):

'the most fundamental lesson of our study is that ordinary people simply doing their jobs, and without any particular hostility on their part, can become agents in a terrible destructive process'.

Unless there is reason to believe that people who go all the way up to 450 volts are especially sadistic and cruel, or are unusually obedient (which 'the "Germans are different" hypothesis' claimed about a whole nation), explanations of obedience must look 'outside' the individual participant. In this way, the emphasis is shifted away from personal characteristics to the characteristics of the *social situation*: most people facing that situation would probably act in a similar (obedient) way. What might some of these situational factors be?

Personal responsibility

Many participants raised the issue of responsibility if any harm came to the learner. Although the experimenter did not always discuss this, when he did say 'I'm responsible for what goes on here', participants showed visible relief. Indeed, when participants are told that they are responsible for what happens, obedience is sharply reduced (Hamilton, 1978).

Milgram saw this *diffusion of responsibility* as being crucial to understanding the atrocities committed by the Nazis, and Eichmann's defence that he was 'just carrying out orders'. It can also explain the behaviour of William Calley, an American soldier who was court-martialed for the 1968 massacre by troops under his command of several hundred Vietnamese civilians at My Lai.

The perception of legitimate authority

As mentioned earlier (see page 120), many participants showed signs of distress and conflict, and so diffusion of responsibility cannot tell the whole story. Perhaps, then, participants saw the experimenter as a legitimate authority, at least up to the point when he said 'you have no other choice, you *must* go on'.

The most common mental adjustment in the obedient participant is to see him/herself as an agent of external authority (the *agentic state*). This represents the opposite of an *autonomous state*, and is what makes it possible for us to function in a hierarchial social system. For a group to function as a whole, individuals must give up responsibility and defer to others of higher status in the social hierarchy. Legitimate authority thus replaces a person's own self-regulation (Turner, 1991). In Milgram's (1974) words:

'The essence of obedience consists in the fact that a person comes to view himself as the instrument for carrying out another person's wishes, and he, therefore, no longer regards himself as responsible for his actions. Once this critical shift of viewpoint has occurred in the person, all the essential features of obedience follow'.

What was it about Jack Williams, the experimenter, which conveyed to participants that he was 'in charge' in the experimental situation?

Authority figures often possess highly visible symbols of their power or status that make it difficult to refuse their commands. In Milgram's experiments, the experimenter *always* wore a grey laboratory coat to indicate his position as an authority figure. The impact of such 'visible symbols' was demonstrated by Bickman (1974). When people were told by a stooge wearing a guard's uniform to pick up a paper bag or give a coin to a stranger, obedience was higher (80 per cent) than when the order was given by a stooge in civilian clothes (40 per cent). Similarly, a stooge wearing a firefighting uniform was obeyed more often than a stooge dressed as a civilian, even though the request (to give someone a dime) had nothing to do with the authority role in question (Bushman, 1984). For Milgram (1974):

'a substantial proportion of people do what they are told to do, irrespective of the content of the act and without limitations of conscience, so long as they perceive that the command comes from a legitimate authority'.

Another major study which demonstrates the impact of uniforms and other symbols of authority is Zimbardo *et al.*'s (1973) 'prison simulation experiment', which is discussed on pages 125–127.

The 'foot in the door' and not knowing how to disobey

According to Gilbert (1981), Milgram's participants may have been 'sucked in' by the series of graduated demands. These began with the 'harmless' advertisement for volunteers for a study of learning and memory, and ended with the instruction to deliver potentially lethal electric shocks to another person. Having begun the experiment, participants may have found it difficult to remove themselves from it.

PAUSE FOR THOUGHT

If the original advertisement had mentioned electric shocks, do you think there would have been many volunteers? In what ways might they have constituted a more *biased sample* than those who participated in the actual experiments?

Presumably, fewer volunteers would have come forward. Those who did may well have been more sadistic than Milgram's sample (assuming that they believed they would be *giving* the electric shocks).

Socialisation

Despite our expressed ideal of independence, obedience is something we are socialised into from a very early age by significant others (including our parents and teachers). Obedience may be an *ingrained habit* (Brown, 1986) that is difficult to resist.

An evaluation of Milgram's research

Milgram's research has caused both considerable interest and controversy, almost from the moment it was first published. Critics have largely focused on three main areas, namely *methodological issues, issues of generalisation*, and *ethical* issues. The last of these is discussed in the *Critical Issue* section of this chapter: see pages 128–132.

Methodological issues

According to Orne & Holland (1968), Milgram's experiments lack *experimental realism*, that is, participants might not have believed the experimental set-up they found themselves in, and knew the learner was not really being given electric shocks. However, a study by Sheridan & King (1972) seems to exclude this possibility.

Key STUDY

Box 6.10 Sheridan & King's (1972) puppy experiment

Students trained a puppy to learn a discrimination task by punishing it with increasingly severe and *real* electric shocks whenever it made an error. Although the puppy actually received only a small shock, the participants could see it and hear its squeals.

After a time, an odourless anaesthetic was released into the puppy's cage, causing it to fall asleep. Although participants complained about the procedure (and some even cried), they were reminded that the puppy's failure to respond was a punishable error, and that they should continue to give shocks. Seventy-five per cent of participants delivered the maximum shock possible.

Orne & Holland (1968) also criticised Milgram's experiments for their lack of *mundane realism*, that is, the results do not extend beyond the particular laboratory setting in which they were collected. They base this claim on the further claim that cues in the experimental setting influenced the participants' perceptions of what was required of them. Obedience, then, might simply have been a response to the *demand characteristics* (see Chapter 7, page 151) of the highly unusual experimental setting. However, naturalistic studies of obedience dispute this.

Key STUDY

Box 6.11 Hofling *et al.*'s (1966) naturalistic study of nurses

Twenty-two nurses working in various American hospitals received telephone calls from a stooge 'Dr Smith of the Psychiatric Department', instructing them to give Mr Jones (Dr Smith's patient) 20 mg of a drug called *Astrofen*. Dr Smith said that he was in a desperate hurry and would sign the drug authorisation form when he came to see the patient in ten minutes' time.

The label on the box containing the *Astrofen* (which was actually a harmless sugar pill) clearly stated that the maximum daily dose was 10 mg. So, if the nurse obeyed Dr Smith's instructions she would be exceeding the maximum daily dose. Also, she would be breaking the rules requiring written authorisation *before* any drug is given and that a nurse be absolutely sure that 'Dr Smith' is a genuine doctor.

PAUSE FOR THOUGHT

What do you think you would have done if you had been one of the nurses?

Of a control group of 22 different nurses asked this same question, 21 said they would not have given the drug without written authorisation, especially as it exceeded the maximum daily dose.

A real doctor was posted nearby, unseen by the nurse, and observed what the nurse did following the telephone call. Twenty-one out of the 22 nurses complied without hesitation, and 11 later said that they had not noticed the dosage discrepancy!

Another common criticism maintains that Milgram's sample was *unrepresentative*. However, altogether Milgram studied 636 people, representing a cross-section of the population of New Haven (the location of Yale University). This was thought to be a fairly typical small American town. However, Milgram admitted that those participants who continued giving shocks up to 450 volts were more likely to see the learner as being responsible for what happened to him, rather than themselves.

These participants seemed to have a stronger *authoritarian character*, which includes a respect for authority as such, and a less advanced level of moral development. However, this was only a matter of *degree*, and there is independent evidence that people who volunteer for experiments tend to be considerably *less* authoritarian than those who do not (Rosenthal & Rosnow, 1966).

PAUSE FOR THOUGHT

Can you think of any other respects in which Milgram's sample could be considered unrepresentative?

Milgram was also criticised for using mainly male participants. However, of the 40 females who did serve as

participants (in experiment 8), 65 per cent went up to 450 volts, comparable to the obedience shown by their male counterparts.

A further methodological criticism concerns the *cross-cultural* replicability of Milgram's findings.

Table 6.3 *Cross-cultural replications of Milgram's obedience experiment (adapted from Smith & Bond, 1998)*

Study	Country	Participants	Percentage obedient
Ancona & Pareyson (1968)	Italy	Students	85
Kilham & Mann (1974)	Australia	Male students Female students	40 16
Burley & McGuiness (1977)	UK	Male students	50
Shanab & Yahya (1978)	Jordan	Students	62
Miranda *et al.* (1981)	Spain	Students	over 90
Schurz (1985)	Austria	General population	80
Meeus & Raajimakers (1986)	The Netherlands	General population	92

Unfortunately, it is very difficult to compare these studies because of methodological discrepancies between them (Smith & Bond, 1998). For example, different types of stooges were used (e.g. a 'long-haired student' in Kilham and Mann's study), some of whom may have been perceived as more vulnerable – or more deserving of shocks – than others. In the Meeus and Raajimakers study, the task involved participants having to harass and criticise someone who was completing an important job application.

Whilst Milgram found no gender differences (as noted above), the Australian female students were asked to shock another *female* (but the learner was always *male* in Milgram's experiments). Also, with the exception of Jordan (Shanab & Yahya, 1978), all the countries studied have been western industrialised nations, so caution should be used when concluding that a universal aspect of social behaviour has been identified. However,

'... in none of the countries studied is obedience to authority the kind of blind process that some interpreters of Milgram's work have implied. Levels of obedience can and do vary greatly, depending on the social contexts that define the meaning of the orders given ...'. (Smith & Bond, 1998)

Issues of generalisation

As noted earlier, Orne & Holland (1968), along with several other researchers, have argued that Milgram's experiments lack mundane realism (or *external* or *ecological validity*). However, Milgram maintains that the process of complying with the demands of an authority figure is essentially the same whether the setting is the artificial one of the psychological laboratory or a naturally occurring one in the outside world.

Whilst there are, of course, differences between laboratory studies of obedience and the obedience observed in Nazi Germany:

'differences in scale, numbers and political context may turn out to be relatively unimportant as long as certain essential features are retained'. (Milgram, 1974)

The 'essential features' that Milgram refers to is the *agentic state* (see page 122).

What do Milgram's studies tell us about ourselves?

Perhaps one of the reasons Milgram's research has been so heavily criticised is that it paints an unacceptable picture of human beings. Thus, it is far easier for us to believe that a war criminal like Adolf Eichmann was an inhuman monster than that 'ordinary people' can be destructively obedient (what Arendt, 1965, called the *banality of evil*).

Yet atrocities, such as those committed in Rwanda, Kosovo and East Timor, continue to occur. According to Hirsch (1995), many of the greatest crimes against humanity are committed in the name of obedience.

Box 6.12 Genocide

Hirsch (1995) maintains that *genocide*, a term first used in 1944, tends to occur under conditions created by three social processes:

- *authorisation* relates to the 'agentic state' (see page 122), that is, obeying orders because of where they come from;

- *routinisation* refers to massacre becoming a matter of routine, or a mechanical and highly programmed operation;

- *dehumanisation* involves the victims being reduced to something less than human, allowing the perpetrators to suspend their usual moral prohibition on killing.

The ingredients of genocide were personified by Eichmann who, at his trial in 1960, denied ever killing anybody. However, he took great pride in the way he transported millions to their deaths 'with great zeal and meticulous care' (Arendt, 1965).

How can we resist obedience?

In 1992, an East German judge sentenced a former East German border guard for having shot a man trying (three years earlier) to escape to the West. The judge's comments echo the spirit of the Nurenberg Accords which followed the Nazi war crimes trials:

'Not everything that is legal is right ... At the end of the twentieth century, no one has the right to turn off his conscience when it comes to killing people on the orders of authorities'. (cited in Berkowitz, 1993)

As noted, it is difficult to disobey authority. However, we are most likely to rebel when we feel that social pressure is so strong that our *freedom* is under threat.

Milgram himself felt that obedience would be reduced by:

- *educating* people about the dangers of blind obedience;

- encouraging them to *question authority*;

- exposing them to the actions of *disobedient models*.

According to Brehm (1966), we need to believe that we have freedom of choice. When we believe that this is not the case and when we believe we are *entitled* to freedom, we experience *reactance*, an unpleasant emotional state. To reduce it, and restore the sense of freedom, we disobey.

Figure 6.10 *Marshall Applewhite, leader of the 'Heaven's Gate' cult, whose members believed that a spaceship would deliver them to the next phase of their lives after they committed suicide. Applewhite and 38 followers consumed lethal doses of phenobarbital and vodka*

ZIMBARDO'S RESEARCH

Almost as famous – and controversial – as Milgram's obedience studies is the *prison simulation experiment* (Zimbardo *et al.* 1973). It was noted earlier (page 123) that this experiment illustrates the impact of uniforms and other visible symbols of authority, and for this reason it is usually discussed in relation to obedience. However, it is also relevant to certain aspects of *conformity*, as well as demonstrating the *power of social situations* on people's behaviour.

Key STUDY

Box 6.13 The prison simulation experiment

Zimbardo *et al.* (1973) recruited male participants through newspaper advertisements asking for student volunteers for a two-week study of prison life. From 75 volunteers, 24 were selected. They were judged to be emotionally stable, physically healthy, and 'normal to average' (based on personality tests). They also had no history of psychiatric problems and had never been in trouble with the police.

Participants were told that they would be *randomly assigned* to the role of either 'prisoner' or 'prison guard'. At the beginning of the experiment, then, there were no differences between those selected to be prisoners and guards. They constituted a relatively homogeneous group of white, middle-class college students from all over America.

The basement of the Stanford University psychology department was converted into a 'mock prison'. Zimbardo *et al.* wished to create a prison-like environment which was as *psychologically real* as possible. The aim was to study how prison life impacts upon both prisoners and guards.

The experiment began one Sunday morning, when those allocated to the prisoner role were unexpectedly arrested by the local police. They were charged with a felony, read their rights, searched, handcuffed, and taken to the police station to be 'booked'. After being fingerprinted, each prisoner was taken blindfold to the basement prison.

Upon arrival, the prisoners were stripped naked, skin-searched, deloused, and issued with uniforms and bedding. They wore loose-fitting smocks with identification numbers on the front and back, plus chains bolted around one ankle. They also wore nylon stockings to cover their hair (rather than having their heads shaved). They were referred to by number only and accommodated in 6 × 9 ft 'cells', three to a cell.

The guards wore military-style khaki uniforms, silver reflector sunglasses (making eye contact with them impossible) and carried clubs, whistles, handcuffs and keys to the cells and main gate. The guards were on duty 24 hours a day, each working eight-hour shifts. They had complete control over the prisoners, who were kept in their cells around the clock, except for meals, toilet privileges, head counts and work.

Figure 6.11
a *A prisoner in one of the three-bedded cells*
b *A prison guard asserting his authority over a prisoner*

After an initial 'rebellion' had been crushed, the prisoners began to react passively as the guards stepped up their aggression each day (by, for example, having a head count in the middle of the night simply to disrupt the prisoners' sleep). This made the prisoners feel helpless, and no longer in control of their lives.

The guards began to enjoy their power. As one said, 'Acting authoritatively can be great fun. Power can be a great pleasure'. After less than 36 hours, one prisoner had to be released because of uncontrolled crying, fits of rage, disorganised thinking and severe depression. Three others developed the same symptoms, and had to be released on successive days. Another prisoner developed a rash over his whole body, which was triggered when his 'parole' request was rejected.

Prisoners became demoralised and apathetic, and even began to refer to themselves and others by their numbers. The whole experiment, planned to run for two weeks, was abandoned after *six days* because of the pathological reactions of the prisoners.

What conclusions can be drawn from the prison experiment?

An outside observer, who had a long history of imprisonment, believed that the mock prison, and both the guards' and prisoners' behaviours, were strikingly similar to real prison life. This supports Zimbardo *et al.*'s major conclusion that it is prisons themselves, *not* prisoners and guards, that make prisons such evil places. As Zimbardo (1973) says:

> 'Not that anyone ever doubted the horrors of prison, but rather it had been assumed that it was the predispositions of the guards ('sadistic') and prisoners ('sociopathic') that made prisons such evil places. Our study holds constant and positive the dispositional alternative and reveals the power of social, institutional forces to make good men engage in evil deeds'.

PAUSE FOR THOUGHT

What does Zimbardo mean by 'Our study holds constant and positive the dispositional alternative ...'?

Volunteers were selected for their emotional stability, 'normality' and so on, and then randomly allocated to the prisoner/guard roles. Therefore, their different behaviours and reactions could *not* be attributed to their personal characteristics (or dispositions). Rather, the differences could only be explained in terms of the different *roles* they played in the context of the mock prison.

According to Banuazizi & Mohavedi (1975), however, the behaviour of both guards and prisoners may have arisen from the *stereotyped expectations* of their respective roles. The participants were 'merely' *role-playing* (based on their prior expectations about how guards and prisoners 'ought' to behave). However, one reply to this criticism is to ask at what point 'mere' role-playing becomes a 'real' experience. As Zimbardo (1971, quoted in Aronson, 1992) says:

> 'It was no longer apparent to us or most of the subjects where they ended and their roles began. The majority had indeed become 'prisoners' or 'guards', no longer able to clearly differentiate between role-playing and self'.

This strongly suggests that their experiences were very real, and that even if they were 'merely' role-playing at the beginning, they were soon taking their roles very seriously indeed!

Section Summary

- Conformity and obedience are similar in some important respects but different in others. In obedience, we are ordered or **directed** to do something by somebody in **higher authority**. Typically, we **deny responsibility** for our obedient behaviour.

- Milgram's obedience research was originally intended to test 'the "Germans are different" hypothesis'. In Milgram's basic procedure, participants are led to believe that they will be delivering increasingly severe electric shocks to another person in a learning experiment. In fact, no shocks are actually given, and neither the learner nor the experimenter is genuine.

- In the **remote-victim condition**, 65 per cent of participants administered the maximum 450-volt shock. In the **voice-feedback condition**, the figure was 62.5 per cent. These results were unexpected. When Milgram asked psychiatrists and students to predict participants' behaviour, few believed anyone would administer the maximum shock.

- Participants were given pre-determined 'verbal prods' by the experimenter when they showed a reluctance to continue. Despite being reassured that no permanent harm was being done to the learner, participants showed great anguish and experienced considerable stress.

- Milgram conducted 16 further variations of the two original studies to determine the factors influencing obedience. **Proximity**, **touch proximity**, **remote authority**, **peer rebellion** and changing the **institutional context** all reduced obedience to various degrees. Having a **peer administer shocks**, however, increased obedience.

- Milgram's participants seemed to believe that the learner was really receiving electric shocks, and so the experiment has **experimental realism**. It is unlikely that **demand characteristics** account for the findings, since obedience has been observed in naturalistic settings. So, Milgram's research also has **mundane realism**.

- When participants are told **they** are responsible for what happens to the learner, obedience is sharply **reduced**. Milgram saw **diffusion of responsibility** as crucial to understanding destructive obedience.

- The perception of the experimenter as a **legitimate authority**, which induces an **agentic state**, also contributes to obedient behaviour. Since obedience is an **ingrained habit** acquired through early **socialisation**, participants might not have known **how to disobey**.

■ **Methodological criticisms** of Milgram's research include the use of mainly male participants. **Cross-cultural replications** of his experiment are difficult to compare because of methodological discrepancies between different studies. However, blind obedience has not been found anywhere, and **social context** influences obedience levels.

■ Zimbardo *et al.*'s **prison simulation experiment** illustrates the impact of uniforms and other visible symbols of authority. It also demonstrates the **power of social situations** on individuals' behaviour.

■ Participants were selected for their emotional stability and general 'normality', and then randomly allocated to the role of prisoner or prison guard. Therefore, their pathological reactions could not be attributed to their personal characteristics. Whilst they may have been merely **role-playing** at the beginning of the experiment, they soon 'became' prisoners or guards.

Self-Assessment Questions

3 a Outline **two** differences between conformity and obedience. *(3 marks + 3 marks)*

b Describe Milgram's *remote-victim* obedience experiment. *(6 marks)*

c Describe **one other** obedience experiment conducted by Milgram. *(6 marks)*

d 'Whilst there are obvious differences between obedience observed in laboratory studies and in Nazi Germany, they may turn out to be relatively unimportant as long as certain essential features are retained.'
To what extent does Milgram's research help us to understand why people obey? *(12 marks)*

4 a Explain what is meant by the terms 'agentic state' and 'experimental realism'. *(3 marks + 3 marks)*

b Describe **one** naturalistic study of obedience. *(6 marks)*

c Outline **two** *methodological* criticisms of Milgram's laboratory studies of obedience. *(3 marks + 3 marks)*

d 'Anyone acting as a participant in an obedience experiment is likely to behave as Milgram's or Zimbardo *et al.*'s participants did.'
To what extent does psychological research support the view that obedience is the product of situational factors, rather than people's personal characteristics? *(12 marks)*

Critical ISSUE

The Development of Ethical Guidelines for Research

ETHICAL ISSUES ARISING FROM THE STUDY OF SOCIAL INFLUENCE

As noted above (see pages 123–125), Milgram's obedience experiments have been criticised in terms of *methodological issues*, *issues of generalisation*, and *ethical issues*. The first two were discussed in the previous section. The third will be discussed in this section. Milgram's experiments undoubtedly helped define many ethical issues and triggered the debate regarding the ethics of research within psychology as a whole. Most of the ethical issues they raise also apply to other areas of social influence research.

PAUSE FOR THOUGHT

Are there any features of Milgram's experimental procedure which you would consider unethical? One way of approaching this is to ask yourself what *you* would have found objectionable/unacceptable, either during or after the experiment, if *you* had been one of his participants.

Protection from harm

One of Milgram's fiercest critics was Baumrind (1964), who argued that the rights and feelings of Milgram's participants had been abused, and that inadequate measures had been taken to protect them from stress and emotional conflict. This refers to the ethical principle of *protection from harm* (both physical and psychological).

Milgram accepted that his participants did experience stress and conflict. However, he defended himself by arguing that Baumrind's criticism assumes that the experimental outcome was *expected* – this was *not* so. Inducing stress was *not* an intended and deliberate effect of the experimental procedure. As Milgram (1974) noted:

'Understanding grows because we examine situations in which the end is unknown. An investigator unwilling to accept this degree of risk must give up the idea of scientific enquiry'.

In other words, an experimenter cannot know what the results are going to be *before* the experiment begins.

We might accept Milgram's claim that there was no reason to believe that participants would *need* protection. However, once he observed the degree of distress in his first experiment, should he have continued with the research programme (17 more experiments)? To justify this, Milgram would have pointed out that:

- At whatever shock level the experiment ended, the participant was reunited with the unharmed Mr Wallace, and informed that no shock had been delivered. In an extended discussion with Milgram, obedient participants were assured that their behaviour was entirely normal, and that the feelings of conflict and tension were shared by others. Disobedient participants were supported in their decision to disobey the experimenter. This was all part of a thorough *debriefing* or 'dehoax', which happened as a matter of course with every participant (see Box 6.14, page 130.)

- The experimenter *did not make* the participant shock the learner (as Baumrind had claimed). Milgram began with the belief that every person who came to the laboratory was free to accept or reject the demands of authority. Far from being passive creatures, participants are active, choosing adults.

There is also the broader ethical issue that concerns *protecting the individual* versus *benefiting society*. This, in turn, is related to the question 'Does the end justify the means?'.

It is worth noting that an ethics committee of the American Psychological Association (APA) investigated Milgram's research shortly after its first publication in 1963 (during which time Milgram's APA membership was suspended). The committee eventually judged it to be ethically acceptable (Colman, 1987). In 1965, Milgram was awarded the prize for outstanding contribution to social psychological research by the American Association for the Advancement of Science.

According to Zimbardo (1973), the ethical concerns are even more pronounced in the prison simulation experiment (see pages 125–127) than in Milgram's experiments:

'Volunteer prisoners suffered physical and psychological abuse hour after hour for days, while volunteer guards were exposed to the new self-knowledge that they enjoyed being powerful and had abused this power to make other human beings suffer. The intensity and duration of this suffering uniquely qualify the Stanford prison experiment for careful scrutiny of violations of the ethics of human experimentation'.

Savin (1973) argued that the benefits resulting from Zimbardo *et al.*'s experiment did not justify the distress, mistreatment and degradation suffered by the participants – the end did *not* justify the means.

PAUSE FOR THOUGHT

How could Zimbardo *et al.* defend themselves against this criticism in a way that Milgram could not?

Their experiment was due to last for two weeks, but when it was realised just how intense and serious the distress, mistreatment and degradation were, it was ended after six days. However, it could be asked why it was not stopped even sooner!

Deception and informed consent

According to Vitelli (1988), almost all conformity and obedience experiments (and more than one-third of all social psychological studies) deceive participants over the purpose of the research, the accuracy of the information they are given, and/or the true identity of a person they believe to be another genuine participant (or experimenter). Deception is considered unethical for two main reasons:

- It prevents the participant from giving *informed consent*, that is, agreeing to participate knowing the true purpose of the study and what participation will involve.

- The most potentially harmful deception is involved in studies, like those of Milgram and Zimbardo *et al.*, in which participants learn things about themselves *as people.*

PAUSE FOR THOUGHT

Given that it is important to understand the processes involved in conformity and obedience (the *end*), can deception be justified as a *means* of studying them?
Identify the deceptions that were involved in Asch's, Milgram's and Zimbardo *et al.*'s experiments? Do you consider any of these to be more serious/unethical than the others, and if so, why?

Critical (I S S U E)

Box 6.14 Can deception ever be justified?

- Most participants deceived in Asch's conformity experiments were very enthusiastic, and expressed their admiration for the elegance and significance of the experimental procedure (Milgram, 1992).

- In defence of his own obedience experiments, Milgram (1974) reported that his participants were all thoroughly *debriefed*. This included receiving a comprehensive report detailing the procedure and results of all the experiments, together with a follow-up questionnaire about their participation. More specifically, the '*technical illusions*', as Milgram calls deception, are justified because they are in the end accepted and approved of by those exposed to them. He saw this, in turn, as justifying the *continuation* of the experiments, which is relevant to the issue of protection from harm discussed above.

- Christensen (1988) reviewed studies of the ethical acceptability of deception experiments and concluded that as long as deception is not extreme, participants do not seem to mind. Christensen suggests that the widespread use of mild forms of deception is justified, first because no one is apparently harmed, and second, because there seem to be few, if any, acceptable alternatives.

- Krupat & Garonzik (1994) reported that university psychology students who had been deceived at least once as participants in research, did not find the experience less enjoyable or interesting as a result. They also said that they would be *less* upset at the prospect of being lied to or misled again (compared with those who had not been deceived).

- Other researchers have defended Milgram's use of deception on the grounds that without it, he would have found results which simply do not reflect how people behave when they are led to believe they are in real situations (Aronson, 1988). In some circumstances, then, deception may be the best (and perhaps the only) way to obtain useful information about how people behave in complex and important situations.

As far as Zimbardo *et al.*'s prison simulation study is concerned, the only deception involved was to do with the arrest of the prisoners at the start of the experiment. They were not told this would happen, partly because final approval from the local police force was not given until minutes before they decided to participate, and partly because the researchers wanted the arrests to come as a surprise.

As Zimbardo (1973) admits, 'This was a breach, by omission, of the ethics of our own informed consent contract', which told participants of everything that was going to happen to them (as far as this could be predicted). It was signed by every one of them, thus giving their permission for invasion of privacy, loss of civil rights, and harassment. Approval for the study had also been officially sought and received, in writing, from the body that sponsored the research, the Psychology Department at Stanford University, and the University Committee of Human Experimentation. This Committee did not anticipate the extreme reactions that were to follow.

Like Milgram, Zimbardo *et al.* held debriefing sessions (both group and individual). All participants returned post-experimental questionnaires several weeks, then several months, later, then at yearly intervals. Many submitted retrospective diaries and personal analyses of the effects of their participation:

> 'We are sufficiently convinced that the suffering we observed, and were responsible for, was stimulus bound and did not extend beyond the confines of that basement prison'. (Zimbardo, 1973)

Codes of conduct and ethical guidelines

Largely as a result of ethically controversial experiments like those of Milgram and Zimbardo, *codes of conduct* and *ethical guidelines* have been produced by the major professional organisations for psychologists. In the USA, this is the American Psychological Association (APA). In the UK it is the British Psychological Society (BPS).

Each organisation has produced several documents that are relevant to different aspects of psychologists' work. Examples include:

- *Guidelines for the Use of Animals in Research* (BPS, 1985);

- *Guidelines for the Professional Practice of Clinical Psychology* (BPS, 1983: see Chapter 1);

- *Ethical Principles for Conducting Research with Human Participants* (BPS, 1990, 1993).

The last of these (for the rest of this chapter abbreviated to '*Ethical Principles*') identifies several guiding principles. Some of the most important are:

- *consent/informed consent*

- *deception*

- *debriefing*

- *protection of participants.*

PAUSE FOR THOUGHT

Do you think it is necessary for psychologists to have *written* codes of conduct and ethical guidelines? What do you consider to be their major functions?

According to Gale (1995), the fact that both the BPS and APA codes are periodically reviewed and revised indicates that at least some aspects do not depend on absolute or universal ethical truths. Guidelines need to be updated in light of the changing social and political contexts in which psychological research takes place. For example, new issues, such as sexual behaviour in the context of AIDS, might highlight new ethical problems. Information revealed by participants can create conflict between the need to protect individuals and the protection of society at large. In spite of the *confidentiality* requirement (see page 132), should a researcher inform the sexual partner of an AIDS-carrying participant? As Gale (1995) points out:

> 'One consequence of such breaches of confidentiality could be the withdrawal of consent by particular groups and the undermining of future reasearch, demonstrating … how one ethical principle fights against another'.

More importantly, changing views about the nature of individual rights will call into question the extent to which psychological research respects or is insensitive to such rights.

One of the earliest formal statements of ethical principles published by the BPS was the *Ethical Principles for Research on Human Subjects* (1978). The *Ethical Principles* (1990, 1993) refers to 'participants' instead. Gale (1995) believes that this change of wording reflects a genuine shift in how the individual is perceived within psychology, from *object* (probably a more appropriate term than '*subject*') to *person*.

This change can be partly attributed to the influence of *feminist* psychologists, who have also helped to bring about the removal of sexist language from BPS and APA journals as a matter of policy.

The Ethical Principles

The introduction to the *Ethical Principles* (1993) states that:

> 'Psychological investigators are potentially interested in all aspects of human behaviour and conscious experience. However, for ethical reasons, some areas of human experience and behaviour may be beyond the reach of experiment, observation or other forms of psychological investigation. Ethical guidelines are necessary to clarify the conditions under which psychological research is acceptable'. [paragraph 1.2]

Psychologists are urged to encourage their colleagues to adopt the Principles and ensure that they are followed by all researchers whom they supervise (including GCSE, A/AS level, undergraduate and postgraduate students):

> 'In all circumstances, investigators must consider the ethical implications and psychological consequences for

the participants in their research. The essential principle is that the investigation should be considered from the standpoint of all participants; foreseeable threats to their psychological well-being, health, values or dignity should be eliminated'. [paragraph 2.1]

Consent and informed consent

According to the *Ethical Principles*:

> 'Participants should be informed of the objectives of the investigation and all other aspects of the research which might reasonably be expected to influence their willingness to participate – only such information allows *informed consent* to be given [paragraph 3.1] … Special care needs to be taken when research is conducted with detained persons (those in prison, psychiatric hospital, etc.), whose ability to give free informed consent may be affected by their special circumstances'. [paragraph 3.5]

PAUSE FOR THOUGHT

You may recall that in Perrin & Spencer's (1981) British replication of Asch's conformity experiment (see page 112), some of the participants were young offenders on probation, with probation officers as stooges. According to paragraph 3.5, would this be acceptable today?

> 'Investigators must realise that they often have influence over participants, who may be their students, employees or clients: this relationship must not be allowed to pressurise the participants to take part or remain in the investigation'. [paragraph 3.6]

In relation to paragraph 3.6., it is standard practice in American universities for psychology students to participate in research as part of their course requirements. So, whilst they are free to choose which research to participate in, they are *not* free to opt out (see Chapter 7, page 152).

Box 6.15 Is there more to informed consent than being informed?

Although informed consent clearly requires being informed of the procedure, participants will not have full knowledge until they have *experienced it*. Indeed, there is no guarantee that the investigators fully appreciate the procedure without undergoing it themselves. In this sense, it is difficult to argue that full prior knowledge can ever be guaranteed. How much information should be given beforehand? How much information can young children, elderly people, infirm or disabled people, or those in emotional distress be expected to absorb?

However, there is more to informed consent than just this 'informational' criterion. The status of the experimenter, the desire to please others and not let them down, the desire not to look foolish by insisting on withdrawing after the experiment is already under way, all seem to detract from the idea that the participant is truly choosing *freely* in a way that is assumed by the *Ethical Principles*.

(Based on Gale, 1995)

Deception

The *Ethical Principles* states that:

'Intentional deception of the participants over the purpose and general nature of the investigation should be avoided whenever possible. Participants should never be deliberately misled without extremely strong scientific or medical justification. Even then there should be strict controls and the disinterested approval of independent advisors'. [paragraph 4.2]

The decision that deception is necessary should only be taken after determining that alternative procedures (which avoid deception) are unavailable. Participants must be *debriefed* at the earliest opportunity (see Box 6.14, page 130).

Debriefing

According to Aronson (1988):

'The experimenter must take steps to ensure that subjects leave the experimental situation in a frame of mind that is at least as sound as it was when they entered. This frequently requires post-experimental 'debriefing' procedures that require more time and effort than the main body of the experiment'.

Where no undue suffering is experienced, but participants are deceived regarding the real purpose of the experiment:

'the investigator should provide the participant with any necessary information to complete their understanding of the nature of the research. The investigator should discuss with the participants their experience of the research in order to monitor any unforeseen negative effects or misconceptions'. [paragraph 5.1]

However,

'some effects which may be produced by an experiment will not be negated by a verbal description following the research. Investigators have a responsibility to ensure that participants receive any necessary de-briefing in the form of active intervention before they leave the research setting'. [paragraph 5.3]

PAUSE FOR THOUGHT

'Active intervention' is more like a 'therapeutic' measure than just 'good manners'. Can you give examples of this second type of debriefing from both Milgram's and Zimbardo *et al*.'s experiments (see pages 129 and 130).

Protection of participants

'Investigators have a primary responsibility to protect participants from physical and mental harm during the investigation. Normally, the risk of harm must be no greater than in ordinary life, i.e. participants should not be exposed to risks greater than or additional to those encountered in their normal life styles'. [paragraph 8.1]

Debriefing represents a major means of protecting participants where emotional suffering has occurred. They must also be protected from the stress that might be produced by disclosing *confidential* information without participants' permission. If participants have been seriously deceived, they have the right to witness destruction of any such records they do not wish to be kept. Results are usually made anonymous as early as possible by use of a letter/number instead of name (Coolican, 1994).

Is protection of participants all that matters?

Whilst 'protection of participants' is one of the specific principles included in the *Ethical Principles*, they are all (including informed consent, deception and so on) designed to prevent any harm coming to the participants, or the avoidance of overt 'sins' (Brown, 1997).

However, Brown (1997) argues that formal codes focus too narrowly on risks to the *individual* participant, in the specific context of the investigation. They neglect broader questions about the risks to the *group* to which the participant belongs. For example, research into racial differences in intelligence has been detrimental to African Americans. Individual black participants were not harmed and might even have found IQ tests interesting and challenging. However, the way the findings were interpreted and used:

'weakened the available social supports for people of colour by stigmatising them as genetically inferior, thus strengthening the larger culture's racist attitudes'.

This demonstrates how it is possible for psychologists to conduct technically ethical research which, at the same time, violates the more general ethic of avoiding harm to vulnerable populations (Brown, 1997).

Section Summary

- The most serious criticisms of Milgram's obedience experiments have been **ethical**. This helped trigger the debate regarding the ethics of research within psychology as a whole.

- Accusations of failing to **protect participants from harm** can be dismissed, because the distress that Milgram's participants experienced could not have been predicted and was not an intended or deliberate effect of the experimental procedure. However, this does not necessarily justify his **continuation** of the research.

- Participants were thoroughly 'dehoaxed' at the end of the experiment. This included reassuring them that their behaviour was normal (if obedient), or supporting them if they disobeyed. Milgram also argued that participants were **free** to obey or disobey.

- Zimbardo believes that the prisoner participants suffered physical and psychological abuse for days at a time, whilst the guards had to face the fact that they had enjoyed abusing them. This relates to the broader issue of **protecting the individual** versus **benefiting society**.

- Whilst **deception** may be commonplace, especially in social psychological experiments, it is unethical if it prevents participants from giving **informed consent**. However, participants who have been deceived generally approve of it retrospectively. Milgram considers this to be a sufficient justification for its use, and others believe that deception may sometimes be the best/only way of obtaining valuable insights into human behaviour.

- The American Psychological Association (APA) and British Psychological Society (BPS) have produced several **codes of conduct** and **ethical guidelines**. These relate to different aspects of psychologists' work, including conducting research with human participants.

- The *Ethical Principles* identifies several guiding principles, most importantly **consent/informed consent**, **deception**, **debriefing** and **protection of participants**.

- The BPS and APA codes and guidelines are periodically revised in the light of changing social and political contexts, such as changing views about individual rights. This indicates that there are no absolute or universal ethical truths. The change from 'subject' to 'participant' itself reflects a change in psychologists' perception of the person.

- Even if the participant has been fully informed about an experimental procedure, this does not guarantee **informed consent**. For example, the experimenter may be in a position of authority over the participant, who may be reluctant to withdraw once the study has started, for fear of looking foolish.

- **Debriefing** must take place at the earliest opportunity following the use of **deception**. The experimenter must ensure that participants leave the experimental situation in at least as positive a frame of mind as when they entered. This might sometimes necessitate **active intervention**, as used by both Milgram and Zimbardo *et al.*

- Informed consent, minimal use of deception, debriefing, confidentiality, destruction of any records, and other ethical principles are all designed to **protect individual participants from physical and mental harm**. As important as this is, there is the danger that research may harm the **group** to which the participant belongs.

Self-Assessment Questions

5 a Explain what is meant by the terms 'informed consent' and 'debriefing'. *(3 marks + 3 marks)*

 b Outline **two** differences between Milgram's and Zimbardo *et al.*'s experiments regarding informed consent. *(3 marks + 3 marks)*

 c Describe **two** *other* ethical issues which have been raised by Milgram's obedience experiments.
(3 marks + 3 marks)

 d 'Without research such as Milgram's, we would have no real understanding of how people behave in complex and important social situations.'

 To what extent can the use of deception be justified in social influence research studies? *(12 marks)*

6 a Explain what is meant by the terms 'deception' and 'protection from harm'. *(3 marks + 3 marks)*

 b Outline **one** reason for the use of debriefing and **one** reason for having codes of conduct/ethical guidelines.
(3 marks + 3 marks)

 c Describe **one** example of how participants were not protected from harm in each of Milgram's and Zimbardo's experiments. *(3 marks + 3 marks)*

 d 'As important as it is to protect individual participants, there are broader ethical issues involved that must also be taken into account.'

 To what extent can codes of conduct/ethical guidelines guarantee that all the major ethical issues involved in human psychological research are properly dealt with?
(12 marks)

CONCLUSIONS

The first part of this chapter discussed research studies into conformity, particularly those of Sherif and Asch. These have usually been interpreted in terms of the influence of majorities. However, Moscovici's re-interpretation of Asch's findings helped to show that minorities can also be influential, making it possible for new ideas and theories to become accepted.

The second part of this chapter then considered obedience experiments, especially those of Milgram and Zimbardo *et al*. Both of these studies demonstrate the power of social situations to make people behave in uncharacteristic ways. This means that it is very difficult to resist authority figures' demands. However, Milgram's research also suggests ways in which resistance can be achieved, so that we might act more independently.

The final part of this chapter looked at the ethical criticisms of social influence research, particularly Milgram's and Zimbardo *et al*.'s experiments. These criticisms relate to some of the most fundamental ethical issues facing psychologists who study human behaviour. Whilst the APA's and BPS's codes of conduct/ethical guidelines are designed to ensure that participants are properly protected, this cannot be guaranteed. They also fail to address wider ethical issues.

WEB ADDRESSES

http://www.psych.upenn./edu/sacsec/text/about.htm
http://longman.awl.com/aronson/student/activities/aschconformityexperiment.asp
http://www.muskingum.edu/~psychology/psycweb/history/milgram.htm
http://www.cba.uri.edu/Faculty/dellabitta/mr415s98/EthicEtcLinks/Milgram.htm
http://www.elvers.stjoe.udayton.edu/history/people/Milgram.html
http://www.stolaf.edu/people/huff/classes/headbook/Milgram.html
http://www.oklahoma.net~jnichols/ethics.html
http://maple.lemone.edu/~hevern/psychref2-4.html
http://www.bps.org.uk/charter/codofcon.htm
http://www.unn.ac.uk/academic/ss/psychology/handbook/99/handbook_/pt21.html

Research Methods

This chapter is about how psychology is *done*. Psychologists make claims about human behaviour and experience, but these claims are not the product of mere 'common sense'. They are developed from, and supported by, evidence produced from *empirical research* ('empirical' means based on real-world observations). Psychological researchers gather data from various types of observation of behaviour. From these they construct theories, and to test those theories they make further predictions and, again, gather data for support. It is through such research that scientific knowledge in psychology is advanced.

This chapter outlines several general approaches to psychological research, from basic designs of the traditional experiment to various non-experimental methods including the questionnaire, survey, interview and direct observation. The strengths and weaknesses of these approaches are explained, along with the advantages and disadvantages of conducting research in the laboratory or the 'field'.

Biases (unwanted influences) can enter into the data-gathering process, and challenge the *validity* of the findings obtained. This is a special problem for psychological research, since people are thinking beings who usually *know* that their behaviour is being observed. In this chapter, several sources of bias are discussed, including those to do with the selected sample (the *kind* of people used in the research study), the *expectations* of researchers and research participants, and the ways in which the variables to be studied are *defined*.

Much research gathers *quantitative* (numerical) data, and psychologists need to understand the techniques used to *summarise* such data (*descriptive statistics*) and to *analyse* various relationships among the data (*interpretive statistics*). Various descriptive statistical techniques are introduced in this chapter and the issue of significance testing is briefly discussed. The description and analysis of *qualitative* (non-numerical) data are also considered.

Quantitative and Qualitative Research

THE SCIENTIFIC NATURE OF PSYCHOLOGY

Research methods concern the *strategies* of scientific research that psychologists employ in order to gather evidence to support theories about human behaviour and experience. Amongst others, researchers use *experiments*, *observational techniques*, *case studies*, *interviews*, and *questionnaires*. Researchers do not select a particular method because they happen to like it. A method is chosen which should produce data in the most unbiased, accurate and

appropriate manner possible. This is essential if psychological research is to be considered *scientific*. Scientific method in psychology involves using objectively gathered data to support or challenge researchers' claims about the world, usually predictions about how people think or behave. If the chosen method is not appropriate, other psychologists will not take a researcher's findings seriously. The researcher tries to use the most appropriate method, taking into account practical, financial and ethical issues. For example, it would be impractical to use questionnaires on babies, and unethical and expensive to rear children in isolation for several years!

Figure 7.1 *Psychological researchers must follow an ethical code of practice*

Box 7.1   Ethical issues in the conduct of psychological research

Throughout this section it should be borne in mind that most psychologists in the UK conduct their research as members of the British Psychological Society (BPS). This has a Code of Conduct for Psychologists and also a set of *Ethical Principles for Conducting Research with Human Participants*. These, and several other guidelines, including those for the use of non-human animals in research, are available in one booklet from the BPS on request. Researchers must agree to, and practice according to, the principles outlined on pages 128–132. *Students who carry out psychological investigations should also adhere strictly to these guidelines.*

Practising research psychologists must also agree to offer professional advice and guidance to research participants who, as it emerges during the course of the research procedure, appear to be suffering with problems that threaten their future well-being. They must make any data available to other colleagues, publish responsibly and monitor the ethical behaviour of colleagues.

What is a research question?

A research question is one that a researcher poses when considering how to support a theory with scientific evidence, or how to extend the scope of findings already obtained. For example, researchers might be considering the general theory that people's physiological state can affect their cognitions about the world. If people are hungry, they might be more likely to notice food, with their attention being drawn to cream cakes rather than mobile phones in adjacent shop windows. To test out this theory, the researchers must create some form of testable *hypothesis*. A hypothesis is a form of assumption or supposition about the way the world is. Here it might be claimed that hungry people tend to recall more food-related events than people who have just eaten a good meal. This is now a position from which to design a study to make an exact test of this hypothesis.

HYPOTHESIS TESTING AND DESCRIPTIVE STUDIES

Not all psychological investigations have the research aim of testing hypotheses. Many studies aim to *explore* or simply *describe* an area of human activity. For example, a researcher might want to find out at what ages, and in what order, children acquire certain aspects of grammar, such as using 'if' or 'the' in their spoken language. A researcher working in a school might wish to investigate the channels of formal and informal communication used between teachers and pupils. Such studies seek to *describe* what they find. Further investigation might involve developing and testing theories *arising from* the descriptive findings.

Box 7.2   Qualitative and quantitative approaches

Quantitative data are measures in numerical form, such as reaction times, whereas *qualitative data* are *unquantified* data, such as recordings of human meanings (speeches, conversation, pictures, advertisements) or visual/verbal descriptions of human behaviour. Both quantitative and qualitative data are forms of *empirical data*, that is, information which has been recorded from research observation.

Qualitative data are obtained when, for example, researchers:

* interview people and keep a record of what they say;
* make observations of people's behaviour and record these verbally or on film (see also Table 7.14, page 163).

Quantitative data are obtained when, for example, researchers:

* record the time people take to perform a task;
* record the number of successes or errors people produce on a task;

- record scores obtained on a psychological test (e.g. verbal reasoning);
- record the number of times people say something (rather than what was said).

Qualitative data may be analysed at a descriptive level. They can also be converted to quantitative data through a process of rating or coding (see pages 162–164). Qualitative data can also be used to test hypotheses, such as whether Japanese adolescents express different kinds of guilt from that expressed by English adolescents. However, this kind of data is most often used as a basis from which to create new theories and understanding. These new theories may be tested quantitatively at a later stage, or researchers may continue with further qualitative work.

Approaches which concentrate on gathering qualitative data, and reporting them in qualitative form, tend to be known as *qualitative approaches*. If quantitative data are gathered, or if qualitative data are converted into quantitative data for statistical analysis, then the approach tends to be termed a *quantitative approach*. Of the methods described below, interviews and observation are most likely to be used in qualitative research, although quantitative data are also often produced. The use of psychological tests and questionnaires is associated with quantitative approaches and the most exclusively quantitative approach is the experiment.

WHAT IS AN EXPERIMENT?: INDEPENDENT AND DEPENDENT VARIABLES

The experiment is generally assumed to be the most reliable and effective method for demonstrating that one variable causes another to change. That is, one variable has an *effect* on another. The term 'effect' is shorthand for *'presumed cause and effect relationship between two variables'*. For example, to demonstrate that chocolate is the factor in a child's diet causing hyperactivity, chocolate might be alternately given and withheld, whilst all other factors in the child's diet are held constant.

In the 'language' of experimental research, we say that we observe the effect of an *independent variable* (chocolate) on a *dependent variable* (hyperactive behaviour), whilst holding all other variables constant. Other factors that *might* affect the dependent variable are known as *extraneous variables*. If any important extraneous variable is operating (such as the amount of sugar the child consumed), the child's aggressiveness cannot

be attributed solely to the chocolate. The sugar might *confound* the apparent effect of chocolate on aggressive behaviour. Uncontrolled variables like this, which can produce alternative explanations of change in the dependent variable, are known as *confounding variables*.

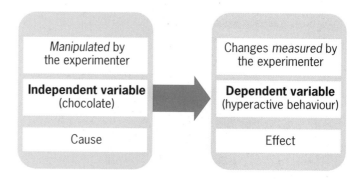

Figure 7.2 *The independent and dependent variables in an experiment*

An example that can be used to illustrate this is Loftus & Palmer's (1974) study, which was discussed in Chapter 2 (see pages 31–32). They asked participants to watch a film of a car accident. Later, the participants were asked a question about what they had seen. For one group, this question was 'About how fast were the cars going when they *smashed into* each other?' For a second group, it was 'About how fast were the cars going when they *hit* each other?'. Members of the 'smashed into' group estimated a higher impact speed than the 'hit' group. In this study:

- the *independent variable* (IV) manipulated was the use of '**smashed into**' or '**hit**';
- the *dependent variable* (DV) was the estimation of **speed** at impact.

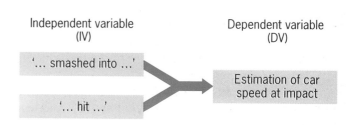

Figure 7.3 *Independent and dependent variables in Loftus & Palmer's (1974) experiment*

To assess the long-term effects of this experimental manipulation a week later, the two groups were asked 'Did you see any broken glass?'. There was none in the film. Thirty-two per cent of the 'smashed into' group reported seeing glass, whereas only 14 per cent of the 'hit' group did so. Twelve per cent of a third group, who only saw the original film and were not asked questions about it, also reported seeing glass after one week. This last group is known as a *control group*. It is used to compare the effects of the IV on the other *experimental groups*. Here, it can be seen that being asked the 'hit' question does not produce any greater mistaken 'remembering' of broken glass a week later, than does being asked no question at all.

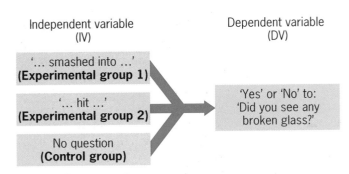

Figure 7.4 *Control and experimental groups in Loftus & Palmer's (1974) experiment*

PAUSE FOR THOUGHT

What would be the IV and DV in an experiment where participants are either kept hungry or given a meal, and then assessed for their recall of food words from a mixed list?

Since hunger was manipulated in order to observe any consequent effect on recall, level of hunger is the IV and number of food words recalled is the DV.

Standardising the procedure and instructions

PAUSE FOR THOUGHT

In Loftus & Palmer's (1974) experiment, what would the researchers have done to ensure that some other variable did not cause the difference in speed estimations?

In an experiment, *extraneous variables* should be held constant or balanced. For instance, a *standardised procedure* would be used in which all participants would be tested in the same place, in the same conditions (e.g. temperature) with the same equipment. The researchers themselves might be the source of some confounding variables. For example, both male and female researchers take longer to collect data from a participant of the opposite sex (Rosnow & Rosenthal, 1997). If data-gatherers are permitted to treat participants differently, this could explain why later differences in the dependent variable

are found. Hence, *standardised instructions* are used wherever possible. This might result in rather robotic experimenter behaviour, but the procedure is then free from the criticism that the experimenter's different treatment of participants might be responsible for any effect found.

Box 7.3   Avoiding bias from participant variables

One important extraneous variable to be controlled in an experiment is the influence of *participant variables*. These are pre-existing differences among people (such as intelligence) which might explain any differences found between groups participating in an experiment. For example, it would be a problem if more *aggressive* drivers had participated in the 'smashed into' condition of Loftus and Palmer's experiment. Such drivers might assume that most people drive as fast as they do. The usual way to control for participant variables is by *randomly allocating all participants to the various experimental conditions*. For each group, every participant has the same chance as any other of being selected into it. This procedure *should* distribute the differences between people relatively evenly across the conditions of the experiment.

QUASI-EXPERIMENTS

Many studies are well controlled and seem to approach the rigour of a true experiment. However, in some respects they lack complete control of all relevant variables, and so are often called *quasi-experiments*. There are two common research situations which would be termed quasi-experiments: those with *non-equivalent groups*, and those which are *natural experiments*.

Non-equivalent groups: participants not randomly allocated to conditions

In many research designs, it is impossible to randomly allocate participants to conditions. For example, suppose an applied educational psychologist wanted to try out a new 'reading boost' programme. Her aim is to measure some children's reading abilities, give them the programme, then check for improvement. She will need a control group for comparison (see above), who will probably have to be an equivalent class in the school. The pupils cannot be allocated to these two conditions *at random*. A problem here is that one class might consist of better readers in the first place.

Natural experiments: treatment not controlled by the experimenter

In the same example as previously described, the researcher herself might not actually manipulate the IV. The reading scheme trials may already be in operation as part of the school's work, and the psychologist might only step in to record results. This kind of quasi-experiment is known as a *natural experiment*, since the conditions would have occurred *naturally* without the existence of the researcher. However, there is still an IV whose effects on reading development (the DV) can be assessed.

Box 7.4   Working in the laboratory or the field – control versus artificiality

Quasi-experiments often occur because researchers need to study phenomena 'in the field'. Here, the 'field' refers to the natural circumstances in which the behaviour occurs, such as the school playground or the office. Such studies are known as *field experiments* (if they *are* experiments) or *field studies*. The conditions of a laboratory study are necessarily artificial (although laboratories themselves are, of course, a part of some people's everyday lives!). To test the hypothesis that coal falls at the same rate as a feather in a vacuum, a hypothesis derived from the laws of gravity, artificial conditions need to be set up. Having supported the hypothesis, the laws of gravity can then be *used* in everyday situations.

People, however, are not pieces of coal. They react to human researchers. The effect on participants' behaviour, caused by their knowing that they are the objects of research, is known as *participant reactivity*. Findings in a laboratory might be particularly affected by people's tendency to be overawed by the setting. They might behave more obediently, more politely, or with greater respect for authority than they might do elsewhere.

NON-EXPERIMENTS: GROUP DIFFERENCE AND CORRELATIONAL STUDIES

Group difference studies occur where there is no specific treatment at all, as in the investigation of sex differences or differences between extroverts and introverts. These studies are not experiments since no specific treatment has been applied to one group. Men and women have spent whole lifetimes being treated differently on a multitude of subtly differing variables. Therefore, it is not reasonable to treat each group as differing specifically on one level of an independent variable.

If a psychological difference is found between two samples of men and women, it is rarely, if ever, possible to claim that the difference is directly related to biological sex. Careful planning must be put into balancing the groups tested for related variables such as differences in age, schooling, personality, economic resources, specific life experiences and so on. If the groups are *not* balanced, then any one or a combination of these variables might be responsible for the difference found. The women might be better educated, the men might come from wealthier families, and so on.

A researcher could never be certain that *all* relevant variables have been balanced. So, even with extensive control and balancing of participant variables, a researcher cannot be certain that a difference between male and female samples is truly a *sex*-difference. The situation is even more ambiguous for personality variable differences, such as extroversion–introversion.

Correlational studies are similar to group difference studies in their lack of experimental rigour, and are very common in psychological research. Strictly speaking, the term *correlation* refers to the degree of statistical relationship between one variable and another. In everyday life we are very used to correlations. For example, we know that the longer people have spent in education, the higher their salaries tend to be (although there are, of course, many exceptions to this general rule).

Instead of conducting an experiment on hungry and satiated participants, as described on page 136, the word list used in that study could be given to randomly selected people, who are asked to recall as many words as they can, and are *then* asked how long it has been since their last meal or decent snack. The research prediction would then become:

The longer time reported since eating, the more food-related words will be recalled from a mixed list.

This is now the prediction of a correlation, and the research study ceases to be an experiment, but becomes a *correlational study*. Hunger is not *manipulated*, but two measures are simply *recorded* (hours since eating and number of food words recalled). Correlations are described statistically on pages 160–162.

The similarity and difference between correlational and group difference studies can be demonstrated by an example of attempting to relate extroversion to social confidence. If *both* variables are measured, they can be *correlated*. Alternatively, respondents might be *categorised* as 'extrovert' or 'introvert', and a *difference between* the two groups tested for (see Figure 7.5).

A correlational study

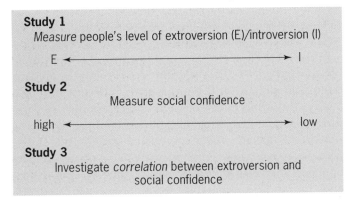

A group difference study

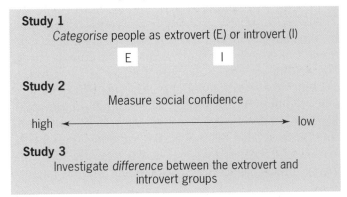

Figure 7.5 *Correlational and group difference studies*

NON-EXPERIMENTAL APPROACHES

As noted previously, experiments have the strong advantage of telling us directly about cause and effect, if conducted carefully. However, not only is it *difficult* to experiment with certain forms of human behaviour (how could you have people fall in love as part of an experiment, for example?), it is also often *unethical*. It would not, for example, be ethical to give some children physical punishment, and others none, in order to see whether the punished children become more aggressive.

PAUSE FOR THOUGHT

Suppose you wanted to investigate the effects of physical punishment on children's development of aggression. How could an ethical and well controlled study be conducted?

You might have come up with one of two general approaches:

- **Looking:** An *observation* could be made of children in their homes and the forms of discipline their parents employ. The children's behaviour in various settings could also be observed and their level of aggressiveness assessed.

- **Asking questions:** Parents could be *interviewed* about their discipline habits and their children's behaviour. The children could also be observed or interviewed. The interview could be rather informal in nature or some form of *questionnaire* could be used.

In either case, ethical principles would require the parents and children to be informed about what exactly was being measured.

Observation

Observation of people's behaviour can be carried out in the field, with the behaviour occurring in an everyday, normal setting. This is known as *naturalistic observation*. Alternatively, observation can occur in a specialised area (e.g. a play observation room). All empirical research involves observation, but here 'observation' refers to the direct observation of relatively unconstrained behaviour as it occurs or as recorded by, for example, a video camera.

Naturalistic observation has the advantage that people may not be particularly affected by the research environment. Additionally, it is possible to keep the researcher's role *undisclosed*, in which case the data gathered cannot be affected by *participant reactivity* effects (see page 139). The data are then genuine samples of normal behaviour, undistorted by the participant's awareness of being studied.

The validity of observational studies

Problems with undisclosed observations

- A serious difficulty with undisclosed observation is the ethical issue of gathering observations on a person without their consent. Naturalistic observation of children's playground behaviour does not seem much of a problem. The behaviour is public, and would occur anyway. However, undisclosed observation of patients' behaviour in a doctor's surgery seems obtrusive, particularly if film recordings are made for later analysis.

- A further ethical issue arises when researchers are *participant observers*, that is, *they are naturalistic observers working as members of the group being observed.* Examples include observing their own work group, or joining a protest committee. Here, group members may disclose confidences with another assumed group member that they might not have shared with a researcher.

- The participant observer also has the problem of making notes and often relies on memory later in the day, with all the associated problems of forgetting and distortion (see Chapter 2).

Problems with disclosed observations

Whether a study is *naturalistic* or *laboratory* based, the participants' awareness of being observed might affect their behaviour. The particular factors of *participant expectancy*, *social desirability* and *demand characteristics* are discussed on page 151.

Problems with naturalistic observation

- Participant observations and those involving only one researcher and/or a unique event (such as a school sports day), are difficult to *replicate*.

- Where there is only one researcher, as in many participant observation studies, it is difficult to check the *authenticity* and *reliability* of the data.

- The naturalistic observer deliberately exerts no control over the observational setting. This leaves many extraneous variables free to vary. For example, the observation of a child in the playground may be distorted by that child having a quiet day or not joining in games as often as usual.

- There can be greater pressure to perform in an ideal manner, since participants know they are in their *normal* role. In a one-off laboratory setting, participants know that a 'bad' performance will have no lasting effect on their lives and can be excused as the result of artificiality and naïveté. The effects of *social desirability* (trying to 'look good') might therefore be stronger in a genuinely social context.

Box 7.5   Observer bias

All observational studies can be affected by *observer bias*. This is really a version of *investigator expectancy* (see Box 7.10, page 151), but here the influence can be very strong indeed. The problem is that each observer can differ in how they perceive, value and label certain behaviours. For example, cultural bias causes many Westerners to label the typical greeting in some Asian cultures as 'deferent' or 'submissive', because a lot of bowing is involved. This behaviour might *look* submissive to Westerners but is *normal* within the cultures that use it. By contrast, the 'high five' greeting used by Western sports competitors and many others might look 'aggressive' to a non-Westerner. More simply, a person raising their arm can be interpreted as 'bidding', 'requesting attention', 'waving', 'making the burglar alarm work', and so on, according to the context and the perceptual bias of the observer (or 'schema' – see page 29).

Recording behaviour through systematic observation

In order to try to reduce possible errors involved in behaviour description, many naturalistic or laboratory observers use some sort of *structured* approach to observation, providing checklists or grids for their trained observers to use (see Figure 7.6). *Systematic observation* or *controlled observation* are terms to describe observation which follows a clearly organised and agreed classification system. Using a coding sheet like that shown in Figure 7.6, observers might make entries for 30 seconds at five-minute intervals whilst observing the same child (*time sampling*), or for 30 seconds on each different child in turn (*point sampling*).

| Child | Time | | Joins in play with rules | Works on joint task | Gives toy – no protest | ... |
	From:	to:				
A	10.05	10.11	X			
	10.12	10.14		X		
	10.15				X	

Figure 7.6 *Possible part of behaviour coding sheet for observers assessing 'co-operative' behaviour in children at play*

Systematic observation has the following advantages:

- subjective interpretations of behaviour are minimised;

- recordings for each observer can be compared for consistency;

- recordings on the same event can be compared across different observers (*inter-observer reliability*);

- use of a structured system prevents the recording of countless trivial and unwanted aspects of behaviour;

- results can be quantified, numerically compared, and tested for *statistical significance*.

However, there are also several disadvantages to this approach:

- not all subjectivity in interpretation can be eliminated;

- behaviour which *might* be important, but has not been included in the observation chart categories, will not be used in the research study;

- behaviour is categorised into units, so the normal *flow* of complex co-ordinated behaviour is not recorded or recognised.

Many *qualitative* researchers would argue that behaviour occurs in a co-ordinated stream, and to categorise it is to lose its basic nature. Such researchers would be more likely to take detailed observations, perhaps by use of continuous notes, a tape recorder, a video camera or the keeping of a *diary*.

Table 7.1 *Comparison of structured, qualitative, naturalistic and participant observation*

Observation type*	Advantages	Disadvantages
Structured	• Can check inter-observer reliability	• Mechanistic
	• Consistent	• May miss important information
	• Lack of bias from selecting different types of behaviour	• Treats behaviour as separable units
	• Extraneous variables controlled if in laboratory setting	• Unnatural behaviour if observed in artificial laboratory setting
Qualitative	• Views behaviour as a whole and in context	• Observer may select different behaviour in different situations
	• Rich, full source of information, especially if in a naturalistic setting	• Harder to check for reliability across observers
		• Lack of replicability
Naturalistic	• Genuine behaviour of participant in known setting, especially if undisclosed	• Variables which may influence observed behaviour are uncontrolled
	• Richer source of information if not structured	• May have 'structured' disadvantages of separating behaviour units and missing important information
Participant	• Observer experiences the participants' natural setting and can interpret observations from their perspective	• Ethical issues and difficulties with information recording if not disclosed
		• Lack of replicability
		• Interpretive bias is strong
		• Lack of observer reliability checks

* Note that the categories are not mutually exclusive; one can have naturalistic participant observation, structured naturalistic observation, and so on.

Asking questions

The questionnaire

PAUSE FOR THOUGHT

Suppose you were given the task of investigating current attitudes among the UK population towards the monarchy. How could you go about attempting to make this assessment?

It is not possible to observe directly someone's attitude towards the monarchy, although we might know that they are proud of their Royal Wedding mug, for example, or that they avoid watching royal events. To obtain more accurate information, people need to be asked questions about what they *think*. However, lengthy interviews will be inefficient since assessing attitudes of the UK population will require use of a *survey* (information-gathering exercise) of a large sample which is as representative as possible (see pages 151–152). Aditionally, little time will be spent with each person, unless the project has a mammoth budget and can afford thousands of interviewers. Therefore, a form of measuring instrument is needed which will make a quick but adequate and efficient assessment of people's attitudes. Such a tool is known as a *questionnaire* or a *psychological scale*. Scales are also used in psychology to measure aspects of personality and of reasoning ability.

Questionnaire items: fixed choice

Questionnaires may use *closed* questions which have specific, limited answers. An example is 'What is your age?'. Alternatively, *open* questions can be used, such as 'Tell me how you feel about animal rights'. Here, the *respondent* (the person being questioned) may answer at any length and in any words. However, used as a tool to measure attitudes, such scales are very often a set of *fixed-choice* closed items, where the respondent must choose one of a number of alternative answers to a question or statement. The simplest choice is 'yes'/'no', but very common is the requirement to choose from among the set of responses shown in Figure 7.7.

Figure 7.7 *Example of a typical response scale* in a questionnaire*

'Members of the Royal Family should not receive money that has been raised from the people's taxes.'

Strongly agree	Agree	Undecided	Disagree	Strongly disagree
5	4	3	2	1

* Response scales like this are often referred to as 'Likert' scales.

Fixed-choice items have the advantage of being *quantifiable*. That is, each answer on the attitude scale can be added up to give a total which indicates the strength of attitude in one direction or the other. For example, people answering 'strongly agree' in Figure 7.7 will end up with a high score, indicating that they are strongly opposed to the monarchy.

The disadvantage of fixed-choice items is that they permit only a *single response* to items already selected by the researcher. Respondents are not able to elaborate on how they feel, give new information, or qualify their answer with 'I do agree, but only ...'.

Box 7.6 The reliability and validity of questionnaires and attitude scales

Any tool that is claimed to measure something must be trustworthy. Psychologists assess the trustworthiness of their measures in terms of their *reliability* and *validity*. The *reliability* of a questionnaire refers to its *consistency of measurement*. *External reliability* can be checked by testing the same group of people twice, after a longish interval, and correlating the two sets of scores. This is known as *test–retest reliability*. Methods of assessing *internal reliability* (whether the questionnaire is consistent within itself) are discussed in Coolican (1999). The *validity* of a questionnaire or attitude scale refers to *the extent to which it measures what it was intended to measure*. If a scale was intended to measure 'attitude to the monarchy', but is later shown to be really measuring 'patriotism', then it would not be considered valid as a measure of attitude to the monarchy. The validity of an 'attitude to the monarchy' scale could be checked by testing a group of people who belonged to a movement dedicated to making Great Britain into a republic. If these people scored quite differently on the scale from randomly selected members of the general public, this would represent some evidence of the scale's validity. Poorly written items will tend to contribute to the lowering of reliability and validity. Some examples of statement types to avoid in questionnaires are given in Table 7.2.

Questionnaire items: open-ended

Open-ended questions, such as 'How do you feel about the monarchy?' have the advantage of making respondents feel satisfied that they have been able to contribute their full views. Such questions are likely to deliver information that researchers may not have thought to ask about. They may give a rich and comprehensive picture of people's feelings and opinions on the topic investigated. However, the information provided can be difficult to summarise and report in its original form. It is also not easy to quantify.

Table 7.2 *Problems with certain kinds of questionnaire item*

Type	Example	Problem
Double-barrelled	The national anthem should be played in cinemas and at football matches.	Respondent is asked to respond to two different questions at once
Leading	Surely the start of the 21st century is a time to abolish the monarchy.	Respondent is 'led on' by the wording to a point where they have to resist to say 'no'.
Factual	The queen is very rich	So what? This is just *true*, so how would agreement demonstrate direction of attitude?
Colloquial	Do you believe in the monarchy?	Colloquial use of 'believe in' can force just a factual answer – 'Yes, it exists'. The questioner *intends* to ask whether the respondent *agrees with* the existence of a monarchy and should make this clear.
Complex	Because Great Britain is moving towards political and financial unification within a federalised European framework, there is no place left for a monarchist political system based originally on feudalism	Too long, too many concepts, and a certain amount of technical usage which the respondent must understand.
Emotive/ Colloquial	Prince Charles should keep his big nose out of other people's business	Relies on emotional appeal and uses slang. Lacks credibility for some respondents, and may annoy them enough not to participate fully.

The interview

Open-ended questions might be used in an *interview* situation where researchers:

- have more time available with each respondent;
- do not wish to impose an exact structure on the information to be obtained;
- want to obtain people's unique and personal views.

Interviews are often used to administer a structured attitude scale or to assess intellectual ability on a one-to-one basis. However, the emphasis here will be upon the more typical *semi-structured interview*, which uses open questioning and has the last two bullet points above as its major goals.

Semi-structured interviews

In a *semi-structured interview*, the investigator starts out with a set of questions to be answered, such as:

> *What would be your reaction if the government were to announce the abolition of the monarchy?*

> *Tell me what you think about the place of a monarch as head of state in modern Britain.*

Notice that these are items which are open, and invite respondents to talk at any length, offering their own opinions and thoughts on the subject.

Central features of the semi-structured interview are that respondents:

- should be helped to feel as relaxed as possible;
- should feel free from evaluation;
- should be helped to respond in as much like a normal conversational manner as is possible.

The hope is that this approach is more likely than others, especially the structured questionnaire, to reveal each respondent's true thoughts and beliefs in detail. The information gathered can be treated as qualitative data, or it can be converted to quantitative data using a version of *content analysis* (see pages 163–164).

Flexibility in the semi-structured interview

In order to make the interview more like a conversation, the interviewer is usually left free to order the questions in a way which makes sense and feels natural at the time. If the respondent naturally moves on to a topic to be covered later, this can be picked up by the interviewer, remembering that skipped questions must be returned to if they do not occur naturally. The interviewer is also free to follow up some points in detail and to clarify others by helping respondents to expand upon what they have said. The aim of these procedures is to obtain the fullest and fairest detail about what respondents wish to say.

PAUSE FOR THOUGHT

What difficulties can you see with the interview procedure just described, compared with structured questionnaires?

A *disadvantage* of the interview approach is that it is more susceptible to the effects of interpersonal variables. Respondents may react differently to different interviewers, and vice versa. Open questions can be asked somewhat differently, or in a leading manner. It is also easier to 'read into' what someone has said in an interview than in response to a fixed-choice question-

naire. This possibly greater variation in the interview context can produce difficulty in making fair and objective comparisons between sets of obtained data.

Table 7.3 *Advantages and disadvantages of interviews and questionnaires*

Advantages	Disadvantages
Interviews	
• Richer, fuller information in respondent's own terms	• Greater effect from interpersonal variables and variation in questioning
• Interviewer can follow up unexpected points and check for intended meaning	• Problems of interpretation
Questionnaires	
• Standardised procedure	• Only simple responses from respondents are available
• Similar treatment of all respondents	• Further information is not tapped
• Less bias from interpersonal factors	• Artificial questioning process and mis-interpretation of questions may produce distorted answers
• Efficient administration	
• Greater reliability and consistency of data analysis	

Figure 7.8 *A sensitive and thorough interviewing technique can elicit rich and highly informative information from interviewees. Professor Anthony Clare's radio programme 'In the Psychiatrist's Chair' has provided some stunning revelations from his famous interviewees through this kind of approach*

Section Summary

- Researchers pose **research questions** in order to seek evidence to support theories. Research studies produce data which can be used to test **hypotheses**, **describe phenomena** or promote **exploration** of a new study area. Research studies may be predominantly **qualitative** (intended to gather meanings) or **quantitative** (intended to gather numerical measurements).

- A **true experiment** controls **extraneous variables**, whilst manipulating an **independent variable** in order to observe causal effects on a **dependent variable**.

- **Confounding variables** are those which, if they are not controlled, might provide alternative explanations of why the dependent variable changed in an experiment.

- In some experiments, there is a **control group** which is used as a **baseline** against which to compare the performance of one or more **experimental groups**.

- **Standardised procedures** and **instructions** should minimise the confounding effects of **extraneous variables**.

- In a **quasi-experiment**, some controls are lacking. Typically, participants are not **randomly allocated** to conditions, and/or the experimenter does not control the independent variable (as in a 'natural experiment'). However, an **identifiable treatment** is applied to one or more groups of people.

- In **non-experimental** research, the relationship between two or more existing variables is often investigated, with one or more variables being categorical (as in a **group difference investigation**) or measured (as in **correlational designs**). **Correlation** is a measure of the extent to which two variables vary together.

- **Observational studies** involve recording relatively unconstrained behaviour in detail. **Naturalistic observation** studies behaviour in the observed person's natural **environment** and, if **undisclosed**, avoids **participant reactivity** effects. It might, however, transgress the ethical principles of **privacy** and **confidentiality**. **Participant observation** involves the researcher interacting in the group being studied.

- Observational studies, especially if naturalistic, can suffer from uncontrolled variables, difficulty of replication, verification and reliability of data, and **observer bias**.

- **Systematic observation** involves the use of a strict **coding system**, trained observers, an organised observational procedure, and checks on **inter-observer reliability**. **Qualitative observation** can involve less structured recording and a fuller account of behaviour and its context.

- **Questionnaires** or **psychological scales** are likely to be used in **surveys** on relatively large and representative samples. **Fixed-choice items** require one of a limited number of predetermined responses from the respondent, and need to be carefully written to avoid bias. **Open-ended answers** provide **qualitative data** which can be **coded** or left as text.

- Psychological questionnaires and scales must be **reliable** (consistent) and **valid** (measure what was intended).

- **Interviews** can be used to administer psychological tests and scales, but are particularly useful for gathering more extended information in a relatively natural and flexible questioning session (known as a **semi-structured interview**).

- Interviews may extract richer, more relevant information than questionnaires, with interviewers able to clarify questions and follow up points. However, questionnaires and scales suffer less from interpersonal and interaction variables, and are standardised measures of behaviour.

Research Design and Implementation

WHY DO RESEARCHERS DO RESEARCH?: RESEARCH AIMS AND HYPOTHESES

Researchers design their studies with certain aims in mind. A qualitative researcher might design research with the aim of investigating communications between patients and receptionists in doctors' surgeries. An observational study might aim to demonstrate that girls' language is as aggressive as boys' in the playground.

This section looks more carefully at the aims and designs of experiments, including typical weaknesses and problems. At the beginning of the last section (see page 136), a possible experiment on hunger and memory was considered. The general aim of this was to support the theory that physiological states can exert an influence on our cognitions about the world. A more specific aim would be to show that hunger affects memory, narrowed down further to the aim of testing the hypothesis that hunger leads to better memory for food-related material. Having thus focused the question, researchers now need to design a research study which will appropriately and effectively test this hypothesis. They need to think about answers to several specific questions, such as:

- How many people should be tested?
- How will they be tested (e.g. should the *same* people be tested when they are hungry and when satiated)?
- What *kind* of memory should be tested?
- How should hunger be defined and measured?

AT HOME WITH THE PEDANTS

Figure 7.9   *Some people just love exact operational definitions*

Box 7.7   Operational definitions

In a scientific study, the same thing must be measured under the same circumstances, and it must be possible for others to *replicate* a piece of research. To achieve this, careful definitions of variables are required. An *operational definition* is one which *defines a variable in terms of the steps taken to measure it*. Hunger could be defined as complete food deprivation for 12 hours (people are not just asked whether they *feel* hungry or not). Memory can be measured by counting how many food-related words each participant recalls from a previously read list of 20 food-related words and 20 other words. The *research hypothesis* or *experimental hypothesis* (that hungry participants recall more food-related material) can be tested with an exact *research prediction*:

Participants deprived of food for 12 hours will recall more food-related words than will participants who have just eaten.

This prediction follows from a *directional hypothesis*, that is, one which states the direction of a difference (hungry participants recall *more* words). A *non-directional hypothesis* claims that a difference exists, but does not make a claim about direction. As an example, suppose a researcher was interested in the effects that an audience has on people's task performance. It might be speculated that *either* people will perform a task *better* with an audience, because they are stimulated and want to perform well, or *worse*, because they are intimidated by being watched. Here a *non-directional* prediction about the outcome of the experiment would be made.

Samples and populations

To be absolutely sure that hunger does cause people to recall more food-related words, the entire population would have to be tested several times. However, this is not at all practical and, in social scientific investigations, a *sample* of people from the *population* of interest is almost always tested. What is obtained, statistically speaking, is a *sample* of scores from an infinite *population* of possible scores. Researchers must assume that their sample of scores has been drawn at *random* from its population. Hopefully, this makes it as *representative* as possible of that population. This is why random allocation to experimental conditions is so important (see page 138).

Now, it will not do simply to show that the hungry participants *happen* to have recalled more food-related words than the satiated participants. If *any* two samples drawn randomly from the same population on a memory task are tested, it is usually found that there is some *slight* difference in performance between them. This difference will occur through random fluctuation and slight differences between people, and is known as *sampling error*.

Supporting hypotheses with significant differences

Researchers need to show that the difference obtained in an experiment is so large that it would not happen just from random sampling error. They want it to be treated as a *significant difference*, that is, a difference which is so large that it is extremely unlikely it would happen if being hungry had no effect on the type of word recalled. With such a large difference it may be accepted, provisionally, that being hungry *was* the cause of the greater number of food-related words being recalled. Statistically, a formal *significance test* must be applied to the two samples of data. This is used to decide between two possibilities, known as the *null hypothesis* and the *alternative hypothesis* (sometimes known as the *experimental hypothesis*).

The *null hypothesis* claims that the two populations from which the two samples have been drawn are the same, that is, being hungry *and* being satiated produce the same population of scores. Researchers would like to dismiss this claim, and claim that there must be *two different underlying populations*, one of scores from satiated participants and one of scores from hungry participants. The *alternative hypothesis* claims that scores in the 'hungry participant' population are generally higher than scores in the 'satiated participant' population. This is the hypothesis that is provisionally *supported* if the null hypothesis is rejected.

Statistical testing in science does not provide proof, it provides *evidence*. In this case, the evidence is in the form of *probability*. Statistical tests calculate the probability of obtaining two samples so different *if they were both drawn from the same population* (that is, if the null hypothesis is true). If this probability is less than 0.05 (a '5% chance'), a *significant difference* is claimed, and the null hypothesis is rejected in favour of the alternative hypothesis (see Figure 7.10). This does not 'prove' that the alternative hypothesis is true. It is simply supported. The result is used as evidence in favour of the research hypothesis. Procedures for showing that a difference is statistically significant are explained in Gross *et al.* (2000).

Step 1: Assume null hypothesis is true (i.e. that the two samples were drawn from the same population)

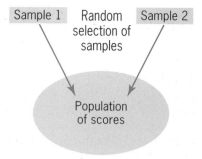

Step 2: Calculate the probability (*p*) of the difference between samples occurring *if the null hypothesis is true.*

Step 3: Make significance decision; use the bolded terms in research report.

Step 4: Final assumption about populations:

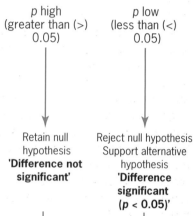
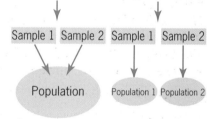

Figure 7.10 *The process of significance testing*

EXPERIMENTAL VALIDITY

Internal validity

Even when a significant difference is obtained, researchers must ask whether it really *was* the independent variable that produced the change in the dependent variable. In other words, is it a genuine 'effect'? Earlier, a psychologist conducting a 'reading boost' programme was described (see page 138). Suppose she just measured a group of children, applied the programme, then measured again and found an improvement. Is this because of the programme or through natural maturity in reading skill? Without a control group for comparison, there would be no way of knowing whether the children would have improved that much regardless of any help from the programme.

The *experimental validity* of a research design refers to the extent to which a *researcher can be sure that the effect apparently demonstrated is real*. This concept can be applied to *all* studies, not just experiments. The concept can be more generally categorised as an issue of *internal validity*. Can we be sure the reading programme improved children's reading ability, or that Loftus & Palmer's (1974) question wording (see page 137) *caused* people to make higher speed estimates? There are usually many possible alternative explanations for an effect. For example, the presence of more aggressive drivers in the 'smashed into' condition might explain the differences in speed estimation, and the natural maturation of the children might explain any improvement in reading performance. Variables which are not controlled in a research design, and which might lead to a mistaken assumption of an effect, are known as '*threats to the validity*' of the findings.

External validity

Even if a definite experimental effect has been demonstrated, researchers still want to know how *general* that effect is. Would it occur in a different environment or among different people? These are questions of *external validity*, of which there are several types, including *population* and *ecological validity*:

- Population validity concerns *the extent to which researchers can be confident that they would obtain the effect among different groups of people*. For example, would the reading programme (see page 138) work on children in a different area, at a different educational level or on bilingual children?
- Ecological validity concerns *the generalisation of the effect from the environment in which it was demonstrated to a different environment*. It is not the case that a study conducted in a naturalistic setting is *automatically* 'more ecologically valid' than one conducted in a laboratory. That depends upon research evidence showing this to be so (see Box 7.8).

implies that it had *low* ecological validity, and perhaps the effect shown could only be obtained in *that* hospital at *that* particular time.

Earlier it was shown that experimental laboratory studies can produce *artificiality*. Many of these probably do lack ecological validity, since they produce effects that *only ever* appear in the laboratory context and probably do not have other applications.

EXPERIMENTAL DESIGNS

Having looked at the issue of experimental validity in general, some of the basic ways in which simple experiments can be designed and run need to be considered. Each of these has strengths and weaknesses, or *threats to validity*. That is, each design can include factors that might cause us to assume an independent variable has affected a dependent variable when, actually, it has not.

Independent groups design

The *independent groups* or *independent samples* experimental design tests different people in each condition of an experiment. This design has certain advantages, which are identified in Table 7.5 (see pages 149–150). However, it has the one major disadvantage that differences between the people in each group, known as *participant variables*, could account for any difference found in the dependent variable. For example, too many aggressive drivers in the 'smashed into' condition of Loftus & Palmer's (1974) experiment might explain the fact that their speed estimations were higher.

Box 7.8 Obedience and ecological validity

Milgram's (1963, 1974) famous obedience demonstration (see Chapter 6, pages 118–125) was shown to have ecological validity *even in the laboratory* because it transferred, with no significantly different effects, to many places and settings, including a commercial office away from the prestigious university laboratory. Other studies carried out in naturalistic settings do *not* necessarily possess great ecological validity if they cannot be replicated in *other* naturalistic settings. Replication of Hofling *et al.*'s (1966) study of obedience in a naturalistic hospital setting has failed to produce similar results (see Box 6.11, pages 123–124). This

Figure 7.11 *Participant variables may confound an experimental effect*

Repeated measures design

An answer to the problem of participant variables is to conduct, wherever possible, a *repeated measures* design experiment. Here, each person participates in *all* conditions of the experiment.

PAUSE FOR THOUGHT

What serious problem might occur if the two initial conditions of Loftus & Palmer's (1974) experiment ('hit' and 'smashed into') had been conducted on the same group of participants?

This would be an unsound strategy since participants would already have answered one question, and could easily guess the experimental hypothesis when presented with the second question. Unwanted effects produced by having participants perform first one, then another condition of an experiment, are known as *order effects*. A solution to the problem of order effects is provided in Box 7.9.

Box 7.9   Order effects and counterbalancing in the repeated measures design

Imagine an experiment in which participants have to solve anagrams first in silence, then with loud music playing. Using the same participants solves the problem of participant variables. The performance of each participant in one condition can be measured *against their own performance in the other condition*. This is the advantage of the repeated measures design but it has other serious weaknesses. For example, the set of words for the second condition must be equal in difficulty to the first set, otherwise the two conditions will not be equivalent.

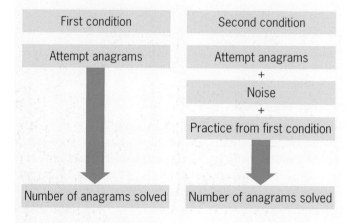

Figure 7.12 *Both noise and practice are present in the second condition of this repeated measures design*

There is, however, a more general problem of *order effects*. Participants' performances could, for example, improve through practice, or deteriorate through boredom or fatigue. The popular way to deal with order effects is to *counterbalance*. Here, half the participants experience the experiment in the order A–B (condition A, silence, then condition B, noise) whilst the rest of the participants receive the order B–A. This will not eliminate order effects, but in most cases it will tend to balance them across the two conditions.

Matched pairs designs

A compromise which deals with both the major weaknesses outlined above (participant variable differences *and* order effects) is to use *matched pairs* (or *matched participants*). In the reading boost example (see page 138), *pairs* of participants could be created, one from the reading boost programme class and one from the class acting as a control group. The members of each pair would be matched as closely as possible on relevant variables such as age, vocabulary and, especially, reading performance at the start of the programme. At the end of the programme, performance on reading can be compared pair by pair. The effects of participant variables have been reduced to a minimum, and it could be argued that *most* of the new reading difference between the pairs must be caused by the programme's influence.

In a true experiment, *all* of the children would be paired on this basis, and then one would be randomly allocated to the experimental programme group and the other to the control group. The study described above, as has been seen, would be classed as a quasi-experiment (see pages 138–139).

Table 7.4 *Arrangement of participants in simple experimental designs*

(Letters represent people – same letter (and number), same person)

Design	Condition 1	Condition 2
	A	F
	B	G
Independent groups	C	H
	D	I
	E	J

(continued on page 150)

(Table 7.4 continued)

Design	Condition 1	Condition 2
	A	A
	B	B
Repeated measures	C	C
	D	D
	E	E
	A1	A2
	B1	B2
Matched pairs	C1	C2
	D1	D2
	E1	E2

Table 7.5 *Advantages and disadvantages of simple experimental designs*

Design	Advantage	Disadvantage
Independent groups	• No order effects	• Participant variables may confound any effects
	• Loss of one participant from one condition does not entail loss of a result from all conditions (see repeated measures).	• More participants needed to fill conditions (for example, 20 participants are needed to get ten results in each of two conditions)
Repeated measures	• No participant variables	• Order effects
	• Fewer participants needed to fill conditions (for example, ten participants provide ten results in *each* of two conditions)	• Loss of one participant entails loss of one result from all conditions.
Matched pairs (participants)	• Participant variable differences minimised	• More participants needed to fill conditions (see independent groups)
	• No order effects	

SOURCES OF BIAS IN EXPERIMENTAL STUDIES

Many threats to the validity of experimental studies have been highlighted by researchers. In general terms, these are sources of *bias* in the proceedings which prevent clear demonstrations of what is causing what.

Confounding

The most common problem is any form of *confounding*. A few examples have been met already. For example, if Loftus & Palmer (1974) had not randomly allocated participants to conditions, they might have found that too many aggressive drivers in the 'smashed into' condition confounded their results. Additionally, having all participants perform any experimental conditions in the same order might lead to improvement because of practice, rather than because of the intended independent variable. Confounding variables, such as participant variables and order effects, can provide alternative explanations for the effect found. If possible, they should be controlled for in the research design. If not, other researchers will criticise the design and claim that the confounding variables might be responsible for the effects that were demonstrated. A goal of many research studies is to try to rule out variables that possibly confounded previous research. When reading about psychological research studies you should always ask yourself 'But what else could have caused that to happen?'.

PAUSE FOR THOUGHT

A researcher wishes to show that caffeine improves performance on a memory task. She shows that participants perform better after drinking a hot cup of coffee than before. Apart from practice or fatigue, what other variables might confound the results?

In this case, it could simply be the hot liquid, not caffeine, that improves performance. It could be some *other* ingredient of the drink, apart from the caffeine, or it could even be just the perception that the researcher is kind and thoughtful!

Piloting the study

Because problems can creep into even the most simple procedure, it is always wise to conduct a *pilot study* before finally settling on the precise instructions and procedure for any research study. This should expose and highlight any difficulties or ambiguities in the procedures. Adjustments can be made for these difficulties before the actual data-gathering process begins. It might also give an idea of how many participants need to be tested to demonstrate a clear effect. It could also show that a study was not worthwhile.

Box 7.10 Investigator and participant expectancy

If a pilot study is not conducted, experimental procedures might not be adequately standardised. A dramatic effect, presumably originating from experimenters' differing treatments, was demonstrated by Rosenthal & Lawson (1964). They randomly allocated rats to students, and told half of them that their rats were 'bright' and the other half that the rats were 'dull'. The 'bright' rats actually did learn more quickly, presumably because of the students' expectancy. This effect was also shown by Rosenthal & Jacobson (1968). Here, randomly chosen children, described to their teachers as likely to make late but sudden gains in educational achievement, actually did make significant progress.

Figure 7.13 *Experimenter bias may subtly alter the outcomes of experiments*

Participants might also be affected in an experiment if they know the expected outcome. To guard against investigator and participant expectancy, experiments can be run as:

- a *single blind*, where participants are not aware which condition they are in, *or*

- a *double blind*, where the data gatherers *also* do not know which condition the participants are in.

Demand characteristics

The term *demand characteristics* was coined by Orne (1962):

'The totality of cues that convey an experimental hypothesis to the subject become significant determinants of the subject's behaviour. We have labelled the sum total of

such cues as the "demand characteristics" of the experimental situation' (page 779).

Orne & Scheibe (1964) showed that features of the experimental situation serve as 'cues' which help participants to interpret what is expected of them. They asked participants to sign a consent form and directed them to a 'panic button'. The participants reacted in a more extreme manner to being left alone in a room for five hours than did other participants who were not given these cues to possible distress. This study supported the view that participants are active thinkers in the research situation, trying to work out what the investigation is all about, and perhaps trying to produce the behaviour expected by the researchers. Such attempts may well distort the behaviour that might otherwise have been observed with 'naïve' participants.

Box 7.11 Social desirability

Participants may well attempt to produce the behaviour that they think is actually desired by the researchers. In Asch's (1952) famous conformity studies (see Chapter 6, pages 109–112), some participants reported that they knew the answers they were giving were wrong, but did not want to 'mess up' the results; they said they thought they might have misunderstood instructions. Here, the demand characteristics of the research setting are affected partly perhaps by a desire to help science produce the 'right' results, and also by a desire to be a 'good participant' – to have one's behaviour seen as *socially desirable*. People also like to be seen to think and do the 'right thing' with regard to, for example, child-rearing or neighbourliness. Hence, social desirability is very likely to intrude as an effect in studies assessing attitudes or typical social behaviour via questionnaire or interview.

Selecting participants: sampling issues

Psychological studies mostly assess *samples* drawn from larger *populations*. Samples are assessed in order to draw tentative conclusions about the underlying population. Therefore, the samples drawn must be *representative*. Sampling is something we often do in our everyday behaviour. For example, if you were trying to decide which bag of nuts to buy for Christmas, you might well sample a few from each bag to check how many were bad or empty. The same principle applies in social research. Samples should therefore be as free as possible from sampling *bias*. If the aim is to generalise results on reading ability from a sample to the population of all eight-year-old children, it is no use selecting a sample consisting of too many girls, exceptional readers, and so on. One way to avoid bias is to sample *at random* from the target population.

Simple random sampling

To sample randomly from a population the following criterion *must* be met:

> *Every item (person) in the population has an equal probability of selection.*

Random samples drawn from the population are extremely rare in experimental psychology. Mostly, researchers use those who volunteer (a type of *self-selecting sample*), those they can cajole into the laboratory, students who have an obligation to participate, or existing groups, such as patients at a clinic.

Figure 7.14 *Focus groups (used increasingly by political parties to gauge public opinion) need to be a representative sample of the population whose views they are intended to reflect*

Random allocation

What *should* occur in any true independent groups experimental design is the *random allocation* of participants to the different conditions. The reasons for this were discussed earlier (see page 138), so outlined below is simply a method for randomly allocating 40 participants to two groups. Typically, all the participants are given numbers and these are then shuffled in a bag or on a computer and the first twenty selected go into one of the groups, the rest into the other. If participants arrive as and when they can be obtained, random allocation is difficult. A near-randomised effect can, however, be achieved by tossing a coin for each participant who arrives until one of two groups has reached 20. The last few *must* now go into the other group, and are thus not randomly allocated.

Stratified samples

A single random sample may not produce good representation of smaller groups within a population, such as left-handers, asthmatics, or those with science and arts A Levels. What can be done is to ensure that important sections of the population *are* proportionately represented in a sample. If 15 per cent of a college population are taking science A levels, 15 per cent of the sample should be selected at random from among science A-level students. This method is known as *stratified random sampling*.

Systematic samples

A non-random alternative for obtaining a representative sample is to select, say, every tenth person from a list (such as a school register). This is *systematic sampling*, and can be made truly random by initially selecting a number from one to ten at random. Suppose the random number selected were four. Every tenth person from the list starting with the fourth (the fourteenth, twenty-fourth, and so on) would then be selected.

Non-random samples: haphazard, opportunity and convenience samples

Selecting participants in a shopping mall *cannot* produce a random sample. Certain people will be avoided, others will avoid the researcher. People at work, in hospital, at school and so on will not be included. Hence, the criterion above is nowhere near satisfied. Such samples may be termed *haphazard*, meaning that they are picked with no conscious bias. A captive group, such as a maths class in a school or college, can be called an *opportunity* or *convenience* sample. *Self-selecting samples* are those where participants select themselves, as when they volunteer to participate in a research study.

Box 7.12 'Experimental biases' apply to non-experiments too!

Experiments can be carried out in the field, and many studies in laboratories are not experiments. However, non-experimental research designs are more likely to be encountered in the field. There are even experiments in which participants do not realise they are participating (e.g. some 'natural' ones), and so there can be no participant reactivity or effect from demand characteristics and social desirability. Nevertheless, all the biasing effects considered above *can* be at work in non-experimental studies and in studies conducted outside the laboratory.

Section Summary

- Researchers develop specific testable and **operationalised hypotheses** from their more general **research aims**. Aims concern the testing or exploration of an idea to provide evidence in support of a theory.

- The **research** or **experimental hypothesis** is the assumption of differences or correlations between variables. The **research prediction** is an associated statement of what is expected to be found among the samples of raw data gathered in a research study.

- The **null** and **alternative hypotheses** are used in **significance testing**, and are claims about the underlying populations from which the samples of data in a study have been drawn. The null hypothesis is the assumption of 'no effect'. It often asserts that population means are equal, or that the population correlation is zero. The alternative hypothesis states that populations are different or that the population correlation is not zero.

- **Significance tests** estimate the probability that samples would be so different (or correlations so large) if the null hypothesis is true. The null hypothesis is rejected when this probability is very low (less than 0.05).

- A study's **internal** or **experimental validity** is the extent to which it is free of design faults and confounding variables that can obscure an independent variable's effect on a dependent variable. **External validity** refers to the degree of generalisation possible from the testing situation (**ecological validity**) or the sample tested (**population validity**).

- The **independent groups** (**samples**) design uses different participants in each condition of an experiment, and has the weakness that **participant variables** can explain differences between conditions.

- The **repeated measures** design tests the same participants in each condition of the experiment, and has the problem that **order effects** might confound any experimental effect. Order effects can be neutralised through **counterbalancing**.

- The **matched pairs** (**participants**) design creates matched pairs of participants and allocates one of each pair at random to each condition.

- **Investigators'** and **participants' expectations** can unwittingly influence the outcomes of research studies. A remedy is the use of a **single** or **double blind control**, where either participants, or both participants and researchers, do not know to which experimental conditions the participants have been allocated.

- **Demand characteristics** refer to participants' reactivity in an experimental situation, in particular their attempts to determine what is being tested.

- **Social desirability** can influence participants to act in accordance with social norms.

- Participants are normally selected as a **sample** from a **population**, in order to be as **representative** as possible of that population. **Random sampling** requires that every person in a population has an equal chance of being selected. **Random allocation** involves ensuring that each participant has an equal chance of being in any condition of an experiment, and should distribute participant variables evenly.

- A **stratified sample** identifies proportions of subgroups required, and samples at random from among these sub-groups. In a **systematic sample** every nth person is selected from a list of people.

- **Haphazard, opportunity, convenience** and **self-selecting samples** are not truly random, and are more often used in psychological research, especially at a student project level. Haphazard samples are picked without conscious bias. Opportunity and convenience samples are formed from those people who are available, and self-selecting samples pick themselves (e.g. volunteers).

- All the biases and weaknesses discussed in the context of experimental studies can apply to most non-experimental studies in exactly the same way.

Data Analysis

DESCRIPTIVE STATISTICS: MAKING MEASUREMENTS OF VARIABLES

Psychological research often tries to demonstrate the effect of one variable upon another, such as the effect of chocolate on hyperactivity, or the effects of physical punishment on children's aggressive behaviour. The term 'variable' implies the possibility of being able to measure what varies. Earlier (see Box 7.7, page 146), it was seen that variables must be *operationalised* in order to be able to measure them. This section is about measuring variables in an effective and appropriate manner.

In Loftus & Palmer's (1974) eyewitness experiment (see page 137), an independent variable was manipulated. The independent variable had two *qualitatively* different levels, the words 'hit' or 'smashed into'. The independent variable in an experiment is very often divided into categories like this, and is therefore not really difficult to 'measure'.

The dependent variable is also very often easy to measure. Loftus and Palmer asked people to estimate the *speed* of the cars at impact in miles per hour. In a memory-recall experiment, the number of words correctly recalled might simply be counted.

PAUSE FOR THOUGHT

Sometimes the measuring task is a little harder. For example, in the reading boost example mentioned on page 138, how could reading ability be measured?

When researchers attempt to measure a complex human characteristic, like reading ability, they must create an *operational definition* (see page 146). Here, the measure of reading ability could be defined in terms of speed, errors made, words not recognised, hesitations, and so on.

It must always be remembered that numerical data are only an *abstraction* from the observed phenomenon. For example, only counting errors in reading ignores the *flow* of reading. In counting answers to questionnaire items, researchers do not have all there is to know about a person's attitude to, say, the monarchy (see page 142). The data that are abstracted from the research are known as a *data set*. Note that 'data' is a *plural* word. Data are *items* of information.

LEVELS OF MEASUREMENT

The data obtained from research observations can be presented in one of three common forms. Researchers can:

- count items in categories (known as *categorical* or *nominal level* data);
- give positions in a group (known as *ranked* or *ordinal level* data);
- give scores on a scale of equal units (known as *interval level* data).

Categorical variables

Nominal level data

Suppose a teacher were doing some administrative work on the names of students in her class. She might organise the students according to the subject they study. She would *classify* them into *categories*, such as (1) French, (2) Physics, (3) History, and so on. Similarly, people can be classified by the kind of job they have, the kind of house they live in, and so on. There may be a *qualitative* difference between the categories used (such as Labour voter, Liberal voter, and so on) or a *quantitative* difference (such as they are in the '0–4-year-old' category or the 'smokes 10–20 a day category'). In either case, such data are organised at a *nominal* level because *any number given to each category is nominal*. It is a label or a *code* for the category and does not work at a mathematical level. The value '2' given to Physics does not mean that this subject is *twice* the value '1' given to French.

Table 7.6 *Categorical variables – nominal level data*

Participants' eating preferences:

Meat eating (1)	Vegetarian (2)	Vegan (3)
127	65	8

No. of cigarettes smoked per day:

None	1–9	10–20	21–30	30+
156	39	45	17	5

Measured variables

Ranked or ordinal level data

Alternatively, the teacher might *order* her students according to the last essay they wrote. She might report that

Higgins came first, Wright second, and so on. Note that with this information we cannot tell *how much* better Higgins' work was than Wright's. We only have the *rank order* of the work, and such ranks are known as *ordinal level* data. To find out what Wright needs to do in order to catch up with Higgins next time, the *mark* that the teacher gave to each essay must be known. If participants are asked to put pictures of people in rank order of attractiveness, we cannot say that the person ranked fourth is twice as attractive as the person ranked eighth. Unlike the scales which measure exact intervals (such as time or weight), there is no universally accepted scale which tells us the distance between people on attractiveness!

Table 7.7 *Measured variables – ranked or ordinal level data*

Perceived order of attractiveness:

Person:	A	B	C	D	E
Rank:	1	3	5	4	2

Participants' recall of words:

Memory score:	7	11	9	12	15	8	4	6
Rank:	3	6	5	7	8	4	1	2

Interval level data

Another administrative task the teacher might perform is adding up the number of days' absence shown for each student. Here, the intervals between points of the scale *are* meaningful, and numbers *can* be compared in a quantitative manner. For instance, Wright's score might be 20 where Higgins' is ten. This means that Wright was absent *twice* as often as Higgins. Scales where the relative distance between different measurement points can be determined are called *interval level* scales. They possess *equal intervals* between measurement units, and these intervals have been *standardised* (that is, there is public agreement on how much each interval represents). Examples are standard measures of weight, height and time. In certain circumstances, these scales may also be termed 'ratio scales' (see Coolican, 1999). Note that the teachers' marks probably have *not* been standardised on a publicly agreed scale. There are debates about whether *psychological* measures represent equal quantities for equal intervals. However, many researchers tend to treat several kinds of psychological measure *as if* they were at an interval level, including:

- number of words correctly recalled as a measure of memory capacity;

- errors made in a reading test;

- psychological scales where large samples of scores are not *skewed* (see page 160).

Table 7.8 *Measured variables – interval level data*

Time (secs.) to read a list of words:

16.2	8.5	9.3	11.2	13.1	9.6	8.5

Participants' recall of words:

Memory score:	7	11	9	12	15	8	4	6

Reducing data to lower levels

Notice that, if we *reduce* interval level data to ranked data, we lose information – how far apart the original values were. We can also reduce interval level data to nominal level by bunching values into categories, as when we call people scoring above 12 on an extroversion–introversion scale 'extroverts', and those below, 'introverts'. Here, we lose *all* information about distances between people within each category.

DESCRIPTIONS OF DATA

Descriptive statistics are tools to summarise sets of data. They should provide a fairly clear picture of trends within the data set. They should also be calculated and presented in such a way that any reader can readily and clearly grasp the claims being made about the data. A reader should not need to ask any further questions.

PAUSE FOR THOUGHT

Give a brief summary of the number of hours you spend studying at home each day.

Unless you are an extremely disciplined and consistent student, you probably found that exercise quite difficult. Most of us do not study a specific and unchanging number of hours per day. You might have said: 'I don't know, let's see, I do five hours some days and skip it entirely on others … say, about two hours or so'. In this statement, there are two rough estimates of measures that can be taken of a data set:

- *central tendency* – the typical or central value (e.g. 'about two hours or so');

- *dispersion* – the extent to which data are spread around the centre (e.g. 'five hours some days and [none] on others').

Measures of central tendency

The mode

The *mode* is the value which occurs most *frequently* in a data set (the most *common* value). The value occurring most frequently in the set of memory scores below is 11, so this is the *mode* of the data set.

Table 7.9 *Words recalled in a memory task*

Numbers of words correctly recalled out of 15.	6 10 8 8 14 7 11 9 13 11 8 11 11 13 7

These data can be arranged in a *frequency table*. It is then easier to see which is the most frequently occurring value:

Table 7.10 *Frequencies of numbers of words recalled in a memory task*

No. of words recalled	6	7	8	9	10	11	13	14
Frequency	1	2	3	1	1	4	2	1

Notice that the mode is the *category* with the greatest number of items, *not* the number of items *in* that category. The mode is the appropriate central tendency measure for data in categories.

The median

The *median* is used at the ordinal level on ranked data. It is the *middle value in a data set* when the values have been *rank ordered*. If the numbers in Table 7.9 are rank ordered, the following is obtained.

Table 7.11

Value:	6	7	7	8	8	8	9	10	11	11	11	11	13	13	14
Rank:	1	2.5	2.5	5	5	5	7	8	10.5	10.5	10.5	10.5	13.5	13.5	15

Notice that to rank order values a rank of 1 is given to the *lowest* value. Where there are several of the same value they *share* the ranks that they occupy. Hence, the two values of 7 occupy the second and third ranks so they share these rank values, receiving a rank of 2.5 each.

Box 7.13 Finding the position of the median

In the example above, there are 15 values altogether, so the median value will be the one in the eighth position. There are seven values below it and seven above it. The median therefore is ten:

This formula can be used to find the position of the median:

$$k = \frac{N+1}{2}$$

where N is the total number of values and the median is in the kth position.

In the example above this is:

$$\frac{15+1}{2} = 8$$

Where there is an even number of values, as in:

$$12 \quad 15 \quad 18 \quad 21$$

the median will be the average of the two central values. The median position here is $(4 + 1)/2 = 2.5$. Hence the median is half way between the second and third values, that is between 15 and 18. The median is 16.5.

The mean

The *mean* is used at the interval level on measured values. It is what is commonly called the 'average', and is calculated by adding up all the scores in a data set and dividing by the total number of scores. So, for the memory scores presented in Table 7.9:

$$6 + 10 + 8 + 8 + 14 + 7 + 11 + 9 + 13 + 11 + 8$$
$$+ 11 + 11 + 13 + 7 = 147$$

$$\frac{147}{15} = 9.8$$

To calculate the mean, use the formula:

$$\bar{x} = \frac{\Sigma x}{N}$$

where $\bar{x}$ is the symbol for the mean, and 'Σ' simply instructs us to *add up* all the instances of what follows it. In this case, all the scores (the 'x's) must be added up.

Table 7.12 *Strengths and weaknesses of central tendency measures*

	Strength	Weakness
Mode	• Simple measure	• Unreliable with small data sets. With one score different in the example above, 8 could have been the mode rather than 11
	• Is equal to one of the scores in the data set; useful with large data sets	• Little affected by *skewed data* (see page 160)
	• Unaffected by a few extreme scores	
Median	• More likely than the mode to be representative of the centre of a small set of values	• May not be an actual value appearing in the data set
	• Unaffected by a few extreme scores	• Can be affected by severely skewed data
Mean	• Most sensitive to all values	• Greatly affected by extreme values in one direction and by skew
	• The numerical centre point of all actual values in the data set	• Usually not an actual value appearing in the data set

Measures of dispersion

Knowing the mean of a set of values is not much use without knowing the amount of variation of the scores *around* the mean. If your tutor told you that the average class mark for the last essay was 56 per cent, you would need to know the kind of *variation* present in the marks to know whether your mark of 62 per cent was exceptionally good relative to the rest, or just a bit above the average.

The range

The *range* of a set of values is simply the distance in units from the top to the bottom value, hence the values must at least appear on an ordinal level scale or higher.

A simple formula to use for the range is:

top value – bottom value + 1.

In Table 7.9 (see page 156), the top value is 14 and the bottom value is 6. The range for this data set is therefore:

14 – 6 + 1 = 9.

Why add one to the difference? Suppose we were looking at the range of rank positions between 5 and 8. How many are there? Although 8 – 5 = 3, there are in fact *four* values included between 5 and 8, these being: 5, 6, 7, 8. In the case of interval measures, when we measure distance we measure to the nearest unit. A value of 173 cm is anything between 172.5 and 173.5 cm *to the nearest cm*. Hence the distance between 5 cm and 8 cm could be a *maximum* of 4 cm (4.5 to 8.5 cm).

A problem with the range is that it tells us nothing about how scores are spread out *within* the range.

The variance and standard deviation

Some scores in Table 7.9 are very close to the calculated mean and some are quite far away from it. The distance of a score from its group mean is known as its *deviation* (*d*). To find the deviation, simply take the mean from the score. Hence, the deviation for the score of 11 is:

11 – 9.8 = 1.2.

In formal terms:

$$d = x - \bar{x}$$

If we want to know how much the scores vary among themselves, we really need some sort of typical or average deviation. The *standard deviation* is something like the average deviation, but not quite. It is a calculation made because, statistically, it is a very useful value. The form of the standard deviation presented below gives a good estimate of the variation that might be expected in the *population* from which the sample was drawn. The formula for this version of the standard deviation is:

$$s = \sqrt{\left(\frac{\Sigma(x - \bar{x})^2}{N - 1}\right)}*$$

and we shall now show how this is done using our sample of memory scores in Table 7.9.

* There is also a version of this formula using only *N* rather than *N* – 1. See Coolican (1999) for an explanation

Box 7.14 Calculation of the standard deviation on the memory scores in Table 7.9

Column 1	Column 2	Column 3
Score (x)	$(x - \bar{x})$	$(x - \bar{x})^2$
6	-3.8	14.44
10	0.2	0.04
8	-1.8	3.24
8	-1.8	3.24
14	4.2	17.64
7	-2.8	7.84
11	1.2	1.44
9	-0.8	.64
13	3.2	10.24
11	1.2	1.44
8	-1.8	3.24
11	1.2	1.44
11	1.2	1.44
13	3.2	10.24
7	-2.8	7.84
$\Sigma = 147$		$\Sigma = 84.40$

$$\bar{x} = \frac{147}{15} = 9.8$$

1 Find the mean. $\bar{x} = 9.8$

2 Take the mean from each score in order to obtain each deviation score $(x - \bar{x})$. See column 2.

3 Square results of step 2 $(x - \bar{x})^2$. See column 3.

4 Add all results of step 3 $(\Sigma(x - \bar{x})^2 = 84.4)$.

5 Divide result of step 4 by $N - 1$ $(84.4 / 14 = 6.03^*)$.

6 Find the square root of step 5 $(\sqrt{6.03} = \mathbf{2.5})$.

* This value is known as the *variance* of a set of values; it is the value found *before* taking the square root of the expression on the right of the equation given on page 157 for standard deviation.

We have a mean of 9.8 and a standard deviation of 2.5. If the standard deviation were *larger* than this value, it would mean that scores in the sample were more widely spread out than they are here. A *smaller* value would indicate closer grouping of scores around the mean. For normally distributed data sets (page 160), about 70 per cent of all scores would fall between +1 and –1 standard deviations from the mean. So, based on the finding for this sample of memory scores, we would estimate that, in a large sample, 70 per cent of scores would fall between 7.3 and 12.3 (that is, between 9.8 – 2.5 and 9.8 + 2.5).

GRAPHICAL REPRESENTATIONS OF DATA

There is another way that the dispersion of scores can be summarised. This involves looking at how they are spread out, or *distributed*, by constructing a visual display of the data.

The histogram and frequency polygon

Figure 7.15 shows a *histogram* of the memory scores shown in Table 7.10. A histogram shows the *frequency* of values, that is, the number of times each value occurred in the data set. The variable being plotted must have originally been measured on at least an interval scale. If data have been collected into categories of that scale (e.g. '11–20 cigarettes per day'), then the histogram shows frequencies for each category. Overall, what should clearly be seen is the *distribution* of the set of scores.

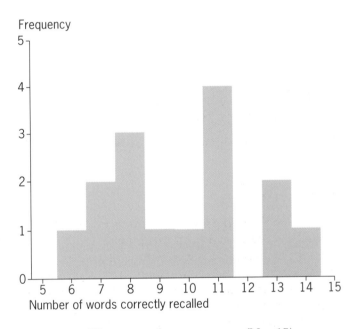

Figure 7.15 *Histogram of memory scores (N = 15)*

There are several important points to note about histograms:

- The columns of a histogram can only represent *frequencies*;
- Frequencies for the *whole* of the data set are shown;
- Empty values within the overall range must be shown. (Hence a 'gap' appears for the value '12' in Figure 7.15, indicating that no one correctly recalled 12 words);
- The columns must be the same width for the same size interval;

- Other than empty values, the overall shape of the curve is *continuous*. Columns are not separated as in a *bar chart* (see below).

Figure 7.16 is a *frequency polygon* of the same memory data. It is produced by drawing a line joining the mid-points of the columns in Figure 7.15. In addition, the lines come down to the mid-points of the empty categories at either end of the distribution.

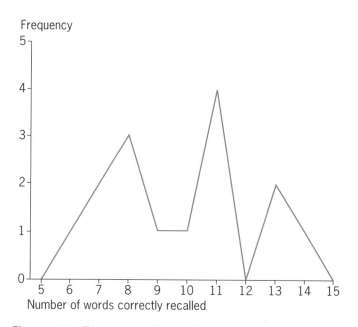

Figure 7.16 *Frequency polygon of memory scores (N = 15)*

The bar chart

The *bar chart* (of which the histogram is a special type) represents values with its bars (columns). In a histogram, these values *must* be frequencies. The columns of bar charts can represent, among other things, totals or percentages in each category, ratios, or group means (the latter being probably the most common in psychological research articles). Figure 7.17 shows the means obtained in an experiment where aggressive and non-aggressive drivers have been asked to estimate the speed of a crashing car and the question wording included the terms 'hit the bollard' or 'smashed into the bollard'.

Figure 7.18 shows the frequencies of people surveyed who reported reading a particular newspaper for more than ten minutes each day on average.

Note that on these bar charts, the columns are *separated* (although we can cluster *sub-groups* together as in Figure 7.17). The columns are separated because the categories on the *x*-axis are *discrete* (there are no values in between them). The *x*-axis categories are often qualitatively different, as in the newspaper example. At other times they might be numbers. For example, the mean memory scores for groups of people given either ten or

20 minutes to learn the words might be shown. However, these numbers (ten and 20) are still *categories*. They *define* each experimental group. There would be no group given, say, 17 minutes to learn. Therefore, it makes sense to separate the columns of the bar chart. The categories on the *x*-axis could also be selected data sets, such as accident figures for 1990 and 2000 for comparison.

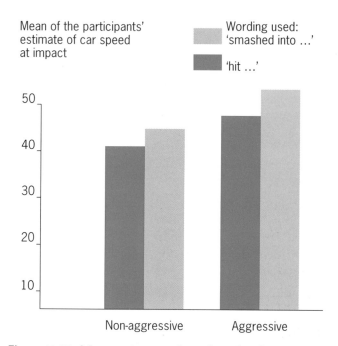

Figure 7.17 *Mean estimates of speed made when aggressive and non-aggressive drivers were told a car 'hit ...' or 'smashed into ...' a bollard*

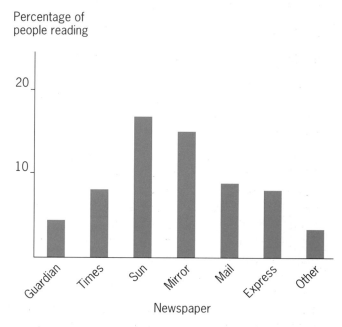

Figure 7.18 *Percentages of people spending more than ten minutes per day reading particular newspapers*

Some important points about statistical charts

When charts or 'figures' are drawn in scientific reports there are several important principles to be followed:

- **The chart must be a useful, fair and clear *summary of data*.** Therefore, a chart which has a bar for each person's score is *not* appropriate (although such charts are a common occurrence in student practical reports). Such a chart is not a *summary*, and is not useful, since the bars can be drawn in any order and the result is an erratic bunch of columns which tell the reader no more than do the raw scores.

- **The *y*-axis (the *vertical* scale, representing amount or frequency) *must* start from zero,** or else be *broken* so that the reader can clearly see that the relative lengths of columns *cannot* be compared. Newspapers often 'cheat' in this respect, but psychological researchers must not.

- **The chart must be plain and simple.** Reports should not contain charts with a multitude of pretty colours and patterns. No extra marks are ever given for aesthetic appeal and sensitive colour contrast. Chart style should not distract from the main purpose of the figure, which is to communicate the pattern in the data set.

- **The chart should have clear headings and labels.** Headings and labels should state *exactly* what is depicted, including a 'legend' where needed (see, for example, Figure 7.17, page 159), and exact units used, without the reader having to hunt through the text for an explanation. '*A chart of memory scores*' is *not* an adequate title for a graph.

- **Never rely on computer software.** Even in this sophisticated age of computer technology, many programs do not produce charts acceptable for coursework reports. Even the best require you to know exactly what you want in terms of headings, labels and legends.

The normal distribution

A frequency chart such as Figure 7.15 (see page 158) shows the *distribution* of all the values in a data set. Distributions of measures of psychological variables very often (but not always) produce this kind of shape, with many scores in the central area and only a few at the extremes. Data sets with many more values at one end of the scale than the other will produce a *skewed distribution*. One particular type of distribution is worth attention here, and is known as a *normal distribution*.

Box 7.15 The use of the normal distributon in psychological measurement

Many distributions of physical measures, such as height and weight, are *approximately* the shape of a *normal distribution*. Because the perfect normal distribution has known statistical properties, it is convenient to assume that underlying populations of such variables do in fact form a normal distribution. In biology, this might be assumed for cucumber length or daisy height. Assuming that a population *is* normally distributed, one important statistical property is that the proportions of values that will fall between 1, 2 and 3 standard deviations above and below the mean are *known*.

Figure 7.19 shows that roughly 68 per cent of all values fall between one standard deviation below and one standard deviation above the mean. Remember, this is *only* true if the distribution is normal. Because of these known statistical properties, many psychological measures (especially personality and intelligence tests) have been constructed on the *assumption* that there is an underlying normal distribution. Tests are then modified until large samples of scores do indeed form a normal distribution. Hence, it is not actually *known* that intelligence forms a normal distribution in the overall population. However, psychological measures of intelligence have been constructed to *create* a normal distribution of scores for large populations.

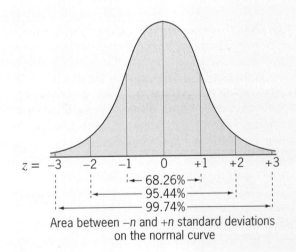

Area between −*n* and +*n* standard deviations on the normal curve

Figure 7.19 *A normal distribution*

Correlation and scattergraphs

Earlier (see page 139) the idea of a *correlation* between two variables was introduced. Statistically, a correlation gives a numerical value (between −1 and +1) to the degree of relationship between two variables. This value (known as a *correlation coefficient*) is higher the more that values on the two variables tend to vary together.

Strong negative correlation	No correlation at all	Strong positive correlation
–1.0	0.0	+1.0
Perfect negative correlation		Perfect positive correlation

Figure 7.20 *The measurement scale for correlations*

Suppose you were interested in young people's smoking behaviour. You might create a psychological scale which assesses people's general attitude towards smoking. You might ask your participants to complete the scale and also to tell you how many cigarettes they tend to smoke per day on average. Suppose you obtained the results shown in Table 7.13. Columns 2 and 3 indicate that the more cigarettes people smoke, the more positive is their attitude towards smoking. Such a relationship is known as a *positive correlation*. In a positive correlation, the higher the value of one variable, *the higher the value tends to be on the other variable*. A *negative correlation* works in the opposite direction. As values on one variable *increase*, values on the other tend to *decrease*. For example, day by day, the higher the temperature, the fewer clothes people tend to wear.

Table 7.13 *Paired scores – number of cigarettes smoked per day and smoking attitude*

Column 1	Column 2	Column 3
Participant	Average number of cigarettes smoked per day	Smoking attitude score
A	5	27
B	8	16
C	0	5
D	25	35
E	20	28
F	1	14
G	10	23
H	15	32

The results from Table 7.13 have been plotted on the *scattergraph* (or *scattergram*) shown in Figure 7.21. Note that here, a person's *two* scores are represented by *one* cross on the scattergraph, and this is placed where the line up from 'cigarettes smoked' meets the line across

from 'attitude score', as shown by the dotted line for participant E. The *shape* of this correlation, upwards from left to right, is produced because high scores are related to high scores, and low to low. When the relationship between scores is very strong, as in this case, the correlation coefficient will be near to 1. In this example, the correlation coefficient is in fact +0.95.

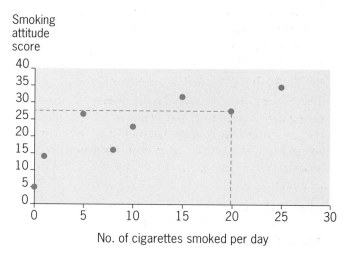

Figure 7.21 *Smoking attitude plotted against number of cigarettes smoked per day*

In a *strong negative* correlation the reverse effect occurs. High scores are paired with low scores and vice versa, producing the kind of scattergram shown in Figure 7.22 and a coefficient near to –1.

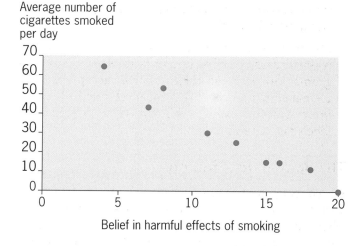

Figure 7.22 *Belief in harmful effects of smoking plotted against number of cigarettes smoked per day*

Where there is little or no correlation between variables, the coefficient will be near to zero, and the scattergraph displays points scattered in a relatively random pattern, as shown in Figure 7.23.

Average number of
cigarettes smoked
per day

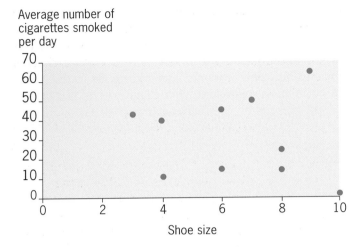

Figure 7.23 *Shoe size plotted against number of cigarettes smoked per day*

Cause and correlation

PAUSE FOR THOUGHT

Suppose that, in a sample of people, a very strong correlation was found between number of cigarettes smoked per day and attitude to smoking. Frequent smokers have a more positive attitude towards smoking, whereas infrequent smokers have a less positive attitude. Does this show that the number of cigarettes smoked *causes* a more positive or negative attitude towards smoking?

The trouble with correlational evidence is that it always brings with it a form of chicken and egg argument. Does smoking fewer cigarettes make one's attitude less favourable, or does a negative attitude cause one to smoke fewer cigarettes? There is almost always an alternative explanation of a demonstrated correlation effect. If A correlates highly with B, it could be that A causes B but it could also be that B causes A. Indeed, both A and B could be effects of some *third* variable, C. For example, perhaps a more negative attitude to smoking *and* smoking fewer cigarettes are both effects of better education, more exposure to knowledge of harmful effects and so on (see Figure 7.24).

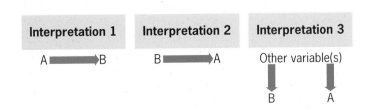

Figure 7.24 *Possible interpretations of a correlation*

ANALYSING QUALITATIVE DATA

Qualitative data are mostly either meanings created by humans (such as speech, text, pictures), or observed behaviour recorded electronically or as a verbal description. An emphasis on meaning rather than number is not new or limited to purely 'qualitative' studies. In Zimbardo *et al.*'s (1973) prison simulation study (see Chapter 6, pages 125–127), the emphasis was upon types of behaviour. In Harlow's (1959) studies of maternal deprivation in monkeys (see Chapter 3, pages 37–38), detailed records were made of the *patterns*, as well as the *frequencies*, of behaviour displayed. Although there were numerical data collected in Asch's and Milgram's conformity and obedience studies (see Chapter 6), participants were also interviewed and asked about the *reasons* for behaving as they did. Without these reasons, the quantitative data tell us that a lot more people conformed or obeyed than we would have expected. They also tell us the conditions under which more people will conform or obey. However, the *qualitative* interview data tell us what people *thought* was going on, and *why* they behaved in ways that very few people would predict. These reasons can themselves be a spur to further quantitative research to test new hypotheses. For example, Milgram moved his research equipment from its original site at Yale University to a downtown office. This was because some participants had said they respected the academic reputation of the University and assumed that professional scientists would not risk human lives (see Chapter 6, pages 121–122).

Figure 7.25 *Quantitative data can be inadequate representations of human meaning*

Two general approaches to the analysis of qualitative data

Historically, there have been two general reactions to the question of what to do with qualitative data.

- The more traditional approach has been to find some way to *turn the qualitative data into quantitative data*, usually using some form of rating system or by coding and categorising.

- Purely qualitative studies deal with the gathered data as *qualitative*. There is usually no statistical analysis and the data are reported in purely verbal terms. This *qualitative approach* is generally taken by those who are strongly opposed to the reduction of qualitative data to quantitative values, on the grounds that too much human meaning is lost in the process.

PAUSE FOR THOUGHT

What kinds of qualitative data can you imagine psychological researchers gathering, either directly from participants or from other indirect sources such as the media?

Table 7.14 is a list of several types of data and their sources that researchers might choose to deal with.

Table 7.14

Publicly available data	Data obtained from individual participants
Newspapers, magazines	Interview contents
Advertising	Story completion
Speeches	Projective tests
Television programmes	Essays
Graffiti (e.g. in toilets)	
Drawings	
Pamphlets	
Art, photographs	

Content analysis: reducing qualitative data to a quantitative level

If a researcher wishes to change qualitative data into a quantitative form it can either be **rated** or **coded** and categorised. Rating systems are used to assess observation or interview content. For instance, researchers might rate the content of interviews with parents about relationships with their children from 1 = close, to 10 = distant.

A traditional and very common approach to qualitative data analysis has been to use some form of *coding system* to categorise occurrences, thereby converting the raw qualitative data into quantitative frequencies; that is, a count is made of the number of times certain selected types of event happen. Several versions of this type of approach come under the general heading of *content analysis*.

Box 7.16 The procedure of content analysis

Suppose that a researcher is interested in the portrayal of children in television advertising. The researcher might sample a certain number of advertisements in order to develop a *coding scheme*. This will tell the researcher's assistants, who will do most of the initial analysis, what to look for in advertisements and how to categorise each event or whole advert. For example, the researcher might classify the role of each child as: consumer, playmate, problem, object of care, and so on.

The research assistants will then be trained in the coding of data and will start the categorising, usually without being aware of the hypothesis under test. This is to ensure that their own biases or expectancies do not somehow guide the data analysis in the direction that the researcher might already be expecting. It is not that researchers distrust their assistants, but that this precaution precludes any future critic from claiming that perhaps the assistants were biased.

Finally, the researcher will move towards an overall *quantitative analysis* of the data, usually in terms of frequencies and percentages. Of interest here, for example, might be the numbers of boys and girls appearing in advertisements for different types of sex-stereotyped plaything.

Purely qualitative analysis

Many contemporary researchers, especially in the areas of social and applied psychology, take a *purely qualitative* approach. Here, statistics usually do not play a large, if any, part in the research findings. What are collected are the types of qualitative data mentioned above, very often interview and observational data, which are presented entirely in qualitative form. Behaviour and speech are treated as a whole. A complete record of behaviour or talk is obtained, and analysis attempts to organise and explain these data, not by reducing them to scores, but by a certain amount of categorising and a search for common 'themes' or ideas. As far as possible, the data are kept in their original form (such as quotations from the actual interview transcript).

The *aims* of qualitative research might be any of the following:

- to explore and describe the data;
- to test hypotheses using the data;
- to generate theories from the data.

The first of these aims will be considered in detail. However, Box 7.17 briefly describes the more complex aims of qualitative research.

Box 7.17 Theory generation and hypothesis testing in qualitative research

Hypothesis testing can be carried out using qualitative data in a way similar to that in which a court case swings on evidence presented verbally by witnesses and defendants. For example, a psychologist researching management styles in a business organisation might predict that alienation would be found in departments where management is distrustful of workers, does not consult them about major changes, does not recognise positive contributions, and fails to deal with those who do not pull their weight. The forms of alienation to be found, however, would not be determined in advance with the use of a structured questionnaire, but would be identified only as they emerge through analysis of interview data.

Theory generation is a rather sophisticated form of qualitative research activity, and detailed accounts can be found in Hayes (1997) and Banister *et al.* (1994). *Grounded theorists* argue that theories can 'emerge' from the investigation and cross-referencing of all data, and that such theories are *local* to the data: they are not grand attempts to explain all similar human behaviour, but an explanation of what was found in a particular study, with some speculation towards more general explanations of similar phenomena.

Exploring and describing qualitative data

There are many different ways of analysing qualitative data but several of them, especially *grounded theory* and *conversation analysis*, will include the following initial steps in searching for themes and categories which emerge from the data. This level of exploring data has been identified by Pidgeon & Henwood (1997) as probably more appropriate for students new to psychology who are conducting relatively simple project work.

Raw qualitative data will usually be in text form, either as written observations or as transcriptions of taped interview data. Transcription is a lengthy and laborious procedure taking several times longer than the interview itself. Simple projects, therefore, might sensibly consist of 15-minute sessions only.

PAUSE FOR THOUGHT

Suppose you wanted to conduct a small research study into a comparison of the self-identities of school and college students of the same age. What interview questions might you construct, and what differences might you expect to emerge in the students' statements?

You might have included questions which asked students to discuss the extent to which:

- they feel they must act as independent learners in command of their own study schedules;
- they feel they are treated as responsible adults by their tutors;
- parents and peers treat them as independent.

Once transcribed, the data would be read through repeatedly, and analysed by searching for common or important themes or ideas that emerge from them.

Several copies of all substantial statements made by participants need to be made, or the data can be manipulated on a computer (for information on software see Coolican, 1999, or http://www.york.ac.uk/inst/ctipsych/web). The statements need to be read and re-read until it is possible to start sorting them into categories. In the example above, we might start by grouping together statements which reflect a 'parental' attitude on the part of school or college tutors. These categories of statement will be revisited later, as further analysis attempts to identify themes which emerge from them, such as factors contributing to 'autonomy', 'tutors as human', or factors reinforcing 'dependence'.

Section Summary

■ Quantitative data can be analysed at a **categorical** or **measured** level. **Categorical data** are **frequencies** grouped into categories with **nominal** values or titles. **Measured data** can be at an **ordinal** level (ranked) or **interval** level (a scale with equal units).

■ Data at a higher level may be reduced to a lower level for analysis. The **level of measurement** of data determines the limits of what kinds of analysis are possible.

■ Common measures of **central tendency** are the **mean**, **median** and **mode**, appropriate for description at the **interval**, **ordinal** and **nominal** levels respectively. The **mean** gives the most accurate measure of central tendency, but is most susceptible to extreme values in one direction. The **median** is less affected by extreme values, and gives a better estimate of centrality than the **mode**, which is the value that occurs most frequently in a data set.

- Common measures of **dispersion** are the **range** and **standard deviation**. The range is the distance in units from the top to the bottom value of a data set. The **standard deviation** is a measure of dispersion around the mean value.

- **Graphical summaries** of data sets must be useful, fair, clear and simple, enabling the reader to see what has happened without consulting accompanying text.

- The **histogram** is a summary of interval level data frequencies (singly or in categories). The **frequency polygon** is a histogram joined at the top centre of each column. **Bar charts** consist of separated columns representing summaries (frequencies, percentages, ratios, and so on) of discrete categories.

- Many human characteristics are found to be distributed according to the shape of the **normal distribution**. Some psychological characteristics are assumed to form a normal distribution, and tests are then constructed to produce such a shape across large samples. Data sets may be **skewed**, with more extreme data to one side of the mode than the other.

- The strength of a **correlation** is measured by a value between –1 and +1. A **positive correlation** refers to a relationship where variables change together in the same direction. A **negative correlation** occurs when high scores tend to be paired with low scores and vice versa. Correlational data can be plotted on a **scattergraph**.

- Correlation is not an indication of **causal direction**. When there is a correlation between A and B, it could be that A causes B, or that B causes A, or that C causes A and B independently.

- **Qualitative data** are non-numerical meanings (e.g. text, observations) gathered either as part of an otherwise quantitative study, or as part of a purely qualitative study, such as participant observation or interview.

- In the more traditional analysis of qualitative data known as **content analysis**, codes are created from pilot data. All data are then coded, and the final analysis presents work on the frequencies or percentages in the coded categories.

- In purely qualitative work, data are analysed at a **qualitative level**. A popular method for this is **grounded theory**, where data are thoroughly searched and cross-referenced with the aim of detecting 'emerging themes' and categories which will eventually account for all the data gathered.

Self-Assessment Questions

1 A psychologist asked the same group of children to draw a picture of Santa Claus and his sack both before and after Christmas. On each occasion, the children were tested at the same time of day, in the same place, and with exactly the same instructions. A measure was taken of the area taken up by Santa's sack. It was found that the mean area *before* Christmas was 16.5 cm^2, whereas the mean area *after* Christmas was 11.4 cm^2. The researcher had predicted that children's schemas of Christmas, and their expectations of presents, would lead to the drawing of bigger sacks before Christmas than after it.

  a Identify the type of experimental design used in this research study. *(1 mark)*

  b Describe **one** strength and **one** weakness of this type of experimental design. *(2 marks + 2 marks)*

  c State the independent variable and dependent variable used in this study. *(1 mark + 1 mark)*

  d Explain why the children were given exactly the same instructions each time they were tested. *(2 marks)*

  e What is meant by the term 'mean' as a descriptive statistic? *(2 marks)*

  f Describe **one** disadvantage of using the mean as a descriptive statistic. *(2 marks)*

  g Explain how the psychologist's expectations about the research may have influenced the results. *(2 marks)*

2 A researcher made an enquiry into the forms of punishment and discipline that a sample of mothers tended to use with their pre-school children. Each mother was interviewed for 20 minutes. The resulting information was recorded on tape and treated as qualitative data. Each mother was also asked to complete two highly reliable questionnaires. One questionnaire measured the mother's attitude to physical punishment. The other assessed the degree to which she recalled being physically punished by her own parents. It was found that there was a correlation of +0.8 between being positive about physical punishment and the degree of being punished as a child.

  a Describe **one** strength and **one** weakness of using interviews in psychological research. *(2 marks + 2 marks)*

  b Explain why it is important for other researchers to be given exact information about the nature of the sample of mothers used in this investigation. *(3 marks)*

  c Explain what is meant by the term 'qualitative data'. *(2 marks)*

d Briefly describe **one** method by which the qualitative data gathered in this study could be analysed. *(3 marks)*

e Explain what is meant by calling a questionnaire 'highly reliable'. *(2 marks)*

f State whether a correlation of +0.8 would be considered weak or strong. *(1 mark)*

CONCLUSIONS

This chapter has looked at the range of basic research methods open to psychologists in their investigation of the nature and causes of human behaviour and experience. Causes are proposed through theories. As in all empirical sciences, evidence to support theories is gathered by testing hypothetical predictions in the real world. Psychologists can set up experiments, observe people or question them.

The experiment is seen as the most effective method in leading to conclusions about cause and effect. However, its use in psychology has been criticised because it can produce rather artificial effects which have little or no application in the real world of human behaviour and interaction. Other methods, although less tightly controlled, might generate more realistic and representative findings.

All methods have strengths and weaknesses. Many of these concern the number of ways in which a false conclusion about effects could be drawn because of the operation of confounding variables, such as participant expectancies, researcher bias, sampling, practice and social desirability. Other limitations come from the level, narrowness or richness of the data gathered and from ethical considerations.

The chapter also looked at some of the ways in which quantitative data can be presented fairly and clearly. It also considered the nature and use of qualitative data, noting that there is a growing use of qualitative research in contemporary psychology.

References

ABERNATHY, E.M. (1940) The effect of changed environmental conditions upon the results of college examinations. *Journal of Psychology*, 10, 293–301.

ABRAMS, D., WETHERELL, M., COCHRANE, S., HOGG, M.A. & TURNER, J.C. (1990) Knowing what to think by knowing who you are: Self-categorization and the nature of norm formation. *British Journal of Social Psychology*, 29, 97–119.

ADLER, A. (1927) *The Practice and Theory of Individual Psychology*. New York: Harcourt Brace Jovanovich.

AINSWORTH, M.D.S. (1967) *Infancy in Uganda: Infant Care and the Growth of Love*. Baltimore, MD: Johns Hopkins University Press.

AINSWORTH, M.D.S., BELL, S.M.V. & STAYTON, D.J. (1971) Individual differences in strange-situation behaviour of one-year-olds. In H.R. Schaffer (Ed.) *The Origins of Human Social Relations*. New York: Academic Press.

AINSWORTH, M.D.S., BLEHAR, M.C., WATERS, E. & WALL, S. (1978) *Patterns of Attachment: A Psychological Study of the Strange Situation*. Hillsdale, NJ: Lawrence Erlbaum Associates Inc.

AINSWORTH, M.D.S. & WITTIG, B.A. (1969) Attachment and exploratory behaviour of 1-year-olds in a strange situation. In B.M. Foss (Ed.) *Determinants of Infant Behaviour*, Vol. 4. London: Methuen.

ALBERGE, D. (1999) Dancers take lessons in eating. *The Times*, 18 August, 11.

ALLEN, V.L. & LEVINE, J.M. (1971) Social support and conformity: The role of independent assessment of reality. *Journal of Experimental Social Psychology*, 7, 48–58.

ALLPORT, G.W. & POSTMAN, L. (1947) *The Psychology of Rumour*. New York: Holt, Rinehart & Winston.

AMATO, P.R. (1993) Children's adjustment to divorce: Theories, hypotheses and empirical support. *Journal of Marriage & the Family*, 55, 23–28.

ANCONA, L. & PAREYSON, R. (1968) Contributo allo studio della a aggressione: la dinimica della obbedienza distructiva. *Archivio di Psicologia Neurologia e Psichiatria*, 29, 340–372.

ANDERSON, J.R. (1995) *Cognitive Psychology and its Implications*. New York: W.H. Freeman & Company.

ANDERSON, L.P. (1991) Acculturative stress: A theory of relevance to black Americans. *Clinical Psychology Review*, 11, 685–702.

ANSHEL, M.H. (1996) Effects of chronic aerobic exercise and progressive relaxation on motor performance and affect following acute stress. *Behavioural Medicine*, 21, 186–196.

ARENDT, H. (1965) *Eichmann in Jerusalem: A Report on the Banality of Evil*. New York: Viking.

ARONSON, E. (1988) *The Social Animal* (5th edition). New York: Freeman.

ARONSON, E. (1992) *The Social Animal* (6th edition). New York: Freeman.

ASCH, S.E. (1951) Effect of group pressure upon the modification and distortion of judgements. In H. Guetzkow (Ed.) *Groups, Leadership and Men*. Pittsburgh, PA: Carnegie Press.

ASCH, S.E. (1952) *Social Psychology*. Englewood Cliffs, NJ: Prentice Hall.

ASCH, S.E. (1955) Opinions and social pressure. *Scientific American*, 193, 31–35.

ASCH, S.E. (1956) Studies of independence and submission to group pressure: 1: A minority of one against a unanimous majority. *Psychological Monographs*, 70, Whole No. 416.

ASKEVOLD, F. & HEIBERG, A. (1979) Anorexia nervosa: Two cases in discordant MZ twins. *Psychological Monographs*, 70, 1–70.

ATKINSON, R.C. & SHIFFRIN, R.M. (1968) Human memory: A proposed system and its control processes. In K.W. Spence & J.T. Spence (Eds) *The Psychology of Learning and Motivation*, Volume 2. London: Academic Press.

ATKINSON, R.C. & SHIFFRIN, R.M. (1971) The control of short-term memory. *Scientific American*, 224, 82–90.

ATKINSON, R.L., ATKINSON, R.C., SMITH, E.E. & BEM, D.J. (1993) *Introduction to Psychology* (11th edition). London: Harcourt Brace Jovanovich.

BADDELEY, A.D. (1966) The influence of acoustic and semantic similarity on long-term memory for word sequences. *Quarterly Journal of Experimental Psychology*, 18, 302–309.

BADDELEY, A.D. (1976) *The Psychology of Memory*. New York: Basic Books.

BADDELEY, A.D. (1981) The concept of working memory: A view of its current state and probable future development. *Cognition*, 10, 17–23.

BADDELEY, A.D. (1990) *Human Memory*. Hove: Lawrence Erlbaum Associates.

BADDELEY, A.D. (1995) Memory. In C.C. French & A.M. Colman (Eds) *Cognitive Psychology*. London: Longman.

BADDELEY, A.D. (1996) Exploring the central executive. *Quarterly Journal of Experimental Psychology*, 49A, 5–28.

BADDELEY, A.D (1997) *Human Memory: Theory and Practice* (revised edition). East Sussex: Psychology Press.

BADDELEY, A.D. & HITCH, G. (1974) Working memory. In G.H. Bower (Ed.) *Recent Advances in Learning and Motivation*, Volume 8. New York: Academic Press.

BADDELEY, A.D., THOMSON, N. & BUCHANAN, M. (1975) Word length and the structure of short-term memory. *Journal of Verbal Learning & Verbal Behaviour*, 14, 575–589.

BANDURA, A. (1969) *Principles of Behaviour Modification*. New York: Holt, Rinehart & Winston.

BANDURA, A. (1984) Recycling misconceptions of perceived self-efficacy. *Cognitive Therapy and Research*, 8, 231–235.

BANISTER, P., BURMAN, E., PARKER, I., TAYLOR, M. & TINDALL, C. (1994) *Qualitative Methods in Psychology*. Buckingham: Open University.

BANUAZIZI, A. & MOHAVEDI, S. (1975) Interpersonal dynamics in a simulated prison: A methodological analysis. *American Psychologist*, 30, 152–160.

BARTLETT, F.C. (1932) *Remembering*. Cambridge: Cambridge University Press.

BAUMRIND, D. (1964) Some thoughts on the ethics of research: After reading Milgram's behavioural study of obedience. *American Psychologist*, 19, 421–423.

BAYDAR, N. & BROOKS-GUNN, J. (1991) Effects of maternal employment and child-care arrangements on pre-schoolers' cognitive and behavioural outcomes. *Developmental Psychology*, 27, 932–945.

BECK, A.T. (1967) *Depression: Causes and Treatment*. Philadelphia: University of Philadelphia Press.

BECK, A.T. (1974) The development of depression: A cognitive model. In R.J. Friedman & M.M. Katz (Eds) *The Psychology of Depression: Contemporary Theory and Research*. New York: Wiley.

BECK, A.T. & WEISHAAR, M.E. (1989) Cognitive therapy. In R.J. Corsini & D. Wedding (Eds) *Current Psychotherapies*. Itasca, ILL: Peacock.

BEE, H. (1992) *The Developing Child* (7th edition). New York: HarperCollins.

BEGLEY, T. (1998) Coping strategies as predictors of employee distress and turnover after organisational consolidation: A longitudinal analysis. *Journal of Occupational & Organisational Psychology*, 71, 305–330.

BEKERIAN, D.A. & BOWERS, J.M. (1983) Eye-witness testimony: Were we misled? *Journal of Experimental Psychology: Learning, Memory & Cognition*, 9, 139–145.

BELL, S.M. & AINSWORTH, M.D.S. (1972) Infant crying and maternal responsiveness. *Child Development*, 43, 1171–1190.

BELSKY, J. & ROVINE, M.J. (1988) Nonmaternal care in the first year of life and the infant–parent attachment. *Child Development*, 59, 157–167.

BERKOWITZ, L. (1993) *Aggression: Its Causes, Consequences and Control*. New York: McGraw-Hill.

BICKMAN, L. (1974) The social power of a uniform. *Journal of Applied Social Psychology*, 1, 47–61.

BLACKMAN, D.E. (1980) Images of man in contemporary behaviourism. In A.J. Chapman and D.M. Jones (Eds) *Models of Man*. Leicester: British Psychological Society.

BOAST, N., COKER, E. & WAKELING, A. (1992) Anorexia nervosa of late onset. *British Journal of Psychiatry*, 160, 257–260.

BOND, R.A. & SMITH, P.B. (1996) Culture and conformity: A meta-analysis of studies using the Asch's (1952b, 1956) line judgement task. *Psychological Bulletin*, 119, 111–137.

BOOTH, A. & AMATO, P.R. (1994) Parental marital quality, parental divorce and relations with parents. *Journal of Marriage & the Family*, 55, 21–34.

BOOTH-KEWLEY, S. & FRIEDMAN, H. (1987) Psychological predictors of heart disease: A quantitative review. *Psychological Bulletin*, 101, 343–362.

BORNSTEIN, M.H. (1989) Sensitive periods in development: Structural characteristics and causal interpretations. *Psychological Bulletin*, 105, 179–197.

BOWER, G.H. & SPRINGSTON, F. (1970) Pauses as recoding points in letter series. *Journal of Experimental Psychology*, 83, 421–430.

BOWLBY, J. (1946) *Forty-Four Juvenile Thieves*. London: Balliere Tindall and Cox.

BOWLBY, J. (1951) *Maternal Care and Mental Health*. Geneva: World Health Organisation.

BOWLBY, J. (1969) *Attachment and Loss*. Volume 1: *Attachment*. Harmondsworth: Penguin.

BOWLBY, J. (1973) *Attachment and Loss*. Volume 2: *Separation*. Harmondsworth: Penguin.

BOWLBY, J., AINSWORTH, M., BOSTON, M. & ROSENBLUTH, D. (1956) The effects of mother-child separation: A follow-up study. *British Journal of Medical Psychology*, 29, 211.

BRADLEY, L.A. (1995) Chronic benign pain. In D. Wedding (Ed.) *Behaviour and Medicine* (2nd edition). St Louis, MO: Mosby-Year Book.

BRANSFORD, J.D., FRANKS, J.J., MORRIS, C.D. & STEIN, B.S. (1979) Some general constraints on learning and memory research. In L.S. Cernak & F.I.M. Craik (Eds) *Levels of Processing in Human Memory*. Hillside, NJ: Erlbaum.

BREHM, J.W. (1966) *A Theory of Psychological Reactance*. New York: Academic Press.

BRIGHAM, J. & MALPASS, R.S. (1985) The role of experience and contact in the recognition of faces of own- and other-race persons. *Journal of Social Issues*, 41, 139–155.

BRITISH PSYCHOLOGICAL SOCIETY (1978) Ethical principles for research on human subjects. *Bulletin of the British Psychological Society*, 31, 48–49.

BRITISH PSYCHOLOGICAL SOCIETY (1983) *Guidelines for the professional practice of clinical psychology*. Leicester: British Psychological Society.

BRITISH PSYCHOLOGICAL SOCIETY (1985) The Committee of the Experimental Psychological Society. Leicester: *Guidelines for the use of animals in research*.

BRITISH PSYCHOLOGICAL SOCIETY (1990) Ethical principles for conducting research with human participants. *The Psychologist*, 3 (6), 269–272.

BRITISH PSYCHOLOGICAL SOCIETY (1993) Ethical principles for conducting research with human participants (revised). *The Psychologist*, 6 (1), 33–35.

BRITISH PSYCHOLOGICAL SOCIETY (1995) *Recovered Memories: The Report of the Working Party of the British Psychological Society*. Leicester: British Psychological Society.

BROWN, H. (1985) *People, Groups and Society*. Milton Keynes: Open University Press.

BROWN, J.A. (1958) Some tests of the decay theory of immediate memory. *Quarterly Journal of Experimental Psychology*, 10, 12–21.

BROWN, L.S. (1997) Ethics in psychology: Cui bono? In D. Fox & I. Prilleltensky (Eds) *Critical Psychology: An Introduction*. London: Sage.

BROWN, R. (1986) *Social Psychology: The Second Edition*. New York: Free Press.

BROWN, R. & KULIK, J. (1977) Flashbulb memories. *Cognition*, 5, 73–99.

BROWN, R. & KULIK, J. (1982) Flashbulb memories. In U. Neisser (Ed.) *Memory Observed*. San Francisco: Freeman.

BROWN, R. & McNEILL, D. (1966) The 'tip-of-the-tongue' phenomenon. *Journal of Verbal Learning & Verbal Behaviour*, 5, 325–337.

BROWN, R.J. (1988) Intergroup relations. In M. Hewstone, W. Stroebe, J.P. Codol & G.M. Stephenson (Eds) *Introduction to Social Psychology*. Oxford: Blackwell.

BROWN, R.J. (1996) Intergroup relations. In M. Hewstone, W. Stroebe & G.M. Stephenson (Eds) *Introduction to Social Psychology* (2nd edition). Oxford: Blackwell.

BRUCE, V. (1998) Fleeting images of shade: Identifying people caught on video. *The Psychologist*, 11(7), 331–337.

BRUCH, H. (1978) *Eating Disorders: Obesity, Anorexia Nervosa and the Person Within*. New York: Basic Books.

BRUCH, H. (1991) The sleeping beauty: Escape from change. In S.L. Greenspan & G.H. Pollock (Eds) *The Course of Life: Volume 4 Adolescence*. Madison, CT: International Universities Press.

BURLEY, P.M. & McGUINESS, J. (1977) Effects of social intelligence on the Milgram paradigm. *Psychological Reports,* 40, 767–770.

BURNE, J. (1999) Don't worry, be happy. *The Guardian* (Supplement), August 24, 8–9.

BUSHMAN, B. (1984) Perceived symbols of authority and their influence on compliance. *Journal of Applied Social Psychology,* 14, 501–508.

BUSS, A.H. & PLOMIN, R. (1984) *Temperament: Early Developing Personality Traits.* Hillsdale, NJ: Erlbaum.

CANNON, W.B. (1927) The James-Lange theory of emotions: A critical reexamination and an alternative theory. *American Journal of Psychology,* 39, 106–124.

CARLSON, N.R. (1987) *Discovering Psychology.* London: Allyn & Bacon.

CHANCE, P. (1984) I'm OK, you're a little odd. *Psychology Today,* September, 18–19

CHEN, P.Y. & SPECTOR, P.E. (1992) Relationships of work stressors and aggression, withdrawal, theft and substance abuse: An exploratory study. *Journal of Occupational & Organisational Psychology,* 65, 177–184.

CHISOLM, K., CARTER, M.C., AMES, E.W.& MORISON, S.J. (1995) Attachment security and indiscriminately friendly behaviour in children adopted from Romanian orphanages. *Development & Psychopathology,* 7, 283–294.

CHRISTENSEN, L. (1988) Deception in psychological research: When is its use justified? *Personality & Social Psychology,* 14, 665–675.

CLARK, K.E. & MILLER, G.A. (1970) (Eds) *Psychology: Behavioural and Social Sciences Survey Committee.* Englewood Cliffs, NJ: Prentice Hall.

CLARK, M.S., MILLBERG, S. & ERBER, R. (1987) Arousal and state dependent memory: Evidence and some implications for understanding social judgements and social behaviour. In K. Fiedler & J.P. Forgas (Eds) *Affect, Cognition and Social Behaviour.* Toronto: Hogrefe.

CLARKE, A.D.B. & CLARKE, A.M. (1998) Early experience and the life path. *The Psychologist,* 11(9), 433–436.

CLARKE-STEWART, K.A. (1989) Infant day care: Maligned or malignant? *American Psychologist,* 44, 266–273.

CLARKE-STEWART, K.A. (1991) A home is not a school. *Journal of Social Issues,* 47, 105–123.

CNATTINGIUS, S., HULTMAN, C.M., DAHL, M. & SPAREN, P. (1999) Very preterm birth, birth trauma, and the risk of anorexia nervosa among girls. *Archives of General Psychiatry,* 56, 634–638.

COHEN, F. & LAZARUS, R. (1979) Coping with the stresses of illness. In G.C. Stone, F. Cohen & N.E. Ader (Eds) *Health Psychology: A Handbook.* San Francisco, CA: Jossey-Bass.

COHEN, G. (1993) Everyday memory and memory systems: The experimental approach. In G. Cohen, G. Kiss & M. Levoi (Eds) *Memory: Current Issues* (2nd edition). Buckingham: Open University Press.

COHEN, S., FRANK, E., DOYLE, W.J., SKONER, D.P., RABIN, B.S. & GWALTNEY, J.M. (1998) Types of stressor that increase susceptibility to the common cold in healthy adults. *Health Psychology,* 17, 214–223.

COLLETT, P. (1994) *Foreign Bodies.* London: Simon & Schuster.

COLMAN, A.M. (1987) *Facts, Fallacies and Frauds in Psychology.* London: Unwin Hyman.

COMER, R.J. (1998) *Abnormal Psychology* (3rd edition). New York: Freeman.

CONRAD, R. (1964) Acoustic confusion in immediate memory. *British Journal of Psychology,* 55, 75–84.

COOLICAN, H. (1994) *Research Methods and Statistics in Psychology* (2nd edition). London: Hodder & Stoughton.

COOLICAN, H. (1999) *Research Methods and Statistics in Psychology* (3rd edition). London: Hodder & Stoughton.

COOLICAN, H., CASSIDY, T., CHERCHER, A., HARROWER J., PENNY, G., SHARP, R., WALLEY, M. & WESTBURY, T. (1996) *Applied Psychology.* London: Hodder & Stoughton.

COOPER, P.J. (1995) Eating disorders. In A.A. Lazarus & A.M. Colman (Eds) *Abnormal Psychology.* London: Longman.

COOPER, R.S., ROTIMI, C.N. & WARD, R. (1999) The puzzle of hypertension in African-Americans. *Scientific American,* 253, 36–43.

COREY, G. (1991) *Theory and Practice of Counselling and Psychotherapy.* Pacific Groves, CA: Brooks/Cole.

CRAIK, F.I.M. & LOCKHART, R. (1972) Levels of processing. *Journal of Verbal Learning & Verbal Behaviour,* 11, 671–684.

CRAIK, F.I.M. & TULVING, E. (1975) Depth of processing and retention of words in episodic memory. *Journal of Experimental Psychology: General,* 104, 268–294.

CRAIK, F.I.M. & WATKINS, M.J. (1973) The role of rehearsal in short-term memory. *Journal of Verbal Learning & Verbal Behaviour,* 12, 599–607.

CRAMB, A. (1997) Stress can be good for the heart, says study. *The Daily Telegraph,* 19 September, 11.

CRISP, A.H. (1967) Anorexia nervosa. *Hospital Medicine,* 1, 713–718.

CRISP, A.H. (1983) Regular reviews: Anorexia nervosa. *British Medical Journal,* 287, 855–858.

CRUTCHFIELD, R.S. (1954) A new technique for measuring individual differences in conformity to group judgement. *Proceedings of the Invitational Conference on Testing Problems,* 69–74.

CRUTCHFIELD, R.S. (1955) Conformity and character. *American Psychologist,* 10, 191–198.

DALEY, A.J. & PARFITT, G. (1996) Good health – Is it worth it? Mood states, physical well-being, job satisfaction and absenteeism in members and non-members of a British corporate health and fitness club. *Journal of Occupational & Organisational Psychology,* 69, 121–134.

DAVIES, T. (1994) Bless his cotton socks. *The Daily Telegraph,* 17 September, 42.

DAVISON, G. & NEALE, J. (1994) *Abnormal Psychology* (6th edition). New York: Wiley.

DE GROOT, A.D. (1966) Perception and memory versus thought: Some old ideas and recent findings. In B. Kleinmuntz (Ed.) *Problem-Solving: Research, Method and Theory.* New York: Wiley.

DEUTSCH, M. & GERARD, H.B. (1955) A study of normative and informational social influence upon individual judgement. *Journal of Abnormal & Social Psychology,* 51, 629–636.

DEVLIN REPORT (1976) Report to the Secretary of State for the Home Development of the Departmental Committee on Evidence of Identification in Criminal Cases. London: HMSO.

EAGLY, A.H. & STEFFEN, V.J. (1984) Gender stereotypes stem from the distribution of men and women into social roles. *Journal of Personality & Social Psychology,* 46, 735–754.

EBBINGHAUS, H. (1885) *On Memory.* Leipzig: Duncker.

ELLIOTT, B.J. & RICHARDS, M.P.M. (1991) Children and divorce: Educational performance before and after parental separation. *International Journal of Law & the Family,* 5, 258–278.

EMMETT, S. (1996) Bulimia cases treble in just five years. *The Independent on Sunday,* 1 December, 1.

ERIKSON, E.H. (1950) *Childhood and Society.* New York: Norton.

EVANS, P., CLOW, A. & HUCKLEBRIDGE, F. (1997) Stress and the immune system. *The Psychologist*, 10, 303–307.

EYSENCK, H.J. (1985) *Decline and Fall of the Freudian Empire*. Harmondsworth: Penguin.

EYSENCK, H.J. & WILSON, G.D. (1973) (Eds) *The Experimental Study of Freudian Theories*. London: Methuen.

EYSENCK, M.W. (1986) Working memory. In G. Cohen, M.W. Eysenck & M.A. Le Voi (Eds) *Memory: A Cognitive Approach*. Milton Keynes: Open University Press.

EYSENCK, M.W. (1993) *Principles of Cognitive Psychology*. Hove: Erlbaum.

EYSENCK, M.W. & KEANE, M.J. (1995) *Cognitive Psychology: A Student's Handbook* (3rd edition). Hove: Erlbaum.

FAIRBURN, C.G., SHAFRAN, R. & COOPER, Z. (1999) A cognitive behavioural theory of anorexia nervosa. *Behaviour Research and Therapy*, 37, 1–13.

FANCHER, R.E. (1996) *Pioneers of Psychology* (3rd edition). New York: Norton.

FEARN, N. (1999) Anorexia via TV. *The Independent*, 27 May, 5.

FESTINGER, L. (1954) A theory of social comparison processes. *Human Relations*, 7, 117–140.

FISKE, S.T. & TAYLOR, S.E. (1991) *Social Cognition* (2nd edition). New York: McGraw-Hill.

FOMBONNE, E. (1995) Anorexia nervosa: No evidence of an increase. *British Journal of Psychiatry*, 166, 462–471.

FRANKENHAUSER, M. (1983) The sympathetic–adrenal and pituitary–adrenal response to challenge: Comparison between the sexes. In T.M. Dembroski, T.H. Schmidt & G. Blumchen (Eds) *Behavioural Bases of Coronary Heart Disease*. Basle: S. Karger.

FRANKENHAUSER, M., LUNDBERG, U. & CHESNEY, M. (1991) *Women, Work and Health: Stress and Opportunities*. New York: Plenum.

FRANKO, D.L. & OMORI, M. (1999) Subclinical eating disorders in adolescent women: A test of the continuity hypothesis and its psychological correlates. *Journal of Adolescence*, 22, 389–396.

FREUD, S. (1923/1984) *The Ego and the Id*. Pelican Freud Library (11). Harmondsworth: Penguin.

FREUD, S. (1926) Inhibitions, symptoms and anxiety. In *Standard Edition of the Complete Psychological Works of Sigmund Freud*, Volume 20. London: Hogarth Press.

FREUD, S. (1949) *An Outline of Psycho-analysis*. London: Hogarth Press.

FRIEDMAN, M. & ROSENMAN, R.H. (1974) *Type A Behaviour and Your Heart*. New York: Harper Row.

GALE, A. (1995) Ethical issues in psychological research. In A.M. Colman (Ed.) *Psychological research methods and statistics*. London: Longman.

GARNER, D.M. (1986) Cognitive–behavioural therapy for eating disorders. *The Clinical Psychologist*, 39, 36–39.

GARNER, D.M., GARFINKEL, P.E., SCHWARZ, D. & THOMPSON, M. (1980) Cultural expectations of thinness in women. *Psychological Reports*, 47, 483–491.

GATHERCOLE, S.E. & BADDELEY, A.D. (1990) Phonological memory deficits in language-disordered children: Is there a causal connection? *Journal of Memory & Language*, 29, 336–360.

GILBERT, S.J. (1981) Another look at the Milgram obedience studies: The role of the graduated series of shocks. *Personality and Social Psychology Bulletin*, 7, 690–695.

GILHOOLY, K. (1996) Working memory and thinking. *The Psychologist*, 9, 82.

GLANZER, M. & CUNITZ, A.R. (1966) Two storage mechanisms in free recall. *Journal of Verbal Learning & Verbal Behaviour*, 5, 928–935.

GLASS, D.C. & SINGER, J. (1972) *Urban Stress*. New York: Academic Press.

GODDEN, D. & BADDELEY, A.D. (1975) Context-dependent memory in two natural environments: On land and under water. *British Journal of Psychology*, 66, 325–331.

GOLDFARB, W. (1943) The effects of early institutional care on adult personality. *Journal of Experimental Education*, 12, 106–129.

GORWOOD, P., BOUVARD, M., MOUREN-SIMIONI, M.C., KIPMAN, A. & ADES, J. (1998) Genetics and anorexia nervosa: A review of candidate genes. *Psychiatric Genetics*, 8, 1–12.

GOWERS, S. & NORTH, C. (1999) Difficulties in family functioning and adolescent anorexia nervosa. *British Journal of Psychiatry*, 174, 63–66.

GREEN, S. (1994) *Principles of Biopsychology*. Sussex: Lawrence Erlbaum Associates.

GREER, A., MORRIS, T. & PETTINGDALE, K.W. (1979) Psychological response to breast cancer: Effect on outcome. *The Lancet*, 13, 785–787.

GROOME, D., DEWART, H., ESGATE, A., GURNEY, K., KEMP, R. & TOWELL, N. (1999) *An Introduction to Cognitive Psychology : Processes and Disorders*. London: Psychology Press.

GROSS, R., McILVEEN, R., COOLICAN, H., CLAMP, A. & RUSSELL, J. (2000) *Psychology: A New Introduction for A Level* (2nd edition). London: Hodder & Stoughton.

HALMI, K.A. (1995) Current concepts and definitions. In G.Szmukler, C. Dare & J. Treasure (Eds) *Handbook of Eating Disorders: Theory, Treatment and Research*. Chichester: Wiley.

HAMILTON, K. & WALLER, G. (1993) Media influences on body size estimation in anorexia and bulimia: An experimental study. *British Journal of Psychiatry*, 162, 837–840.

HAMILTON, V.L. (1978) Obedience and responsibility: A jury simulation. *Journal of Personality & Social Psychology*, 36, 126–146.

HAMPSON, P.J. & MORRIS, P.E. (1996) *Understanding Cognition*. Oxford: Blackwell.

HARBURG, E., ERFURT, J.C., HAUENSTEIN, L.S., CHAPE, C., SCHULL, W.J. & SCHORK, M.A. (1973) Socioecological stress, suppressed hostility, skin colour, and black-white male blood pressure: Detroit. *Psychosomatic Medicine*, 35, 276–296.

HARLOW, H.F. (1959) Love in infant monkeys. *Scientific American*, 200, 68–74.

HARLOW, H.F. & SUOMI, S.J. (1970) The nature of love – simplified. *American Psychologist*, 25, 161–168.

HARLOW, H.F. & ZIMMERMAN, R.R. (1959) Affectional responses in the infant monkey. *Science*, 130, 421–432.

HARROWER, J. (1998) *Applying Psychology to Crime*. London: Hodder & Stoughton.

HARTLEY, J. & BRANTHWAITE, A. (1997) Earning a crust. *Psychology Review*, 3 (3), 24–26.

HARTLEY, J. & BRANTHWAITE, A. (2000) Prologue: the roles and skills of applied psychologists. In J Hartley & A Braithwaite (Eds) *The Applied Psychologist* (2nd edition). Buckingham: Open University Press.

HASSETT, J. & WHITE, M. (1989) *Psychology in Perspective* (2nd edition). Cambridge: Harper & Row.

HAY, P.J., GILCHRIST, P.N., BEN-TOVIM, D.I., KALUCY, R.S. & WALKER, M.K. (1998) Eating disorders revisited. II: Bulimia nervosa and related syndromes. *Medical Journal of Australia*, 169, 488–491.

HAYES, N. J. (1997) *Doing Qualitative Analysis in Psychology*. Hove: Psychology Press.

HAYWARD, S. (1996) *Applying Psychology to Organisations*. London: Hodder & Stoughton.

HAYWARD, S. (1998) Stress, health and psychoneuroimmunology. *Psychology Review*, 5 (1), 16–19.

HAYWARD, S. (1999) Stress, health and the immune system. *Psychology Review*, 5 (3), 26–27.

HEBB, D.O. (1949) *The Organisation of Behaviour*. New York: Wiley.

HENWOOD, K. & PIDGEON, N. (1995) Grounded theory and psychological research. *The Psychologist*, 8(3), 115–8.

HETHERINGTON, E.M. & STANLEY-HAGAN, M. (1999) The adjustment of children with divorced parents: A risk and resiliency perspective. *Journal of Child Psychology & Psychiatry*, 40(1), 129–140.

HINNEY, A., HERRMANN, H., LOHR, T., ROSENKRANZ, K., ZIEGLER, A., LEMKUHL, G., POUSTKA, F., SCHMIDT, M.H., MAYER, H., SIEGFRIED, W., REMSCHMIDT, H. & HEBEBRAND, J. (1999) No evidence for an involvement of alleles of polymorphisms in the serotonin1Dbeta and 7 receptor genes in obesity, underweight or anorexia nervosa. *International Journal of Obesity & Related Metabolic Disorders*, 23, 760–763.

HIROTO, D.S. & SELIGMAN, M.E.P. (1975) Generality of learned helplessness in man. *Journal of Personality & Social Psychology*, 31, 311–327.

HIRSCH, H. (1995) *Genocide and the Politics of Memory*. Chapel Hill, NC: The University of North Carolina Press.

HODGES, J. & TIZARD, B. (1989) Social and family relationships of ex-institutional adolescents. *Journal of Child Psychology & Psychiatry*, 30, 77–97.

HOFLING, K.C., BROTZMAN, E., DALRYMPLE, S., GRAVES, N. & PIERCE, C.M. (1966) An experimental study in the nurse–physician relationships. *Journal of Nervous & Mental Disorders*, 143, 171–180.

HOGG, M.A. & VAUGHAN, G.M. (1998) *Social Psychology* (2nd edition). Hemel Hempstead: Prentice Hall Europe.

HOLLAND, A.J., HALL, A., MURRAY, R., RUSSELL, G.F.M. & CRISP, A.H. (1984) Anorexia nervosa: A study of 34 twin pairs and one set of triplets. *British Journal of Psychiatry*, 145, 414–418.

HOLMES, D.S. (1994) *Abnormal Psychology* (2nd edition). New York: HarperCollins.

HOLMES, T.H. & RAHE, R.H. (1967) The social readjustment rating scale. *Journal of Psychosomatic Research*, 11, 213–218.

HORWOOD, L.J. & FERGUSSON, D.M. (1999) A longitudinal study of maternal labour force participation and child academic achievement. *Journal of Child Psychology & Psychiatry*, 40(7), 1013–1024.

HOUSTON, J.P., HAMMEN, C., PADILLA, A. & BEE, H. (1991) *Invitation to Psychology* (3rd edition). London: Harcourt Brace Jovanovich.

HUNTER, I.M.L. (1964) *Memory, Facts and Fallacies*. (2nd edition) Harmondsworth: Penguin.

JACOBSON, E. (1938) *Progressive Relaxation*. Chicago: University of Chicago Press.

JAHODA, M. (1958) *Current Concepts of Positive Mental Health*. New York: Basic Books.

JAMES, W. (1890) *The Principles of Psychology*. New York: Henry Holt & Company.

JENKINS, J.G. & DALLENBACH, K.M. (1924) Oblivescence during sleep and waking. *American Journal of Psychology*, 35, 605–612.

JOHNSON, J.H. & SARASON, I.G. (1978) Life stress, depression and anxiety: Internal/external control as a moderator variable. *Journal of Psychosomatic Research*, 22, 205–208.

JONES, M.C. (1925) A laboratory study of fear: The case of Peter. *Pedagogical Seminary*, 31, 308–315.

JUDD, J (1997) Working mothers need not feel guilty. *Independent on Sunday*, 27 November, 5.

JUNG, C.G. (1964) (Ed.) *Man and his Symbols*. London: Aldus-Jupiter Books.

KAGAN, J., KEARSLEY, R. & ZELAGO, P. (1978) *Infancy: Its Place in Human Development*. Cambridge, MA: Harvard University Press.

KAHN, H. & CUTHBERTSON, B.A. (1998) A comparison of the self-reported mental and physical distress of working and full-time homemaker mothers – A UK pilot study. *Stress Medicine*, 14, 149–154.

KAMINER, H. & LAVIE, P. (1991) Sleep and dreaming in Holocaust survivors: Dramatic decrease in dream recall in well-adjusted survivors. *Journal of Nervous & Mental Diseases*, 179, 664–669.

KANNER, A.D., COYNE, J.C., SCHAEFER, C. & LAZARUS, R.S. (1981) Comparison of two modes of stress measurement: Daily hassles and uplifts versus major life events. *Journal of Behavioural Measurement*, 4, 1–39.

KENDLER, K.S., MCLEAN, C., NEALE, M., KESSLER, R., HEATH, A. & EAVES, L. (1991) The genetic epidemiology of bulimia nervosa. *American Journal of Psychiatry*, 148, 1627–1637.

KENNEDY, D. (1997) Anorexia is linked to brain deficiency. *The Times*, 14 April, 5.

KENRICK, D.T. (1994) Evolutionary social psychology: From sexual selection to social cognition. *Advances in Experimental Social Psychology*, 26, 75–121.

KEPPEL, G. & UNDERWOOD, B.J. (1962) Proactive inhibition in short-term retention of single items. *Journal of Verbal Learning & Verbal Behaviour*, 1, 153–161.

KIECOLT-GLASER, J.K., MARUCHA, P.T., MALARKEY, W.B., MERCADO, A.M. & GLASER, R. (1995) Slowing of wound healing by psychological stress. *The Lancet*, 346, 1194–1196.

KILHAM, W. & MANN, L. (1974) Level of destructive obedience as a function of transmitter and executant roles in the Milgram obedience paradigm. *Journal of Personality & Social Psychology*, 29, 696–702.

KOBASA, S.C. (1979) Stressful life events, personality, and health: An inquiry into hardiness. *Journal of Personality & Social Psychology*, 37, 1–11.

KOBASA, S.C.O. (1986) How much stress can you survive? In M.G. Walraven & H.E. Fitzgerald (Eds) *Annual Editions: Human Development*, 86/87. New York: Dushkin.

KOLUCHOVA, J. (1972) Severe deprivation in twins: A case study. *Journal of Child Psychology & Psychiatry*, 13, 107–114.

KOLUCHOVA, J. (1991) Severely deprived twins after 22 years observation. *Studia Psychologica*, 33, 23–28.

KOVEL, J. (1978) *A Complete Guide to Therapy*. Harmondsworth: Penguin.

KREBS, D. & BLACKMAN, R. (1988) *Psychology: A First Encounter*. New York: Harcourt Brace Jovanovich.

KREMER, J. (1998) Work. In K. Trew & J. Kremer (Eds) *Gender and Psychology*. London: Arnold.

KRUPAT, E. & GARONZIK, R. (1994) Subjects' expectations and the search for alternatives to deception in social psychology. *British Journal of Social Psychology*, 33, 211–222.

LAMB, M.E., STERNBERG, K.J., HWANG, P. & BROBERG, A (Eds) (1992) *Child Care in Context*. Hillsdale, NJ: Erlbaum.

LAMB, M.E., THOMPSON, R.A., GANDER, W. & CHARNOV, E.L. (1985) Infant–Mother Attachment: *The Origins and Significance of Individual Differences in Strange Situation Behaviour*. Hillsdale, NJ: Erlbaum.

LARSEN, K.S. (1974) Conformity in the Asch experiment. *Journal of Social Psychology*, 94, 303–304.

LARSEN, K.S., TRIPLETT, J.S., BRANT, W.D. & LANGENBERG, D. (1979) Collaborator status, subject characteristics and conformity in the Asch paradigm. *Journal of Social Psychology*, 108, 259–263.

LASK, B. & BRYANT-WAUGH, R. (1992) Childhood onset of anorexia nervosa and related eating disorders. *Journal of Child Psychology & Psychiatry*, 3, 281–300.

LAUER, C.J., GORZEWSKI, B., GERLINGHOFF, M., BACKMUND, H. & ZIHL, J. (1999) Neuropsychological assessments before and after treatment in patients with anorexia nervosa and bulimia nervosa. *Journal of Psychiatric Research*, 33, 129–138.

LAZARUS, R.S. (1999) *Stress and Emotion: A New Synthesis.* London: Free Association Books.

LAZARUS, R.S. & FOLKMAN, S. (1984) *Stress, Appraisal, and Coping.* New York: Springer.

LEE, S., HSU, L.K.G. & WING, Y.K. (1992) Bulimia nervosa in Hong Kong Chinese patients. *British Journal of Psychiatry*, 161, 545–551.

LEFCOURT, H.F., DAVIDSON, K., PRKACHIN, K.M. & MILLS, D.E. (1997) Humour as a stress moderator in the production of blood pressure obtained during five stressful tasks. *Journal of Personality & Social Psychology*, 31, 523–542.

LEGGE, D. (1975) *An Introduction to Psychological Science.* London: Methuen.

LEVINGER, G. & CLARK, J. (1961) Emotional factors in the forgetting of word associations. *Journal of Abnormal & Social Psychology*, 62, 99–105.

LEWINSOHN, P.M., HOPS, H. & ROBERTS, R.E. (1993) Adolescent psychopathology: I. Prevalence and incidence of depression and other DSM-3-R disorders in high school students. *Journal of Abnormal Psychology*, 102, 133–144.

LLOYD, P., MAYES, A., MANSTEAD, A.S.R., MEUDELL, P.R. & WAGNER, H.L. (1984) *Introduction to Psychology – An Integrated Approach.* London: Fontana.

LOFTUS, E.F. (1975) Leading questions and the eyewitness report. *Cognitive Psychology*, 1, 560–572.

LOFTUS, E.F. (1979) Reactions to blatantly contradictory information. *Memory and Cognition*, 7, 368–374.

LOFTUS, E.F. (1997) Creating False Memories. *Scientific American*, September, 50–55.

LOFTUS, E.F. & LOFTUS, G. (1980) On the permanence of stored information in the human brain. *American Psychologist*, 35, 409–420.

LOFTUS, E.F. & PALMER, J.C. (1974) Reconstruction of automobile destruction: An example of the interaction between language and memory. *Journal of Verbal Learning & Verbal Behaviour*, 13, 585–589.

LOFTUS, E.F. & ZANNI, G. (1975) Eyewitness testimony: The influence of wording on a question. *Bulletin of the Psychonomic Society* 5, 86–88.

LOFTUS, G. (1974) Reconstructing memory: The incredible eyewitness. *Psychology Today*, December, 116–119.

LOGIE, R.H. (1995) *Visuo-Spatial Working Memory.* Hove: Lawrence Erlbaum.

LOGIE, R.H. (1999) Working Memory. *The Psychologist*, 12(4), 174–178.

LOGIE, R.H., WRIGHT, R. & DECKER, S. (1992) Recognition memory performance and residential burglary. *Applied Cognitive Psychology*, 6, 109–123.

LONG, B.C. & KHAN, S.E. (Eds) (1993) *Women, Work and Coping: A Multidisciplinary Approach to Workplace Stress.* Canada: McGill-Queens University.

LORENZ, K.Z. (1935) The companion in the bird's world. *Auk*, 54, 245–273.

MACCOBY, E.E. (1980) *Social Development – Psychological Growth and the Parent-Child Relationship.* New York: Harcourt Brace Jovanovich.

MACLEAN, P.D. (1982) On the origin and progressive evolution of the triune brain. In E. Armstrong & D. Falk (Eds) *Primate Brain Evolution.* New York: Plenum Press.

MAIN, M. (1991) Metacognitive knowledge, metacognitive monitoring, and singular (coherent) versus multiple (incoherent) models of attachment: Findings and directions for future research. In C.M. Murray Parkes, J.M. Stephenson-Hinde & P. Marris (Eds) *Attachment Across the Life-Cycle.* London: Routledge

MAIN, M. & WESTON, D.R. (1981) The quality of the toddler's relationship to mother and to father: Related to conflict behaviour and the readiness to establish new relationships. *Child Development*, 52, 932–940.

MAIN, M., KAPLAN, N. & CASSIDY, J. (1985) Security in infancy, childhood and adulthood: A move to the level of representation. In I. Bretherton & E. Waters (Eds) *Growing Points of Attachment Theory and Research.* (Monographs of the Society for Research in Child Development, Volume 50, Serial No. 209.) Chicago: University of Chicago Press

MALINOWSKI, B. (1929) *The Sexual Life of Savages.* New York: Harcourt Brace Jovanovich.

MANN, L. (1969) *Social Psychology.* New York: Wiley.

MARMOT, M., BOSMA, H., HEMINGWAY, H., BRUNNER, E. & STANSFIELD, S. (1997) Contribution of job control and other risk factors to social variation in health disease incidence. *The Lancet*, 350, 235–239.

MARMOT, M. & WILKINSON, R. (1999) *Social Determinants of Health.* Oxford: Oxford University Press.

MARRONE, M (1998) *Attachment and Interaction.* London: Jessica Kingsley Publishers.

MARUSIC, A., GUDJONSSON, G.H., EYSENCK, H.J. & START, R. (1999) Biological and psychosocial risk factors in ischaemic heart disease: Empirical findings and a biopsychosocial model. *Personality and Individual Differences*, 26, 285–304.

MASLOW, A. (1968) *Towards a Psychology of Being* (2nd edition). New York: Van Nostrand Reinhold.

McCORMICK, L.J. & MAYER, J.D. (1991) Mood-congruent recall and natural mood. Poster presented at the annual meeting of the New England Psychological Association, Portland, ME.

MEEUS, W.H.J & RAAIJMAKERS, Q.A.W. (1986) Administrative obedience: Carrying out orders to use psychological-administrative violence. *European Journal of Social Psychology*, 16, 311–324.

MEICHENBAUM, D. (1976) Towards a cognitive therapy of self-control. In G. Schawrtz & D. Shapiro (Eds) *Consciousness and Self-Regulation: Advances in Research.* New York: Plenum Publishing Co.

MEICHENBAUM, D.H. (1997) The evolution of a cognitive-behaviour therapist. In J.K. Zeig (Ed.) *The Evolution of Psychotherapy: The Third Conference.* New York: Brunner/Mazel.

MELHUISH, E.C. (1993) Behaviour Measures : A measure of love? An overview of the assessment of attachment. *Association of Child Psychology & Psychiatry Review & Newsletter*, 15, 269–275.

MEMON, A. & WRIGHT, D.B. (1999) Eyewitness testimony and the Oklahoma bombing. *The Psychologist*, 12(6), 292–295

MILGRAM, S. (1963) Behavioural study of obedience. *Journal of Abnormal & Social Psychology*, 67, 391–398.

MILGRAM, S. (1965) Liberating effects of group pressure. *Journal of Personality & Social Psychology*, 1, 127–134.

MILGRAM, S. (1974) *Obedience to Authority*. New York: Harper & Row.

MILGRAM, S. (1992) *The Individual in a Social World* (2nd edition). New York: McGraw-Hill.

MILLER, E. & MORLEY, S. (1986) *Investigating Abnormal Behaviour*. London: Erlbaum.

MILLER, G.A. (1956) The magical number seven, plus or minus two: Some limits on our capacity for processing information. *Psychological Review*, 63, 81–97.

MILLER, G.A. & SELFRIDGE, J.A. (1950) Verbal context and the recall of meaningful material. *American Journal of Psychology*, 63, 176–185.

MINUCHIN, S., ROSMAN, B. & BAKER, L. (1978) *Psychosomatic Families*. Cambridge, MA: Harvard University Press.

MIRANDA, F.S.B., CABALLERO, R.B., GOMEZ, M.N.G. & ZAMORANO, M.A.M. (1981) Obediencia a la antoridad. *Pisquis*, 2, 212–221.

MOOS, R.H. (1988) *Coping Response Inventory Manual*. Social Ecology Laboratory, Department of Psychiatry, Stanford University and Veterans Administration Medical Centers. Palo Alto, Califormia.

MORRIS, C.D., BRANSFORD, J.D. & FRANKS. J.J. (1977) Levels of processing versus transfer appropriate processing. *Journal of Verbal Learning & Verbal Behaviour*, 16, 519–533.

MORRIS, J.N. (1953) Coronary heart disease and physical activity of work. *The Lancet*, 2, 1053–1057.

MORRIS, P.E., TWEEDY, M. & GRUNEBERG, M.M. (1985) Interest, knowledge and the memorising of soccer scores. *British Journal of Psychology*, 76, 415–425.

MOSCOVICI, S. (1976) *La Psychoanalyse: Son Image et Son Public* (2nd edition). Paris: Presses Universitaires de France.

MOSCOVICI, S. & FAUCHEUX, C. (1972) Social influence, conforming bias and the study of active minorities. In L. Berkowitz (Ed.) *Advances in Experimental Social Psychology*, Volume 6. New York: Academic Press.

MOSCOVICI, S. & LAGE, E. (1976) Studies in social influence III: Majority versus minority influence in a group. *European Journal of Social Psychology*, 6, 149–174.

MUMFORD, D.B., WHITEHOUSE, A.M. & PLATTS, M. (1991) Sociocultural correlates of eating disorders among Asian schoolgirls in Bradford. *British Journal of Psychiatry*, 158, 222–228.

MURDOCK, B.B. (1962) The serial position effect in free recall. *Journal of Experimental Psychology*, 64, 482–488.

MURRAY, I. (1999) Men are 'forgotten' anorexics. *The Times*, 18 August, 11.

NOBILI, L., BAGLIETTO, M.G., DE CARLI, F., SAVOINI, M., SCHIAVI, G., ZANOTTO, E., FERRILLO, F. & DE NEGRI, M. (1999) A quantified analysis of sleep electroencephalography in anorectic adolescents. *Biological Psychiatry*, 45, 771–775.

NOLAN, J. & MARKHAM, R. (1998) The accuracy–confidence relationship in an eyewitness task: Anxiety as a modifier. *Applied Cognitive Psychology*, 12, 43–54.

NORTON, C. (1999) Sperm count linked to stress. *The Independent*, 9 September, 11.

ORNE, M.T. (1962) On the social psychology of the psychological experiment: with particular reference to demand characteristics and their implications. *American Psychologist*, 17, 776–783.

ORNE, M.T. & HOLLAND, C.C. (1968) On the ecological validity of laboratory deceptions. *International Journal of Psychiatry*, 6, 282–293.

ORNE, M.T. & Scheibe, K.E. (1964) The contribution of non-deprivation factors in the production of sensory deprivation effects: The psychology of the 'panic button'. *Journal of Abnormal & Social Psychology*, 68, 3–12.

PARKE, R.D. (1981) *Fathering*. London: Fontana.

PARKER, I., GEORGACA, E., HARPER, D., McLAUGHLIN, T. & STOWELL-SMITH, M. (1995) *Deconstructing Psychopathology*. London: Sage.

PARKIN, A.J. (1993) *Memory: Phenomena, Experiment and Theory*. Oxford: Blackwell.

PARKIN, A.J., LEWINSON, J. & FOLKARD, S. (1982) The influence of emotion on immediate and delayed retention: Levinger and Clark reconsidered. *British Journal of Psychology*, 73, 389–393.

PERRIN, S. & SPENCER, C. (1981) Independence or conformity in the Asch experiment as a reflection of cultural and situational factors. *British Journal of Social Psychology*, 20, 205–209.

PETERSON, L.R. & PETERSON, M.J. (1959) Short-term retention of individual items. *Journal of Experimental Psychology*, 58, 193–198.

PETKOVA, B. (1997) Understanding eating disorders: A perspective from feminist psychology. *Psychology Review*, 4, 2–7.

PIDGEON, N. & HENWOOD, K. (1997) Using grounded theory in psychological research, in N.Hayes (Ed.) *Doing Qualitative Analysis in Psychology*. Hove: Psychology Press.

PINES, A. (1984) Ma Bell and the Hardy Boys. *Across the Board*, July/August, 37–42.

QUINTON, D. & RUTTER, M. (1988) *Parental Breakdown: The Making and Breaking of Intergenerational Links*. London: Gower.

REBER, A.S. (1985) *The Penguin Dictionary of Psychology*. Harmondsworth: Penguin.

RICHARDS, M.P.M. (1995) The International Year of the Family – family research. *The Psychologist*, 8, 17–20.

ROBERTSON, J.& ROBERTSON J. (1967–73) Film Series, *Young Children in Brief Separation*: No 3 (1969). John, 17 months, 9 days in a residential nursery. London: Tavistock.

ROGERS, L., RESNICK, M.D., MITCHELL, J.E. & BLUM, R.W. (1997) The relationship between socioeconomic status and eating-disordered behaviours in a community sample of adolescent girls. *International Journal of Eating Disorders*, 22, 15–23.

ROSENHAN, D.L. & SELIGMAN, M.E. (1984) *Abnormal Psychology*. New York: Norton.

ROSENTHAL, R. & JACOBSON. L. (1968) *Pygmalion in the Classroom: Teacher Expectation and Pupils' Intellectual Development*. New York: Holt.

ROSENTHAL, R. & LAWSON, R. (1964) A longitudinal study of the effects of experimenter bias on the operant learning of laboratory rats. *Journal of Psychiatric Research*, 2, 61–72.

ROSENTHAL, R. & ROSNOW, R.L. (1966) *The Volunteer Subject*. New York: Wiley.

ROSNOW, R.L. & ROSENTHAL, R. (1997) *People Studying People: Artifacts and Ethics in Behavioural Research*. New York: W.H. Freeman.

ROTTER, J.B. (1966) Generalised expectancies for internal versus external control of reinforcement. *Psychological Monographs*, 30 (1), 1–26.

RUDERMAN, A.J. (1986) Dietary restraint: A theoretical and empirical review. *Psychological Bulletin*, 99, 247–262.

RUSSELL, G.F.M. (1979) Bulimia nervosa: An ominous variant of anorexia nervosa. *Psychological Medicine*, 9, 429–448.

RUTTER, M. (1981) *Maternal Deprivation Reassessed* (2nd edition). Harmondsworth: Penguin.

RUTTER, M. (1989) Pathways from childhood to adult life. *Journal of Child Psychology & Psychiatry*, 30, 23–25.

SAVICKAS, M.L. (1995) Work and adjustment. In D. Wedding (Ed.) *Behaviour and Medicine* (2nd edition). St Louis, MO: Mosby-Year Book.

SAVIN, H.B. (1973) Professors and psychological researchers: conflicting values in conflicting roles. *Cognition*, 2 (1), 147–149

SCARR, S. & THOMPSON, W. (1994) Effects of maternal employment and nonmaternal infant care on development at two and four years. *Early Development & Parenting*, 3(2), 113–123.

SCARR, S. (1998) American child care today. *American Psychologist*, 53(2), 95–108.

SCHACHTER, S. (1951) Deviation, rejection and communication. *Journal of Abnormal & Social Psychology*, 46, 190–207.

SCHAFFER, H.R. (1971) *The Growth of Sociability*. Harmondsworth: Penguin.

SCHAFFER, H.R. (1996a) *Social Development* Oxford: Blackwell.

SCHAFFER, H.R. (1996b) Is the child father to the man? *Psychology Review*, 2(3), 2–5.

SCHAFFER, H.R. & EMERSON, P.E. (1964) The development of social attachments in infancy. *Monographs of the Society for Research in Child Development*, 29 (Whole No. 3).

SCHAFFER, R. (1998) Deprivation and its effects on children. *Psychology Review*, 5(2), 2–5.

SCHURZ, G. (1985) Experimentelle Überprüfung des Zusammenhangs zwischen Persönlichkeitsmerkmalen und der Bereitschaft der destruktiven Gehorsam gegenüber Autoritaten. *Zeitschrift für Experimentelle und Augewandte Psychologie*, 32, 160–177.

SELIGMAN, M.E.P. (1975) *Helplessness: On Depression, Development and Death*. San Francisco: W.H. Freeman.

SELYE, H. (1936) A syndrome produced by diverse nocuous agents. *Nature*, 138, 32.

SELYE, H. (1976) *The Stress of Life* (revised edition). New York: McGraw-Hill.

SELYE, H. (1980) The stress concept today. In I.L. Kutash (Ed.) *Handbook on Stress and Anxiety*. San Francisco: Jossey-Bass.

SHALLICE, T. & WARRINGTON, E.K. (1970) Independent functioning of verbal memory stores: A neurophysiological study. *Quarterly Journal of Experimental Psychology*, 22, 261–273.

SHANAB, M.E. & YAHYA, K.A. (1978) A cross-cultural study of obedience. *Bulletin of the Psychonomic Society*, 11, 267–269.

SHERIDAN, C.L. & KING, R.G. (1972) Obedience to authority with an authentic victim. Proceedings of the 80th Annual Convention, *American Psychological Association*, Part 1, 7, 165–166.

SHERIF, M. (1935) A study of social factors in perception. *Archives of Psychology*, 27, Whole No. 187.

SHERIF, M. (1936) The *Psychology of Social Norms*. New York: Harper & Row.

SHULMAN, H.G. (1970) Encoding and retention of semantic and phonemic information in short-term memory. *Journal of Verbal Learning & Verbal Behaviour*, 9, 499–508.

SISTRUNK, F. & McDAVID, J.W. (1971) Sex variable in conforming behaviour. *Journal of Personality & Social Psychology*, 2, 200–207.

SKINNER, B.F. (1990) Can psychology be a science of mind? *American Psychologist*, 45, 1206–1210.

SLUCKIN, W. (1965) *Imprinting and Early Experiences*. London: Methuen.

SMITH, P.B. (1995) Social influence proceses. In M. Argyle & A.M. Colman (Eds) *Social Psychology*. London: Longman.

SMITH, P.B. & BOND, M.H. (1998) *Social Psychology Across Cultures* (2nd edition). Hemel Hempstead: Prentice Hall Europe.

SOLSO, R.L. (1995) *Cognitive Psychology* (4th edition). Boston: Allyn & Bacon.

SPENCER, C. & PERRIN, S. (1998) Innovation and Conformity. *Psychology Review*, 5(2), 23–26.

SPERLING, H.G. (1946) 'An experimental study of some psychological factors in judgement.' (Master's thesis, New School for Social Research.)

SPITZ, R.A. (1945) Hospitalism: An inquiry into the genesis of psychiatric conditions in early childhood. *Psychoanalytic Study of the Child*, 1, 53–74.

SPITZ, R.A. (1946) Hospitalism: A follow-up report on investigation described in Vol. 1, 1945. *Psychoanalytic Study of the Child*, 2, 113–117.

SPITZ, R.A. & WOLF, K.M. (1946) Anaclitic depression. *Psychoanalytic Study of the Child*, 2, 313–342.

STEIN, S., CHALHOUB, N. & HODES, M. (1998) Very early-onset bulimia nervosa: Report of two cases. *International Journal of Eating Disorders*, 24, 323–327.

STROBER, M. & KATZ, J.L. (1987) Do eating disorders and affective disorders share a common aetiology? *International Journal of Eating Disorders*, 6, 171–180.

SUE, D., SUE, D. & SUE, S. (1994) *Understanding Abnormal Behaviour* (4th edition). Boston: Houghton-Mifflin.

SUI–WAH, L. (1989) Anorexia nervosa and Chinese food. *British Journal of Psychiatry*, 155, 568.

SUOMI, S.J. & HARLOW, H.F. (1977) Depressive behaviour in young monkeys subjected to vertical chamber confinement. *Journal of Comparative & Physiological Psychology*, 80, 11–18.

SWEENEY, K. (1995) Stay calm and heal better. *The Times*, 21 December, 5.

SZASZ, T.S. (1960) The myth of mental illness. *American Psychologist*, 15, 113–118.

TAYLOR, S. (1990) Health psychology: The science and the field. *American Psychologist*, 45, 40–50.

TEMOSHOK, L. (1987) Personality, coping style, emotions and cancer: Towards an integrative model. *Cancer Surveys*, 6, 545–567 (Supplement).

TIZARD, B. (1977) *Adoption: A Second Chance*. London: Open Books.

TIZARD, B. & HODGES, J. (1978) The effects of early institutional rearing on the development of eight-year-old children. *Journal of Child Psychology & Psychiatry*, 19, 99–118.

TIZARD, B. & REES, J. (1974) A comparison of the effects of adoption, restoration to the natural mother and continued institutionalisation on the cognitive development of four-year-old children. *Child Development*, 45, 92–99.

TOUYZ, S.W., O'SULLIVAN, B.T., GERTLER, R. & BEAUMONT, P.J.V. (1988) Anorexia nervosa in a woman blind since birth. *British Journal of Psychiatry*, 153, 248–249.

TULVING, E. (1968) Theoretical issues in free recall. In T.R. Dixon & D.L. Horton (Eds) *Verbal Behaviour and General Behaviour Theory*. Englewood Cliffs, NJ: Prentice-Hall.

TULVING, E. (1972) Episodic and semantic memory. In E. Tulving & W. Donaldson (Eds) *Organisation of Memory*. London: Academic Press.

TULVING, E. (1974) Cue-dependent forgetting. *American Scientist*, 62, 74–82.

TULVING, E. & PEARLSTONE, Z. (1966) Availability versus accessibility of information in memory for words. *Journal of Verbal Learning & Verbal Behaviour*, 5, 389–391.

TULVING, E. & THOMPSON, D.M. (1973) Encoding specificity and retrieval processes in episodic memory. *Psychological Review*, 80, 352–373.

TURNER, J.C. (1991) *Social Influence*. Milton Keynes: Open University Press.

UHLIG. R. (1996) Superwaif Sindy 'is shaping future of girls aged eight'. *The Daily Telegraph*, 14 September, 9.

VAN AVERMAET, E. (1996) Social influence in small groups. In M. Hewstone, W. Stroebe & G.M. Stephenson (Eds) *Introduction to Social Psychology* (2nd edition). Oxford: Blackwell.

VAN IJZENDOORN, M.H. & DE WOLFF, M.S. (1997) In search of the absent father: meta analyses of infant–father attachment: A rejoinder to our discussants. *Child Development*, 68, 604–609.

VAN IJZENDOORN, M.H. & KROONENBERG, P.M. (1988) Cross-cultural patterns of attachment: a meta-analysis of the strange situation. *Child Development*, 59, 147–156.

VAN IJZENDOORN, M.H. & SCHUENGEL, C. (1999) The development of attachment relationships: Infancy and beyond. In D. Messer & S. Millar (Eds) *Exploring Developmental Psychology: From Infancy to Adolescence*. London: Arnold.

VAUGHN, B.E., GOVE, F.L. & EGELAND, B.R. (1980) The relationship between out-of-home care and the quality of infant-mother attachment in an economically disadvantaged population. *Child Development*, 51, 1203–1214.

VITELLI, R. (1988) The crisis issue reassessed: An empirical analysis. *Basic and Applied Social Psychology*, 9, 301–309.

WADE, C. & TAVRIS, C. (1993) *Psychology* (3rd edition). New York: HarperCollins.

WADE, T., NEALE, M.C., LAKE, R.I. & MARTIN, N.G. (1999) A genetic analysis of the eating and attitudes associated with bulimia nervosa: Dealing with the problem of ascertainment in twin studies. *Behaviour Genetics*, 29, 1–10.

WALLACE, B. & FISHER, L.E. (1987) *Consciousness and Behaviour* (second edition). Boston: Allyn & Bacon.

WATERS, E. (1978) The reliability and stability of individual differences in infant–mother attachments. *Child Development*, 49, 483–494.

WATSON, J.B. (1913) Psychology as the behaviourist views it. *Psychological Review*, 20, 158–177.

WATSON, J.B. (1919) *Psychology from the Standpoint of a Behaviourist*. Philadelphia: J.B. Lippincott.

WATSON, J.B. & RAYNER, R. (1920) Conditioned emotional responses. *Journal of Experimental Psychology*, 3, 1–14.

WATTS, J. (2000) Dare to be different, Japanese are urged. *The Guardian*, 21 January.

WAUGH, N.C. & NORMAN, D.A. (1965) Primary memory. *Psychological Review*, 72, 89–104.

WEISS, J.M. (1972) Psychological factors in stress and disease. *Scientific American*, 226, 104–113.

WELLS, G.L. (1993) What do we know about eyewitness identification? *American Psychologist*, 48, 553–571.

WESSLER, R.L. (1986) Conceptualising cognitions in the cognitive-behavioural therapies. In W. Dryden & W. Golden (Eds) *Cognitive-Behavioural Approaches to Psychotherapy*. London: Harper & Row.

WICKENS, C.D. (1972) Characteristics of word encoding. In A. Melton & E. Martin (Eds) *Coding Processes in Human Memory*. Washington, DC: Winston.

WICKENS, C.D. (1972) *Engineering Psychology and Human Performance* (2nd edition). New York: HarperCollins.

WILCOX, J.A. (1990) Fluoxetine and bulimia. *Journal of Psychoactive Drugs*, 22, 81–82.

WILLIS, R.H. (1963) Two dimensions of conformity–nonconformity. *Sociometry*, 26, 499–513.

WISEMAN, C.V., GRAY, J.J., MOSIMANN, J.E. & AHRENS, A.H. (1992) Cultural expectations of thinness in women: An update. *International Journal of Eating Disorders*, 11, 85–89.

WOLPE, J. & RACHMAN, S. (1960) Psychoanalytic evidence: A critique based on Freud's case of Little Hans. *Journal of Nervous & Mental Disease*, 131, 135–145.

WOOLEY, S. & WOOLEY, O. (1983) Should obesity be treated at all? *Psychiatric Annals*, 13, 884–885.

WRIGHT, D.B. (1993) Recall of the Hillsborough disaster over time: Systematic biases of 'flashbulb' memories. *Applied Cognitive Psychology*, 7, 129–138.

WYNN, V.E. & LOGIE, R.H. (1998) The veracity of long-term memory: Did Bartlett get it right? *Applied Cognitive Psychology*, 12, 1–20.

YAGER, J., HATTON, C.A. & LAWRENCE, M. (1986) Anorexia nervosa in a woman totally blind since the age of two. *British Journal of Psychiatry*, 149, 506–509.

YUILLE, J.C. & CUTSHALL, J.L. (1986) A case study of eyewitness memory of a crime. *Journal of Applied Psychology*, 71, 291–301.

ZILBOORG, G. & HENRY, G.W. (1941) *A History of Medical Psychology*. New York: Norton.

ZIMBARDO, P.G. (1973) On the ethics of intervention in human psychological research with special refernce to the 'Stanford Prison Experiment'. *Cognition*, 2 (2), 243–255.

ZIMBARDO, P.G. (1992) *Psychology and Life* (13th edition). New York: Harper Collins.

ZIMBARDO, P.G., BANKS, W.C., CRAIG, H. & JAFFE, D. (1973) A Pirandellian prison: The mind is a formidable jailor. *New York Times Magazine*, 8 April, 38–60.

ZIMBARDO, P.G. & LEIPPE, M. (1991) *The Psychology of Attitude Change and Social Influence*. New York: McGraw-Hill.

ZIMBARDO, P.G. & WEBER, A.L. (1994) *Psychology*. New York: HarperCollins.

Index

Page numbers in **bold** indicate definitions of words/concepts.